growing the
MIDWEST
garden

growing the
MIDWEST
garden

ED LYON

Timber Press
Portland · London

Frontispiece: A Milwaukee, Wisconsin, private garden exemplifies
outstanding Midwest gardening. Opposite: No stereotypes here. Bedazzle
any garden with unique plant materials such as these succulent jewels.
Page 6: 'Autumn Cascade', a weeping cultivar of native black tupelo,
at her autumn finest.

Photography credits appear on page 300. Map on page 25 ©Benchmark Maps
Cover image photographed at The Flower Factory, Stoughton, Wisconsin,
one of the Midwest's finest perennial nurseries.

The Haseltine Building
133 S.W. Second Avenue, Suite 450
Portland, Oregon 97204-3527
timberpress.com

Printed in China
Book design by Jane Jeszeck/www.jigsawseattle.com
Library of Congress Cataloging-in-Publication Data
ISBN 13: 978-1-60469-466-6 (paperback)
ISBN 13: 978-1-60469-495-6 (hardcover)

Lyon, Ed, 1957- author.
  Growing the Midwest garden/Ed Lyon.—First edition.
    pages cm
  Includes index.
  ISBN 978-1-60469-495-6 — ISBN 978-1-60469-466-6 1. Gardening—Middle West.
I. Title.
  SB453.2.M53L96 2015
  635.0977—dc23
                        2014038515

To Darrell (Dylan) Wayne Hart,

whose love, respect, and support are the reasons

for any successes I may achieve.

Contents

FOREWORD

IN A WORLD that is increasingly global, gardening remains a local endeavor. The concept of the right plant for the right place is one of the tenets of gardening, so understanding the unique traits of your location, such as soil, weather, hardiness zone, and natural ecosystems is vital to successful gardening. At the heart of Ed Lyon's *Growing the Midwest Garden* are the experiences of a real gardener who has spent a lifetime honing his knowledge and craft, while never forgetting that where you live determines how you garden.

Ed has compiled an informative and experiential tome that will be invaluable to regional gardeners at all levels of accomplishment, from the nascent to the experienced. He boils down location information into the various ecotypes within the Midwest so that gardeners can more easily understand where they live and how that impacts the way they garden. Ed keeps the tone light, even humorous, when explaining climate zones, soils, fertilizing, watering, and even demystifies some common garden myths along the way. Although this is not a design book, Ed deftly covers common garden design elements, too. In the end, what makes this book so valuable is that Ed Lyon is a raconteur of gardening wisdom and experience. His successes and failures will ring true to longtime gardeners while bolstering the confidence of those just starting out.

For those of you who haven't had the pleasure of meeting Ed, you'll get to know him as you read this book because he writes like he talks, with an easy, friendly, and helpful demeanor. He's amassed a wealth of knowledge and experience for gardeners to tap into. After all, who better to advise you on Midwestern gardening than a Midwestern gardener—in this case, we'll forgive Ed his Mid-Atlantic upbringing!

As a longtime proponent of regional plant trials and a native Midwesterner, I especially appreciate the local and regional tenor of the book. In our global economy, plants come to us from everywhere but are often untested widely. Regional trials help gardeners make informed decisions on the best plants for their area. Ed has compiled an impressive list of tried-and-true garden plants plus many more uncommon plants that will entice gardeners to explore and push the boundaries. He has melded a compendium of good garden plants with an encyclopedia of gardening practices specifically tailored to the Midwest. Simply put, I've waited a long time for this book.

—RICHARD G. HAWKE
PLANT EVALUATION MANAGER
CHICAGO BOTANIC GARDEN

Gardens should exude joy, which Mexican hat fully expresses.

PREFACE

HORTICULTURE IS MY SECOND career. When I lost my agribusiness job in the 1990s, like many people at that time, I realized it might be a good time to return to college for a new career. I researched a number of fields and realized that what I had always considered a hobby—gardening—had developed into an obsession. That insight directed me to a plant-based focus and I worked toward an M.S. degree in horticulture. I think the value of this book is that a hands-on amateur turned "expert" is dispensing the advice. When I advise others I am quick to tell them that they will learn far more from my mistakes than my successes. This might be my definition of gardening.

As a horticulturist, I will forever be in debt to my father for teaching me about native vegetation. It was an integral part of our lives that instilled deep love and appreciation for nature and would eventually change my career. I doubt I will ever feel at home without the proximity of trees and the scent of dried leaves.

Growing up on a small dairy farm near Cooperstown, New York, I remember my father lamenting that the property bordering our farm contained black locust (which produced the best fence posts), but it missed our land entirely. In contrast, we were

the only farm with mature, fruit-bearing butternuts (oh, how I miss Mom's butternut cake!). We didn't think consciously about it as youngsters but we had already learned that plants prefer specific environments and what flourished in one area didn't thrive in others. When I took dendrology (a fancy name for the botanical, versus horticultural, study of trees), we learned how site specific tree species can be. I returned home after that class and took a reminiscent walk through the "back forty." I noticed that musclewood and ironwood grew only in the wooded border, sugar maple and beech populated the eastern hillside, and eastern hemlock dominated the north. Black alder and American sycamore were happy along stream banks but only smaller shrubs effectively established roots in swampy muck. Tamarack and white oak defied the challenges of wet feet until they eventually reached a size where roots forced shallow due to excess water could no longer sustain their weight. They had toppled with giant circular plates of root-bound soil jutting skyward. This exposed more sunlight for shrubby willows and arrowwood viburnum; Davids to fallen Goliaths.

Trees may have been the most obvious evidence of plants evolving and adapting to specific, culture-influenced sites, but there were plenty of examples of perennial plant acclimatization as well. Foam flower wasn't a popular garden plant when I was a farm boy, but by the time I was gardening as an adult it had become a favorite. I discovered it abundantly in two forms in the glen growing between stream and dry upland woodland. Fortuitously, it was

I am a horticulturalist, but I am also a gardener with dirt under my nails.

A view from the "back forty" on the New York family farm.

spring and the plant was in bloom; I was delighted to see clumping *Tiarella cordifolia* intermixed with running *T. cordifolia* var. *cordifolia*.

My woodland traipsing is a lesson in culture for gardeners. It is when we see how specific these plants site themselves in their natural environment that we better understand their cultural needs in cultivation. The fact that foam flower populations ended before reaching the upper woodland explains why that plant fails to thrive in dry shade gardens. Home gardens are contrived versions of what we find in nature and it is necessary to understand the conditions each species needs replicated to grow well. Breeding cultivars of naturally occurring species improves traits; however, plants have taken

centuries to evolve and adapt to specific sites and a few generations of breeding isn't going to dramatically change basic cultural needs.

My mother's influence was the calming effect of growing vegetables. She had a vegetable garden close to an acre in size that provided a bounty of fresh produce all summer: two freezers packed full, jars of preserved fruits, and vegetables that were visual delights lining shelves in the basement. I was a typical boy who loved animals—I had my own flock of

OPPOSITE TOP White beech to the left and eastern hemlock to the right, creating segregated populations on the farm.
BOTTOM The foam flower I found growing in its native environment on the farm.

13

Flowers were few and far between on my first nasturtium plants, but the plants were huge.

bantam chickens—but didn't think I liked vegetables. However, I did show some interest in Mom's planting activities at about age twelve. She recognized the curiosity, ordered a Gurney Seed Company one-cent seed packet for kids, and encouraged me to plant the seeds in a plot adjacent to my chicken shed.

A boy on a dairy farm knows all about manure as fertilizer, so I amended my little plot with rich, aged chicken dung. My seed packet contained a number of large, round nasturtium seeds. I had no idea what this pea-like seed would produce and wouldn't know until researching it later that nasturtium prefers lean soils for ideal flowering. Mine grew like a proverbial weed, producing massive, waist-high "shrubs" (I was twelve, remember). They didn't flower much at all; it would be years before I would learn that vegetative growth from highly available nitrogen produces foliage at the expense of bloom. It hardly mattered, as my first attempt at growing something had produced colossal plants! This was my first lesson that if you want to get someone excited about gardening, their initial efforts need to be successful, exciting, and rewarding. My mom praised my gardening prowess—smart lady—and the following year that little plot was simply not enough and I was side-by-side with her in the vegetable garden.

Another life lesson on the value of gardening is the personal connections that it can facilitate. When I was around sixteen, my grandfather and I had reached the point of nearly despising one another until we bonded over gardening. I told him about adding Epsom salts to tomatoes and he was exuberant when his plants grew massively larger than mine. Just like my experience with the nasturtiums, he didn't care that the yield was low, it was more about the success and the huge plants he grew. We competed over size and yield, discovered new vegetables, and delighted in sharing harvests with others. By the time I left for college my grandfather and I

had become friends. I thank gardening to this day because two years later he died from a brain tumor.

The benefits of gardening are numerous. Ornamental plants provide opportunities for enjoyment, inspiration, creativity, and satisfaction. They add value, curb appeal, and outdoor living opportunities to homes, along with offering privacy and personality. Edible plants furnish healthy sustenance. Native plants supply food and habitat, sustaining natural systems. Gardening also evokes memories of loved ones, reminds me of childhood influences, and reconnects me to nature and my early development. Connections . . . it is my hope that they become part of your gardening experience as well.

I learned early to appreciate even the smallest of forest floor plants such as princess-pine (*Lycopodium obscurum*) and emerging ferns.

INTRODUCTION

Fans of Stephen King will know that he connects with readers by talking directly to them using the affectionate term "Constant Reader" because he realizes they continue to read his books. I'm hoping that you use this book as a go-to gardening reference, thus becoming my "Constant Gardener." Because gardening is experiential, I believe best advice comes from those who have dirt under their nails. I share advice based on as much actual experience as possible, mostly mine, but sometimes from other gardeners and horticulturalists. I have attempted to simplify complex topics, remove as much dryness as possible, and base as much on real life as I can.

Successful gardens start with durable plants.

I WILL TAKE YOU through the book as King does his Constant Reader and I hope we will develop a rapport that makes you excited about gardening.

The best incentive for long-term gardening is early success. If conditions beyond your knowledge and control frustrate you, you are likely to think you are a poor gardener (the proverbial "brown thumb"). Discouraged novices quit and never feel the satisfaction gardening can add to their lives. Here is an analogy. For a number of years I worked part-time in the camping department of a sporting goods store and outfitted many families that were going camping for the first time. In Wisconsin, the first outing is often Memorial Day weekend, which can be cold, rainy, and unpleasant. If I did not outfit newbies with the right tent, sleeping bags, and clothing, and it rained—the tent leaked, the sleeping bags got soaked, and they woke wet and cold—all those supplies probably never saw the light of day again. Gardening is much like this. If you aren't outfitted with knowledge, the right plants, the correct tools, a basic understanding of soil science, and other factors, you may become an "unhappy camper" and give up gardening. After all, it isn't something one *has* to do. Solving challenges should be rewarding rather than obstacles or failures, if one is forearmed with knowledge. My greatest reward in teaching is to see the look of relief on peoples' faces when they realize an existing problem is not because they are poor gardeners, and enlightenment when they comprehend how to correct issues.

In the following chapters I will discuss the most basic concepts of good gardening practices in the Midwest. I want you to discover what makes the Midwest unique from the rest of the country and understand that variations exist within it. I will spend time on the most overlooked (yet most essential topic) of soils and culture, and cover pests and diseases. I'll broach low-impact gardening and weave it all together with appealing design. Midwesterners face gardening challenges unlike other parts of the country, but we have our own plant palette of exciting plants indigenous to our region alone. The plant section contains more than two hundred selections of annuals, perennials, trees, and shrubs to round out the book.

Gardening is one of the most enjoyable activities available that connects us with the natural world. However, it presents many challenges for amateur and even advanced gardeners. It is implausible to think that one book will have every solution and even the best botanical/horticultural minds will never achieve a fraction of possible plant science knowledge. But don't let that intimidate you. Just be aware that horticulture is not stagnant and it is beneficial to your own best practices to stay abreast of new information. Attend talks and events where professionals are willing to share new information, patronize independent garden centers that hire staff who stay current with new research, pick the brains of successful gardeners on home garden tours, build a library of garden resource books, and subscribe to regional gardening magazines. The Internet has come a long way with available horticultural knowledge but I still find it suspect and rarely use it as single source. Consider the credentials of the source.

It is my hope that this book will increase garden successes in spite of Mother Nature's hindrances. Know there will always be some failures. Embrace them and make them learning experiences. Forge forward, Constant Gardener!

Gardening should provide amusement as well as enjoyment. *Gomphocarpus physocarpus* has a common name that is easy to imagine.

ACKNOWLEDGING YOUR ROOTS

Gardening in the Midwest

GARDEN EDUCATION IN THE MIDWEST must start with some introduction as to what makes it different from the rest of the country. Most of my gardening experience concentrated on field crops and vegetable gardening, until my early thirties when I moved to Madison, Wisconsin, and seriously started ornamental gardening. I embarked on the experience like most homeowners, believing that as long as I bought plants appropriate to the area's cold hardiness zone, they would thrive similarly whether I was in New York or Wisconsin. After several years of watching rhododendrons and blueberries flounder, tea roses flower sporadically, and conifer foliage scorch in winter—all plants that had flourished with minimal care in New York—it dawned on me that there had to be more to garden success than zone. In my progression from amateur to professional, I have developed such conviction that regional differences truly are the most important gardening factors, all of my current teaching, writing, and speaking now reference it in some way.

When I started gardening as an adult and transitioned from vegetables to ornamentals, I had some past knowledge and experience. That is not true for

The contour of the Midwest ranges from thousands of acres of flat prairies and plains to bluffs and escarpments formed by glacial action.

many in the generations following my age group. Some of you may be starting at a disadvantage, with little plant and soil biology knowledge, much less the concept that regionality will heavily influence your gardening efforts.

The cliché "forewarned is forearmed" applies well to gardening, but education, education, *education* is even more useful. You will discover it is easy to find unlimited information about plant materials from books, magazines, Internet, classes, and other venues, but the first obstacle is to understand regional differences and put gardening information into that context. I guarantee that the basic information you learn about coral bells, for example, will need to be adjusted based on the area of the country where you live and garden. Variations in color, size, and form of 'Georgia Peach' will be dramatic enough that it may look like a different plant in Portland, Oregon, than in my Midwest garden. And survival—well that's an additional factor!

THE MIDWEST: A BREAKDOWN

The Midwest is unlike any other area of the continent for gardening and includes dramatically different areas with their own geographical, environmental, and cultural idiosyncrasies. That may seem both obvious and an understatement; however, I find that this basic fact is often overlooked by beginning, and

A first-year *Heuchera* 'Georgia Peach' shines in Terra Nova's display garden in Portland, Oregon.

A plant of the same age in my Wisconsin garden takes on a different color.

sometimes advanced, gardeners. What exactly do we mean by "Midwest"? The term has as many cultural connotations as it does geographical, but for the purpose of this book, it describes an area including North Dakota, South Dakota, Nebraska, Kansas, Minnesota, Iowa, Missouri, Wisconsin, Illinois, Indiana, Michigan, and Ohio, along with southern Manitoba, Ontario, and Saskatchewan. I will continue to simplify this very complex and diverse area by referring to it simply as the Midwest.

The Midwest falls into two major ecoregions: the temperate broadleaf and mixed forest ecoregion, and the temperate grasslands, savannas, and shrubland ecoregion. Both stretch expansively from Canada to southern borders of our region, which means that even though the habitats are the same, they span hardiness zones. The characteristic habitat of the former is dominated by broadleaf trees and includes oaks, beeches, maples, and birches, with a mix of conifers including pines, firs, and spruces. The latter is a terrestrial biome whose vegetation consists of grasses and/or shrubs. So we start our regional breakdown knowing that whereas trees dominated the ecosystem of the eastern broadleaf and mixed forest region, to the west shortgrass prairies prevailed in semi-arid areas and tallgrass prairies dominated areas of higher rainfall. Soil types also define and separate vast areas of this region. Let's break down our region further by geographic, climatic, and cultural factors.

The expansive size of the Midwest creates significant variations in temperature, soil types, rainfall, humidity, and other climatic influences. Just within the state borders of Wisconsin, for example, there is enormous variation in geographical, environmental, and cultural factors. We see extremes in soil texture and porosity from hard-pan, acidic clay soils in the northeast to high-alkaline, limestone-based escarpments in the southwest, to pure sand in the central portion of the state. USDA cold hardiness zones range from 3 to 6. These are only a few examples of fluctuations within a portion of a larger region.

In order to break down the Midwest region further, I use five identifiable range designations that others have already named: South of the Boreal, Great Lakes, Prairie, Plains, and Lower Midwest.

Few regions in the country vary as dramatically in climates as the Midwest, with cold hardiness zones from 2 to 7. Extreme heat and extreme cold, drought and floods, tornados and straight-line winds, humid and arid—the gamut runs amok here.

A range can be defined as the region throughout which a kind of organism or ecological community naturally lives or occurs, as well as the distance between possible extremes. Ranges cross state boundaries and vary considerably in expanse. Keep in mind, too, that transitional zones exist between the ranges, every range will have variable localities, and every locality will have its idiosyncratic micro-climates. You now know why culture becomes the dominant theme of this book.

The Midwest: Geographic Historical Perspective

The Midwest was heavily shaped and influenced by glaciers that not only carved out the Great Lakes but also shaped the gently rolling plains. The retreating glaciers formed a massive lake whose dried bed now includes part of North Dakota and Minnesota's Red River Valley. Glacier carving and retreat meant that the mountains of the Midwest would never be large; even the Ozarks are old, worn to rolling hills of clay and limestone. I marvel at bluffs and hills created by the nation's largest river systems—the Mississippi, Missouri, and Ohio Rivers—carving and winding their way through rolling landscapes. The glacier carved these rivers and deposited debris that provides alluvial richness in one area but scraped, limited-soil rocky escarpment in others. In general, middle America is considered flat; even our highest mountains are called the Black Hills.

Although the Midwest doesn't contain major mountain ranges, it possesses extremely large rivers and lakes.

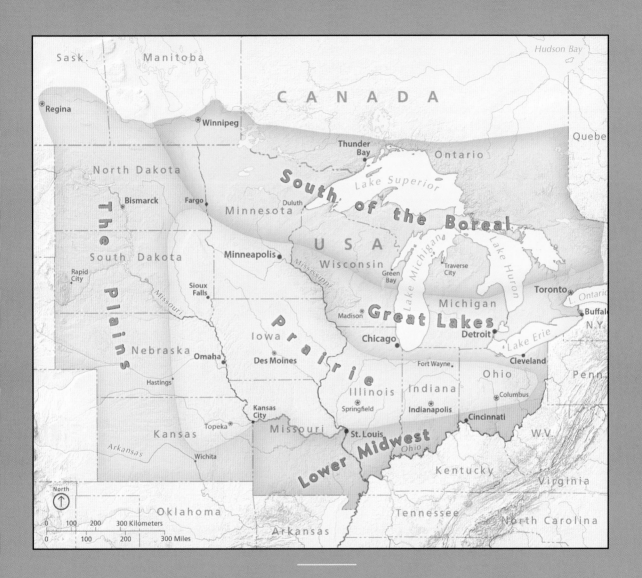

The Midwest area covered in this book is truly "middle America." Distinctively different topography and environmental variations define five large ranges within the Midwest. The lines that differentiate ranges here do not exist as distinct borders; rather there are transitional zones of gradual change from one range to another.

No clear lines separate ranges or regions. For instance, this Kansas City garden sits near the borders of what I define as Lower Midwest and the Plains. Temperatures may be moderate and springs early, but there are no guarantees that snow and ice won't remain once plants start blooming.

South of the Boreal

I remember a history class description of the eastern half of North America when it was first discovered by our forefathers. The topography they faced was reportedly characterized by a squirrel's ability to travel from the eastern seaboard to the Mississippi River, from tree to tree, never touching the ground. Old-growth forests are gone but this range—extending from south of Lake Winnipeg in Manitoba eastward into southern Ontario and northern Minnesota, Wisconsin, and Michigan—is reminiscent of the feeling they must have evoked. The northern border of this area is the boreal forest with vegetation composed primarily of conifers. Winters are long and annual precipitation is moderate to high.

Those of us in southern Wisconsin joke with our northern neighbors that they have two seasons: winter and August.

Gardening in these climes develops appreciation for color intensified by cooler temperatures, and many plants struggling with fungal foliar afflictions in the south remain clean and healthy in lower humidity. Deeper and more reliable snow cover provides consistent winter protection for perennials, and the soils tend to be better drained, often even sandy. I was invited to speak in Marquette, Michigan, once and as I was making the drive, I was wondering how I was going to generate excitement about an area I assumed was cold longer than it was warm. However, as I neared the Michigan border,

I noticed home gardens with lupines, poppies, and delphiniums. Gardeners in my area would love to grow these flowering perennials, but give up on them because they fail in our heavy soils. I believe I made the crowd quite happy when I announced that they were succeeding with plants that wouldn't survive in Madison!

Because this range is less populated and has avoided heavy agricultural tillage, the soils tend to be more fertile, have escaped major disturbance and compaction, and still support the necessary biological soil food web. Rich, brown forest soils, or alfisols, are created from autumn leaf-fall, providing abundant and rich humus, which decays rapidly in spring with rains and melting snow. The farther south in the range, the more the broadleaf trees dominate and conifers thin out. Deciduous trees utilize more soil nutrients, and decaying foliage binds nitrogen and other essential elements. This is part of the reason that soil pH increases where conifers ebb and aluminum and iron are not readily available to plants.

The Great Lakes

True lake effect is what defines the Great Lakes range, along with climatic and soil differences. The range encompasses the southern halves of Wisconsin and Michigan; northern Indiana, Illinois, and Ohio; as well as a portion of Ontario between Lakes Huron and Erie. On the north and west sides of these massive water masses, the soils contain less organic matter and are cooler. The vegetation is similar to that of the South of the Boreal range where conifers are a dominating force. The southern borders are warmer and progress from sand dunes to marshland to deciduous forests and rich soils that support agriculture. Some of the largest wholesale nurseries were established in areas such as Lake County, Ohio, and along Lake Michigan's western shore because of superb soils and moderated climates.

South of the Boreal, residents garden with plants that flourish in a short season and cool summer temperatures.

Lake effect is usually used in reference to snow, but it is a broader precipitation term. Lake effect moisture is created when a mass of cold air moves over a body of warmer water and creates an unstable temperature profile in the atmosphere. This causes the formation of clouds that eventually develop into rain or snow showers. The side of the lake where the wind starts will be drier and have less snow cover, the side of the lake where the wind ends will receive more moisture and, as a result, have the title "snow belt." When clouds that picked up moisture over the lake hit land, the change in terrestrial temperature causes the system to start dropping that moisture. Consistent snow cover and adequate moisture make the eastern and southern shores more moderate; springs warm up slower, which most plants prefer. Even though spring starts cooler, seasonal temperatures average ten degrees warmer and temperatures remain warmer into fall, thus avoiding early killing frosts. The western and northern borders warm up earlier in the spring due to the moderating effects of the huge expanse of water, but are cooler and drier through the growing season and into fall. The lakes

affect all of the bordering states to some degree, but the most dramatic effects occur within sixty or so miles of their borders.

As one moves away from the proximity of the lakes, undisturbed soils are fairly deep and rich in organic matter. The predominant woodland is dry deciduous forest. "Dry" is important because shade gardeners in the Great Lakes region struggle with the concept that shade is not moist. On average, summers tend to be hot and humid; winters provide fairly consistent ground moisture and snow cover, but very low humidity. The growing season is long enough for most perennials and vegetables, and the four seasons are very distinct and somewhat equal in duration.

The Prairie

Shortgrass and tallgrass: these two word combinations define this range. Portions of Ohio, Indiana, Illinois, Iowa, Missouri, and Minnesota were home to the original tallgrass prairie, the "sea of grass" that pioneers encountered in their western expansion. Adequate moisture allows grasses and forbs to reach impressive heights, but they start to diminish by the time they reach the eastern portions of Kansas, Nebraska, and the Dakotas. Here start hundreds more miles of flat topography, now through shortgrass prairie, better adapted to drying winds, harsher winters, and scorching summers. Other than some patches of forest in the east, prairie grasses determined soils and land use. Grasses defined Midwest hardiness with extremely deep roots that made them vigorous and long-lived. Over time, the accumulation of organic matter created dense and deep sod that was exploited by man as he turned it into agriculture.

OPPOSITE Gardening in the Great Lakes range is heavily influenced by proximity to four of the five lakes.

TOP Rich, grass-formed soils (where still prevalent) are the deepest of the Prairie range, supporting some of the tallest grasses and perennials. ABOVE If you think tropical and exotic are possible only in southern climes, take a look at this private home in Minneapolis.

These were some of the most fertile soils on the continent. A minuscule fraction of original prairie still exists and today's gardener deals with soils that were likely tilled at some point, which means poorer soil structure than areas north. Cities, towns, and suburban areas are still surrounded by acres of flat farmland. Climate fluctuates less and temperatures are more moderate in the eastern portion, but overall this range typically experiences hot, sultry summers and cold, arid winters. Desiccating winds are a larger consideration and this part of the Midwest is more likely to experience drought.

The Plains

When I researched public gardens of the Midwest, this range came up significantly short. Geological history of Saskatchewan south through the western Dakotas, Nebraska, and Kansas tells a harsh story. The same glacier that gently carved drumlins (elongated hills formed by glaciers) and moraines (less geometrically defined glacial masses), depositing rich sediment in the north-central Midwest where I live, crushed the land mass of the Plains and created streams and canyons with thin soils. Shortgrass and midgrass prairies dominated areas with soils so shallow and dry that woody plants failed to establish and thrive. Pre-agricultural history included lightning-induced grass fires, sweeping winds, chilling winters, and hot, dry summers.

Gardeners of this range, I bow to you. The gardening issues I complain about pale in comparison to your challenges: open land with few windbreaks for dry, hot summer winds that turn desiccating and frigid in winter; thin soils that were further compromised by tillage and high pH; and shallow soils that make it hard to support canopy trees. It is no wonder I struggle to find gardening venues and resources on the western edge of the Midwest. But gorgeous and inspirational gardens are created by intrepid gardeners who embrace these challenges, by either maximizing native plants or modifying their conditions for resilient ornamentals, or even combining the two. Since the gardening season can be short, it is an opportunity to embrace saucy annuals and exotic tropicals for fast growth and continuous color.

The Lower Midwest

Topography rules the Lower Midwest, which includes the southernmost reaches of Ohio, Indiana, Illinois, and Missouri. The flat plains of the northern border transition to oak- and hickory-covered hills, formed by streams and rivers carved through an upland plateau. West of the Mississippi River, the Ozark Mountains boast the only real peaks of the Midwest populated in oaks and pines, gently cascading down to the prairie edge of northern Missouri. Winter temperatures are the most moderate of the Midwest and moisture is generally not an issue. The siting between northern areas (where spring and fall are short due to cold), and southern areas (where those seasons are fleeting due to heat) means that all four seasons last longer and each is fairly moderate. Extremes give way to more subtle transitions.

Settlers from the Southeast had a major influence on this area. Native redbuds, sugar maples, sweet gum, and flowering dogwoods balance imported southern Magnolia and crepe myrtle, as new residents built plantations reminiscent of home. Towering, tall trees such as the native tulip tree were as important for shading stately homes in humid summers as they were to lining long drives to the estates.

LOCALITY AND MICROCLIMATE

Successful gardening requires a firm understanding of region, but it is equally important to further acknowledge the variability of effects found within

The Plains range combines some of the most severe fluctuations in temperature with some of the poorest soils. Gardeners here have to be as determined as the native plants, like these in the South Dakota Badlands.

ranges, and even smaller, within localities and microclimates. Let's start with locality: the area or neighborhood in which you live. This may still involve large areas. I consider rural, suburban, or urban part of your locality. For instance, I garden on older Main Street, within a small village with new subdivisions, ten miles from downtown Madison, and a mile from rural farm fields and forested woodland. In spite of the proximity of all five of these areas within a ten-mile radius, each has dramatically different gardening conditions.

Think about differences in soils alone on each site. The wood lot probably has fairly undisturbed soils, created by falling leaves and debris and active microbes. The soil texture of the farm fields have been highly modified from years of tillage and contamination by fertilizers and pesticides. My 1897 Victorian house had a hand-dug basement, so surrounding soil is original to the site. The subdivisions were built at a time when contractors removed valuable topsoil, sold it for profit, replaced it with poor soils from excavating the basements, and added back 4 to 6 in. of topsoil, likely not even original to the site. Downtown Madison homes may still sit on original soils, but years of mechanical compaction, urban renewal, proximity to massive areas covered in asphalt and concrete, heavy salt and chemical use, and other factors have created yet different soil

Moderate seasons with early springs and short winters balance hot, humid Lower Midwest summers.

composition. Here we have five sites that are in the same region, range, and locality, but have dramatically different situations in soils alone. We haven't even broached differences in sun, shade, wind, runoff, and other mitigating factors.

Microclimate is a term that is used to describe local atmospheric locations where the climate differs from surrounding areas. Many things can affect that variation but gardeners picked up the term and modified it to cultural conditions that influence their gardens. The difference must be significantly favorable enough to plant sensitivities that would cause them to fail to thrive or die in the surrounding unprotected landscape. A microclimate can be created as simply as providing blockage from desiccating wind. A wall, hedge, side of the house, fence: all of these can protect a wind-sensitive plant from drying or chilling breezes. Suburban and urban yards tend to be microclimates compared to surrounding rural countryside. Buildings and canopy trees provide blockage from sweeping winds; large amounts of concrete and asphalt within the municipality keep frosts at bay longer, heating the area up quicker in spring; and the sides of homes, walls, and fences hold warmth within the yard.

I consider the ability to heavily modify soils an important form of microclimate as well. Amending garden beds to dramatically increase organic matter content, improve porosity and texture, encourage deep rooting for winter survival and drought tolerance, entice beneficial microbial and biotic activity, and promote natural fertility also allows one to grow plants that would otherwise fail outside the perimeters of the garden. I boast zone 6 plants in my zone 5 garden by providing ideal soil conditions, which make as much or, in some cases, more difference than protecting the top portions from the elements. My adjoining neighbors could not grow the same plants with the soils in their yards.

The farm fields in the foreground were exposed to several hundred years of soil modification before the homes in the background were built. None of the original ecosystem remains.

THE ALLURE OF ZONE

The single word "zone" is shorthand for "USDA plant hardiness zone." This originally referred only to the average annual extreme *minimum* temperature that a designated plant is expected to survive. Recently we recognized that plants possess heat stress limits, so the American Horticultural Society developed an AHS heat zone map. Since cold hardiness zones have been the standard for a much longer time period, and cold temperatures tend to be more critical to plant survival for much of the country, I use "zone" in reference to the USDA map. You folks in the Lower Midwest may utilize both. Hardiness zones are based on a thirty-year period of the past, not the lowest average temperature that has ever occurred or might occur in the future. There have been several versions of this map, with the most recent update in 2012.

As you can imagine, weather data recording has become more sophisticated over time, so the more years of data collection, the more accurate the information. As it is, the data for the 2012 map does not include even the most recent years, it supports data collected from 1976 through 2005. Visit the USDA's site at planthardiness.ars.usda.gov where you can select your state as an expanded view. The 2012 USDA Plant Hardiness Zone Map is based on the average annual minimum winter temperature, divided into 10-degree F zones. Each zone is further divided into "a" and "b" 5-degree subzones ("a" is colder). A sophisticated algorithm was used to interpolate low-temperature values between actual weather reporting stations, so it is considered more accurate than previous versions. Thus a hardiness zone is a geographically defined area in which plants are capable of surviving the minimum temperatures of that zone. For example, a plant that is described as hardy to zone 5a means that it can withstand a minimum temperature of −20 degrees F. That plant would be expected to die if temperatures dropped below that for any duration of time. A more "winter hardy" zone 4a plant would tolerate dropping to −30 degrees F.

The 2012 map generated a great deal of conversation when it was released because many areas of the Midwest were adjusted upward; for instance, the area in which I live went from 4b (−25 to−20 degrees F) to zone 5a (−20 to −15 degrees F). This means we could in theory grow plants more sensitive to cold temperatures than in the past because the new map showed average minimum temperatures had risen over time. My volunteers noticed the change immediately, and I received a lot of emails asking what that meant. I jokingly responded that everyone needed to go out to their gardens and have a stern talk with their zone 5 plants, telling them there was no longer any valid reason they shouldn't survive! Additionally, it does not preclude an isolated zone 4 winter in zone 5 that will kill plants that had survived average winters.

I don't know if we have been remiss as horticulturists or if it is the result of how plants are marketed (I expect a combination of both), but we have inadvertently trained our garden consumers into believing that zones are the definitive criteria for plant survival. We market ornamental plants with the implication that if they match zone, they will thrive. But many factors other than just zone influence plant survival in your garden: soil structure (porosity, density, pH, and texture), organic matter content, soil biology, winter protection, microclimates, fertility, and other cultural influences.

For an example of why zone is not the definitive factor for determining plant hardiness, let's take a look at Oswego, New York, and Denver, Colorado—both are the same zone 5 as my garden in Madison, Wisconsin. Plants in Oswego, which sits near Lake Ontario with deep, friable, rich, and porous soils, are covered in lake-effect snows all winter, protecting them from temperature extremes and wind with spring water excess draining away from plant crowns and friable soils preventing soil heaving. Around Denver, plants are indigenous to deep, well-drained, gravelly or sandy soils; winter winds are free of damaging humidity; and deep roots allow winter survival even without snow cover. My garden plants are subjected to heavy clay soils, extremely wet springs that turn into droughty summers, heaving soils in spring, and winters with alternating snow, rain, and ice. These three locations have dramatically different conditions and very few zone 5 plants could thrive in all three.

Provenance

Another lesser-known influence is provenance. Provenance is a term gardeners rarely hear that is infrequently used in general marketing. Many plants are indigenous to very large native ranges and, as a result, develop their own individual populations

Eastern redbud's expansive native range (zones 5 to 9) makes it the poster child for provenance issues. When trees end up in Midwest retail outlets, it is generally impossible to identify the seed source. Redbuds from zone 8 Georgia populations, for example, haven't evolved or adapted to cold winters and will not survive zone 5.

with specific cultural restrictions and hardiness. The coldest zone for which they will be labeled is the northernmost range, not the entire population. This becomes an issue because it is usually impossible to determine seed source at the retailer. Your best solution lies in two options. One is to patronize local independent garden centers and nurseries that have some idea of the lineage of the plants they purchase for resale. It is highly unlikely that mass merchandisers have any idea of the seed source of their plants. They utilize brokers who buy plants from all over the country based on price, not location or provenance. The other option is to look for cultivars, if they exist, developed in your zone. Breeding and plant selection can improve plant hardiness.

Provenance tends to be used as a term for woody plants and not perennials because it affects cold survival as well as cultural factors. We tend to blame cultural conditions different from the native site as the primary reason for unthrifty perennials,

On Changing Plant Habits

There is only so much plant biology you can change. Botany teaches us plant processes and interactions—in short, how a plant works. Complex plant biology has taken millions of years to develop. Plants adapt slowly over eons to find their niche in unique geographical, climatic, and environmental conditions. Carnivorous plants such as pitcher plants adapted to capturing insects. In highly acidic conditions, such as northern Midwest peat bogs, plants cannot take up enough nitrogen to survive. A plant that adapts to capture insects digests them for necessary nitrogen that the roots are unable to provide. Now we have a plant that has adapted to grow where other plants can't and it thrives without competition. This is a biological function the plant cannot change. Take away its source of insect nutrition and it will die in the peat.

The word ornamental is used to describe plants selected for features that make them more interesting or more durable in the domesticated garden than they were in nature. Exotic refers to non-native. Selecting for genetic differences in color, form, shape, or other garden-worthy virtues does not change their biological requirements. It may make them more disease and insect resistant, more robust, and more tolerant of environmental factors; that is the general goal of plant breeding. But some factors take years and years to change significantly. Knowing the biological history of a plant and where it is naturally indigenous will tell you a great deal about how it is likely to perform in your garden, and why it behaves the way it does. Although exceptions exist, most plants remain adversely sensitive to cultural conditions different from those of their native environments.

but cultural requirements are part of that plant's evolution and adaptation within its provenance. Cultural considerations are easier to modify than cold tolerance.

EXCEPTIONS TO THE RULES

The same plant can thrive in one garden and fail in another. The primary reason is that educated and experienced gardeners provide as close to ideal conditions as possible, understanding the needs of each plant. However, from time to time you will run across gardeners who defy the rules. I worked for almost ten years with a nursery where I lost count of the times I would advise someone against a plant because it would not survive locally—only to have them return at some point to tell me it was thriving in their garden. It happens! As horticulturalists, we

have to advise according to what is the norm, not the rare unexplainable exceptions.

Genetic mutations can also result in plants flouting their zone. It is exciting to find plants thriving where they shouldn't, because it is possible it might be due to a genetic modification that makes the plant superior. Sometimes propagating from that plant will create a new cultivar that carries the same exceptional trait; sometimes it is not a genetic advancement at all but an unexplainable fluke. Many new and improved cultivars come from such outliers; others disappoint. Flowering dogwood is not reliably hardy in the Madison area but one tree in the city has grown into a healthy, mature specimen. Numerous attempts have been made to propagate from this tree in the hopes that it has a naturally occurring genetic mutation that makes it hardy. But as far as I know, no progeny any hardier than the species has been generated, so it remains an enigma.

Sometimes survival in defiance of zone is as simple as the plant hasn't been trialed sufficiently to accurately gauge its true adaptive abilities to new growing sites. When plant exploration brings a new plant into the country, suppliers have to provide a hardiness designation as part of necessary marketing tools. There is no better way to gauge it than by the climatic conditions where it was found. That is a logical place to start, but different cultural conditions in another area could either improve or decrease its hardiness in the new environs. In such cases, it can sometimes take years for anecdotal evidence to change its zone designation in the new location.

Regardless of the many reasons we find outliers to the rules, the most common reason a plant will defy its zone is that we provide it with ideal or better conditions than where it was indigenous. I am successfully growing zone 6 plants in my zone 5 garden because I have provided cultural conditions that make up for the zone deficiency. As one advances gardening skills, this is a challenge embraced as "fun"; succeeding gives us a great sense of accomplishment. I have also killed a lot of plants. I have not been able to find the source of this quote, but I once heard it said, "Plants don't die. We kill plants." That quote keeps me humble as a gardener. Plants die because we plant them in the wrong site, don't provide the essentials, or neglect them. But they also fail because of factors beyond our control: unseasonable temperatures and weather conditions; pests and diseases; rodents and deer; contaminants from neighbors, droughts, and floods; and numerous other variables. Nature is not easy to control, so gardening at the mercy of elements isn't necessarily for the faint of heart, but, in the same regard, successes will provide you with rewards and satisfaction worth the effort. Don't be afraid to experiment. The

Epimedium (barrenwort) is a relatively recent import to U.S. gardens that required experimentation to determine hardiness outside its native Asian ranges.

term "pushing the envelope" is used commonly to describe discovering ways to succeed with plants not considered hardy. It takes gardening to a new level and it is fun to brag when it works. If it doesn't, consider it knowledge gained. Like many gardeners, I joke that I won't give up on a particular plant until I've killed it three times!

Cultural Considerations

GARDENING IN ANY REGION includes geographical, environmental, and cultural considerations. This chapter addresses cultural conditions. I begin at the root of the matter with the importance of soil and soil quality: the very foundation of successful gardening. Then I delve into low-impact gardening by addressing practices with low impact on the human body and garden space as well as minimal negative impact on the environment. I finish with the scourges of the garden: the insects, diseases, and pests no gardener escapes entirely and which change continually over time. Unlike the geographical and environmental conditions, the cultural issues discussed in this section are ones we can modify, change, or avoid.

IT STARTS WITH THE EARTH

Midwest gardeners cannot ignore soils. In the northern portion of the region, typical summers are hot, so soils dry out easily and are prone to drought. In contrast, winters freeze ground solid; frost depths are often measured in feet. Weather fluctuations cause soils to heave in winter-to-spring transition,

No matter how overused *Echinacea purpurea* and *Rudbeckia fulgida* var. *sullivantii* 'Goldsturm' may seem, they have proven their worth as durable Midwest garden plants.

ripping root systems apart, killing more plants than cold temperatures. Key to plant survival is deep rooting: for drought survival, to combat heaving, and for overall durability. In the Lower Midwest, winters are milder and frosts are less damaging but hot, humid summers are equally brutal on plants that lack the deep organic matter that provides good drainage and even moisture to roots. In my estimation, soil depth and quality are the most critical determinants to gardening success.

Soil is a Living Thing

The subtle awareness that soil is living will change how you work in garden soil forever. As my first soils professor memorably impressed upon me, soil is not dirt! Dirt is inert material with highly variable composition that may or may not include soil components. I expect it comes as no surprise to gardeners that soils have complex chemical and physical properties (including minerals, water, and air), but few people think of soil as a biological system that contains biotic (living and once-living organisms) components. This makes it a living food web. Don't let "complex" intimidate you: all natural systems are complexly integrated. However, some basic truths should guide your gardening efforts without you having to become a soil scientist. Once you understand the multifaceted systems that define quality

Organically rich, deep, friable soils are ideal for setting deep roots that survive winter, drought, and compaction.

When purchasing or creating garden soil, make sure it contains both mineral and organic matter.

soils, and understand the biotic portion, thinking and using "soil" instead of "dirt" will serve as a subconscious reminder that we manage living systems very differently than we do inert.

The Parents: Minerals and Organic Matter

The first ingredient of soil is parent bedrock that has eroded into minerals that clump into aggregates. The other ingredient is organic matter: anything that was once living (plant or animal), has died, and become part of a layer of decomposition (compost). Gardeners should keep forefront in their minds that organic matter is the critical portion of the biological equation that provides nutrients naturally to plants and allows soils to retain moisture. Soil value and properties are determined by the quality and quantities of both minerals and organic matter.

Soil did not evolve simply as two layers, bedrock on bottom and organic matter on top. Soil scientists refer to soil horizons, defining (1) an A horizon as surface layer, predominantly organic matter and dark in color, (2) a B horizon with clay and iron oxide accumulation leached down from A and, (3) a C

horizon as solid parent bedrock material. In nature, new material is constantly added to the A horizon, the layer most important to you as a gardener. Foliage and branches drop, plants die, surface rocks erode, and animals defecate and die. Organic matter accumulation is in a constant state of decomposition, which is accelerated by living organisms, heat, and water. Keeping this layer deep, porous, and friable (crumbly, not solid) is important to leach clays, oxides, and other deleterious materials beyond the reach of roots. Soil surface is constantly eroded by wind, water, and human activities. Soil creation from deeper bedrock parent material through weathering is extremely slow. It is important to think of soil in three dimensions, and to understand that soil has depth as well as area.

Inadequate organic matter is the number one culprit causing issues I encounter when advising gardeners. It is unlikely you will ever have too much organic matter or no need to replenish. Most gardens start on sites stripped of deep, indigenous A horizons that are already years in deficit. Gardeners do not acknowledge that organic matter disappears over time. Hot temperatures and excessive watering accelerate decomposition. Gardens in the Lower Midwest will need organic matter replenishment far more often than those in northern ranges.

I often joke about the most common cultural descriptor you will find listed as ideal for most garden plants: "evenly moist, well-drained soils." Think about that oxymoronic combination. How often are your garden soils draining adequately while staying consistently and evenly moist? This is especially true for the Midwest's hot, dry summers. I spend a considerable amount of time watering to achieve "evenly moist" soils. Conversely, plants appreciate less water in winter. The best way to reach this ideal is with high levels of organic matter. Organic matter retains water while providing adequate pore space for drainage.

Pores are Important

Let's take the difference between soil and dirt one step further. The soil ingredients we've discussed so far are solid. But the remaining two components of soil are liquid (water) and gas (air). Soil is composed of solid particles (minerals and organic matter) and pore space (water and air). Water is inherently logical. Gardeners understand soils require moisture; too much or too little causes death. Moisture content is dependent upon amount of organic matter and pore space. Organic matter attracts and binds water. Pores allow movement. Too little pore space means soils won't drain adequately; oversaturation for extended periods causes flooding. Too much pore space allows water to drain too quickly and causes drought conditions. Ideal soils for agriculture and gardening contain equal ratios of air space to solid particle. That balance creates excellent porosity, allowing for moisture retention for healthy roots, while providing adequate drainage.

Another reason we need adequate pore space is

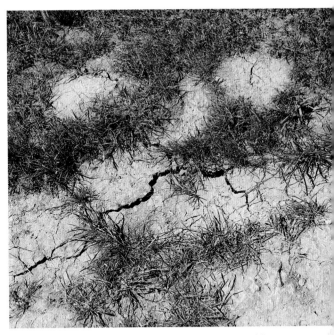

Soils deficient in organic matter compact and deter healthy root growth. As evident here, they hold no water reserve in time of drought.

a function of soil structure: friability. Soil structure has become a hot topic in recent years, as we learn the adverse effects of soil compaction. Structure influences soil particle aggregation. Structure, along with texture (the size of mineral particles), affects pore size and space. Dense or compacted structure greatly reduces the amount of air and water that can move through soil and restricts root penetration. The more we research, the more we realize the impact of compaction; even minimal amounts over time have larger implications than previously thought. The most practical and successful way to increase pore space is, you guessed it, to add organic matter. To summarize porosity, pore space is important for drainage, oxygen content, and friability. The size, distribution, and shape of the solid particles and the size and number of pore spaces characterize every soil type.

Soil Texture

Mineral particles range in size from fine to coarse, with clay as finest, then silt, and finally sand as the most coarse. The percentage of each in soil determines what we call soil texture; whether a soil is classified as sandy, silty, clayey, or a combination. Because of the disparity in particle size, an ideal soil will not contain equal percentages of each. A balanced soil is considered loam, containing 40 percent sand, 40 percent silt, and 20 percent clay.

Sand particles are the only ones large enough to be seen with the naked eye. Sandy soil has a gritty feel (coarse textured) when rubbed between fingers. Silt particles are smaller and feel powdery (like flour) and do not hold together well when wet, although they are more cohesive than sandy soils. Clay is the smallest particle with many minute pore spaces. This may seem counterintuitive, but remember: more particles per unit means more total exterior surface area, thus more pore space. The problem is that those pores are minuscule spaces, too small for air and water movement. Water fills the spaces but is not able to flow. Soils with a high number of clay particles have very high water-holding capacity and are very fine textured, making them feel smooth and sticky (like soap) when wet.

In the simplest terms, too much sand means too much drainage with no water retention, too much clay means no drainage with no root penetration. Sand particles are large with uneven edges, creating large pore spaces, whereas infinitesimally small-sized clay is so uniform it packs together extremely tightly. To emphasize further the relative size of particles, imagine you are holding a clay particle the size of a grain of salt in your hand. A silt particle next to it would be the size of a mint. A sand particle would be the size of a stove! (The ratio is about 1:26:1025.)

This is important information for gardeners dealing with dense, clay-heavy soils. Most areas of the region have areas with clay soils but this challenge is most prevalent around homes, especially those constructed after the 1950s. This is when the method of new home building changed to stripping the topsoil and storing for later resale, digging out the clay subsurface and spreading it across the property, then bringing back a few inches of topsoil to cover it. Few homes built in recent history possess their original topsoil, and most contain substantially altered soil layers compacted by heavy equipment and featuring unearthed deep clay.

One would think the solution would be to add larger particles such as sand to create larger pores. In fact, some products such as gypsum and others labeled as "clay busters" are sold with this misleading claim. To understand the fallacy, return to the infinitesimally small size of clay particles. In order to

Benefits of Organic Matter

- Provides fertility and nutrients, especially nitrogen, as it is decomposed by microorganisms.
- Binds soil particles together so they resist erosion.
- Improves soil structure and porosity which allows water, air, and nutrients to move readily to living organisms.
- Strong absorber of pollutants such as pesticides, organic wastes, and heavy metals.

You can improve existing beds by annual and semi-annual compost applications around plants. Plants "rise" with annual applications; you will not bury them over time. I use wood mulch in spring because of its season-long attributes of water retention, weed blocking, and soil-crusting prevention.

adequately mix clay, silt, and sand, you need to break each into fully separated particles. One small clump of clay could contain hundreds of thousands of particles. In addition, clay particles are ionically bonded, making them even more difficult to separate. So you will be mixing clumps of clay with sand, which is very similar to the process of making concrete. Never let anyone convince you to rototill or otherwise blend coarse components into clay. You will end up with a worse situation that will be even harder to correct.

The only forces capable of separating clay particles are natural dynamisms, which may take centuries, or the activity of living organisms. Earthworms, nematodes, microbes, and other biotic organisms effectively separate particles over time and their detritus adds organic matter in minute spaces that human interaction can never separate. These organisms cannot survive in clay, so introducing them requires providing food and a medium that allows mobility: organic matter. Improving heavy

My fall compost application serves also as protective winter cover; plants emerge easily through this porous material.

soils takes time. Begin the process by adding layers of compost regularly to the top of your existing soil. Do not attempt to mix. Living organisms will multiply every year and start breaking down particles, mixing transitional zones between compost and clay. Year by year, the transition zone will improve in a downward process. Once improved, plant roots will begin penetrating what had been previously impassable and assist the clay-busting process. Adding layers of compost is called berming and allows plants to establish over poor soils. When starting new beds on poor soils, berming creates deep, friable soils to provide plants with adequate growth until the transition zone improves.

Under severe clay conditions, it works best to create new beds with berms as high as reasonable and affordable for the space. Several feet, if you can do it, will give your plants depth for a good start, and survival while the clay-to-compost zone is improving. For new beds, I recommend a mix of 50 percent loam and 50 percent compost. Many garden centers or commercial supply companies will make mixes to specification. Often a product called "topsoil" is sold as loam but quality can be highly variable and may be high in mineral content and low in (or devoid of) compost. If you are not sure of the quality of the product, ask for a small sample (even if you have to purchase it) and take it to a local Cooperative

Extension office, soil lab, or similar organization for evaluation. Cooperative Extension offices often have mailing envelopes available if distance is a concern.

To improve existing beds with plants you don't wish to disturb, utilize the process of adding compost twice annually. It will take longer, but you will see significant progress in a few years. I add roughly 4 in. in spring and another 4 in. in fall. I use wood mulch in spring and compost in fall. Because each form of compost has benefits and drawbacks, I vary fall applications annually. For instance, leaf compost may be followed the next year by mushroom compost, which might be followed by composted manure. The composted forms increase the breakdown of wood mulch, improving overall quality at a fairly rapid rate compared to nature.

Conversely, some soils of the Midwest such as the Central Sands region of Wisconsin are heavily sand based. Rather than holding excess water, these soils present the difficulty of retaining moisture. The fix remains the same, however—add compost. It is faster and easier to remedy than clay because sand particles are so easy to separate and distribute in a mix. If you are in such an area and have access to topsoil, I would recommend adding a 20 percent topsoil to 80 percent compost ratio to your sandy soils.

Another word of caution. Avoid any so-called shredded or pulverized topsoil. Remember what you just learned about clay. The smaller and more uniform we make soil particles, the closer it resembles clay. Shredding soil destroys critical texture and structure. Add water to shredded soil with no added compost, and you have concrete-like conditions! "Chunky" topsoil may not be visually attractive, but it indicates that soil still has structure. Excessive rototilling and working of soil also pulverizes soil over time into small, uniform particles.

Color it Brown

Soil color reflects many soil properties and is widely used when classifying soils, but isn't generally a factor that gardeners consider. Farmers are aware of color because it influences plant growth through

TOP Pulverized soils look fine and silky but lack the structure necessary for a wide variety of macro and micro pores.
ABOVE Quality soil should be rich brown with high organic matter content, and demonstrate texture with variably sized components.

The high organic matter content in my soils melts snow before other yards on my street.

The soils in the Allen Centennial Gardens' French Garden beds appeared thin and gray and annuals were no longer growing lushly, so I knew it was time for serious remediation. I removed the existing soil and mixed 50/50 with organic matter and replaced. Note the improved color and texture.

effect on soil temperature. Dark-colored soils absorb more heat from the sun than lighter-colored soils. In spring, dark soils will be first to melt snow cover and provide early warmth for emerging plants. This makes a significant impact on how early farmers can work fields, so you can see it would also be beneficial to vegetable gardens and spring perennials. The color of soil surface horizons is related to how much organic matter is present. The snow cover on my organically rich garden melts as much as a week earlier than the neighborhood. Invariably, people will ask me if I have some form of underground heating!

A change in soil color indicates an alteration in mineral composition or amount of water present. Gray-colored soils usually indicate insufficient or declining organic matter because there is a heavier percentage of mineral to compost. When I notice thin gray soils, I know I need to add significant amounts of compost. Gray can also indicate over-saturated soils with anaerobic conditions.

Just What Is Compost?

We generally use the word compost—also called black gold—to describe human-created organic matter produced from recycled biotic materials to be used as fertilizer and soil amendment. Composting is a fairly simple process and many types of mechanical home systems are now available. Here's an important fact. A system does not insure good compost; ingredients and process do. Most people believe creating compost is as simple as throwing any type of organic refuse—from table scraps to grass clippings and leaves—into a pile and letting it heat with occasional turning. I was appalled to hear a famous garden writer quip, "There is no such thing as bad compost." I am here to tell you that is untrue.

Like soil, quality compost needs to be friable, porous, and able to sustain living beneficial micro-organisms, fauna, and bacterial activity. Improperly

Many home composting systems are available, but the ingredients are far more important than the composter. You can create excellent compost in inexpensive home systems. Make sure your system is easy to access to turn the ingredients.

balanced and treated compost can create habitats for deleterious organisms harmful to soil. Beneficial composting organisms require four equally important ingredients to work effectively similar to soils: carbon-based materials, nitrogen, oxygen, and water. Composting also requires heat.

Carbon is the basis for energy for microbial oxidation that produces the heat, as well becoming part of the organic matter. Carbon is the "brown" portion of compost, such as dry leaves, straw, hay, newspapers, and aged wood mulch.

Nitrogen is necessary for growth and to reproduce more organisms to oxidize carbon. It comes from "green" or food-based "wet" materials such as grass clippings, green plant material, leftover fruits and vegetables, coffee grounds, egg shells, and animal manure.

Oxygen is necessary for oxidizing carbon and stimulating the decomposition process. Dense, wet masses of compost do not provide enough oxygen for necessary aerobic processes for living organisms.

Water is required in decomposition processes but must be managed in correct amounts to maintain activity without causing anaerobic conditions.

Correct ratios of individual components provide beneficial bacteria with nutrients and conditions to heat the pile. A large amount of water will be released as vapor-depleting oxygen; this is why you need to occasionally turn the ingredients. As the pile continues to heat to higher temperatures, it will require more added air and water. The intent is to reach and maintain temperatures around 140 degrees F until components start breaking down. A proper air to water balance is critical to maintaining high temperatures. Too much air, water, or carbon with too little nitrogen slows the process. Now you can see why I don't consider home composting easy.

Recommendations for the most efficient composting call for a carbon to nitrogen ratio of about 30 to 1. Most plant and animal materials contain both carbon and nitrogen in varying amounts, so recommendations are two parts carbon to one part nitrogen to reach a near ideal balance. When constructing layered compost bins or garden beds use 1 inch of nitrogen-based to 2 in. of carbon-based materials. A thermometer to measure and monitor heat is useful. Compost can be used for planting once 140 degrees drops to around 100.

Mulch Can Be Compost, but Compost Isn't Always Mulch

Mulch is a term generally used for a layer of material added to the surface of ground for reasons other than adding organic matter, although the composition is usually organic and becomes compost as it degrades. Occasionally inorganic materials are used for mulching but I do not recommend them. They are generally not conducive to healthy plant growth, can be difficult to maintain once airborne weeds establish, and need to be replaced over time. It makes sense to use organic mulches because they add overall value and quality to soil as they decompose into compost.

The number one reason for mulching is to reduce weeds invading garden beds (although that philosophy is somewhat false because the highest percentage of weeds results from airborne seed). Mulch also conserves soil moisture and prevents soil crusting, allowing water to penetrate while reducing evaporation, preventing erosion and drought injury, and reducing water needs. It regulates soil temperatures by keeping roots cooler in extreme heat and further protects from winter injury. It provides

Lasagna Gardens

Lasagna gardens aren't new, but became popular with the release of Patricia Lanza's 1998 *Lasagna Gardening* book. This is not a garden planted with ingredients for making vegetarian lasagna. Lasagna gardening is really no different than the process of adding compost to your home garden; it is about creating quality soil in layers, except you build this all at once.

This form of gardening eliminates the need to dig up existing turf and is especially useful for poor soils or soilless surfaces such as asphalt or concrete. The practice is to lay down layers of the same nitrogen- and carbon-rich ingredients we discussed for composting. However, you don't periodically aerate lasagna gardens or need to watch moisture levels. It takes a few months of "baking" but creates a rich growing medium quickly. If you provide a lasagna garden with constructed sides, you have a raised bed.

The goal is to create the right combination of carbon and nitrogen, exactly as described in composting. Many diagrams of lasagna gardens look complicated because they may show a dozen ingredients. They demonstrate the various components available, but a good lasagna garden can be developed with only a few components, as long as you follow the carbon-to-nitrogen ratio.

Start by putting down thick layers of newspaper or one or two thicknesses of corrugated cardboard as the base. This kills the underlying grass and/or weeds while the top layers are "cooking." Apply 4 to 6 in. of carbon-rich items shredded into small pieces. Add 2 to 3 in. of nitrogen-rich material. Repeat the layers, making them at least 1 to 2 ft. deep; the mound height drops as layers decompose. Covering with black plastic provides heat, accelerating the process, but isn't necessary. Layers heat up to 140 degrees F as the decomposition begins and you cannot plant at this point. In around two weeks, temperatures should drop to 100 degrees F (it will feel a little warm to your touch when you insert your hand) and you should be able to plug seedlings and create furrows for seed. In subsequent years, continue to add layers to supplement decomposing organic matter.

aesthetic value, visually defining and separating individual plants and planting areas. Decomposed mulch offers nutrients as well as structure and nutrition for microorganisms. Finally, it creates buffer zones between plantings and lawn, limits mower damage to plants, and eliminates competition with turf.

Mulches can be used as winter protective cover. I apply a thick protective layer of leaves in fall that provides insulation when snow cover (which provides perennial plants with a layer of insulation from wind, cold, and desiccation) is not present. Mulch used as winter protection is much coarser and deeper than mulch used as soil amendment, and compresses down into a thick, dense mat under the weight of snow. Even though it is valuable organic matter, it is too heavy for plant emergence, so most of it has to be removed around the time of spring ephemeral emergence. The layer you remove can then go to a compost bin and later be returned to the garden as compost.

Mulch is an aesthetically pleasing way to define garden beds and provides numerous other benefits.

In late November, after rodents have found their winter homes, I apply a thick layer of leaves as further insulation. In the spring, most of the layer needs to be removed.

Wood mulch urban myths

You may have heard warnings not to use shredded bark as mulch because it ties up fertility. This is an example of misconstrued facts. It is true that microorganisms break down lignin in wood, tying up nitrogen in the process. However, this stops once wood is decomposed. Consider the location of the wood mulch: on the soil surface. Where are nitrogen-seeking roots? Well below the soil surface. They are utilizing nitrogen from surrounding compost. By the time nitrogen-limited wood mulch becomes the organic matter around roots, there is no longer nitrogen tie-up. Research has shown that nitrogen is not tied-up when soluble fertilizer passes through mulch, either.

No Room for Barriers

To understand why I abhor landscape fabric, begin with a synonym: weed barrier. Ironically, it does not effectively prevent weeds but *does* become an effective barrier to the basics necessary to quality soil! The theory behind this weed prevention claim is that noxious plants invade your garden spaces either from below or by creeping in. Although a few weeds do encroach this way, the largest percentage arrives airborne (most drift in with wind, some drop from trees, and many are deposited through bird and animal feces). I could live with the fact that fabric doesn't prevent weeds if using it created no more harm than unnecessary labor and expense. But landscape fabric creates an impermeable barrier between layers of soil. Fabric limits movement of water and oxygen between the compost on top and existing A, B, and C layers below. Over time, the soil beneath becomes anaerobic and compacted. The physical movement of organisms crucial to breaking down organic matter into released nutrients disappears under the fabric, because they also need oxygen and drainage to survive. Shut out living organisms and soil becomes an inert system.

Avoid fabric and create beds of deep, healthy soil giving ornamental plants the vigor to outcompete weeds. A 4- to 6-inch layer of mulch added annually keeps weeds at bay and contributes to soil quality as it decomposes. One of the sad facts of life is that there will always be weeds! I have used my share of landscape fabric over the years, and pulled it out after years of being in the ground. The nasty, compacted, destroyed soil I always find on the underside is alarming.

Impermeable barriers such as plastic destroy underlying soil even faster. Solid plastic, black or clear, is recommended only as a method to non-chemically kill soil pathogens and weeds. Called soil solarization, plastic sheeting is placed over soil to capture heat from the sun to kill weeds, fungi, bacteria, and some nematodes. It is not recommended for more than two years and is so effective it kills beneficial life as well as injurious. Once the plastic is removed it is generally recommended to add quality compost to the area, to jump start the necessary microbial and animal life into activity again.

Weed barriers limit and ultimately destroy healthy soil conditions and may become unsightly over time.

This misinformation gave bark mulch such a bad reputation that at one point I eliminated it altogether, giving favor to other composted materials as more fertile and friable. However, I forgot the water evaporation reduction benefit of wood mulch. Even though my soils were highly fertile and porous, they dried out too quickly and increased watering needs dramatically. Now I use bark mulch in spring and some form of heavily composted organic matter in fall. This alternating of materials has improved water retention without compromising drainage and fertility.

An advantage of bark mulch is low cost and availability; however, cypress mulch is egregiously unsustainable and should not be used. I want to warn you about a cheap source of wood mulch. Many municipalities pick up and shred woody debris left curbside. It is often available at no charge. It is shredded extremely coarse, which makes it hard to place around plants. A high percentage is freshly cut so it is "green," which means it needs at least a year of additional time to break down and decompose into useful compost. In many cases this wood has been removed from a home site because trees or shrubs succumbed to disease, insect damage, or death. Insects and disease can be transferred to your garden in green, unheated, non-composted material. Shredded wood mulches from professional suppliers have been partially composted and heat-treated to minimize disease and insect content. Research has proven that insidious verticillium wilt can survive treatment, but most commercial wood mulch does not contain wood from verticillium-susceptible trees; municipal piles may.

It Is Good To Have Chemistry

Soil pH is the most common chemistry-based issue. In the simplest terms, low pH is acidic and high pH is alkaline. Most people realize that pH ranges between 0 and 14. However, soils range from approximately 4.5 to 8.5; lower or higher creates extreme conditions in which plants cannot survive. Some plants grow equally well across a wide pH scope, others are preferential and don't thrive outside a limited scale. Most ornamental plants prefer nearly neutral (6.0 to 7.0). The Midwest has a number of pockets of either acidic or alkaline soils and an excellent map is available at nac.unl.edu/atlas/Map_Html/Stable_and_Productive_Soils/Regional/SoilpH/pH1.JPG. Note that the strongly acidic areas tend to be the Lower Midwest, central and northern Wisconsin, and areas of the western Dakotas. The western shorelines of Lakes Michigan, Huron, and Erie as well as a stretch of the Prairie states from western Ohio to northeastern Illinois, and a very large swath from Saskatchewan and Manitoba, down through large tracts of the Plains states are all labeled 6.7 to 7.7. This is a huge range for pH; 6.7 is nearly neutral and desirable whereas 7.7 is quite alkaline.

Acidic soils are corrected by adding agricultural lime or amendments, such as dolomite and wood ash. Mediation toward neutral is generally fairly quick and easy although strongly acidic soils may require annual applications. Alkaline soils are much more difficult to depress, and are also challenging to maintain once reached. Areas of high pH have high lime water content which acts to continually raise pH. Even though the pH scale is divided into equal increments, each incremental drop in pH scale is ten times more difficult to lower. A pH of 5.5 is ten times more acidic than 6.5, but one hundred times more acidic than 7.5, and one thousand times more acidic than 8.5; the effort to reduce that pH is equally incremental.

Gardeners in high- or low-pH areas often employ a great deal of effort, time, and money to change pH and maintain it at different levels. This is fine if you are up to that challenge. My gardening locality can

High pH restricts iron uptake, causing chlorosis. This pin oak (*Quercus palustris*) should have rich, dark green foliage.

exceed 8.0, and we kill a great deal of acid-loving rhododendrons, blueberries, and azaleas because we cannot lower and maintain pH to their ideal. If we do manage to lower pH enough for survival, they still fail to achieve the ideal size, vigor, and yields they would in naturally low pH soils. The best advice is to embrace plant materials that thrive in your area without excessive effort and enjoy those that don't when visiting other areas of the country.

Soil pH is important because it affects availability of soil nutrients. Many nutrients are not readily available to plants in soils with pH extremes. For instance, plants have reduced ability to utilize iron in alkaline conditions. As a result, they become chlorotic (iron-deficient) and need supplemental iron. Generally, nutrient deficiencies show up as common symptoms easily looked up and readily corrected if discovered and diagnosed quickly. If simple symptomatic diagnoses are unclear, use diagnostic labs.

Always remember existing soils are heavily influenced by regional mineral and biotic factors. The combination of two primary soil conditions—the bedrock composition and the predominant vegetation—determines structure, texture, color, density, pH, fertility, and all other soil properties.

Fertilizing and Watering

Good cultural practices encourage root depth and improve Midwest plant survival. Two of the largest mistakes homeowners make limiting root depth are improper fertilization and watering.

Annuals and vegetables do require fairly heavy and regular applications for fertility, as it takes a great deal of energy to maximize vegetative growth, yields, and continuous flowering. Water-soluble fertilizers work well in these situations if you follow directions for timing and application rates. But perennials and woody plants do not require the same degree of fertility, and excess fertility causes plant cells to grow faster and in an elongated fashion. This results in weak stems and plants that will lodge (flop) under rains or other adverse conditions.

Inorganic, water-soluble fertilizers are formulated for quick uptake. They generally provide the three primary nutrients considered important for plant growth and flowering, nitrogen (N), phosphorus (P), and potassium (K), and the ratio of each in a formulation is listed in the order N-P-K. For example, a water-soluble fertilizer labeled 21-5-20 contains 21 percent nitrogen, 5 percent phosphorus, and 20 percent potassium. Water-soluble fertilizers may also contain secondary nutrients such as calcium, magnesium, and sulfur as well as micronutrients, depending on formulations for specific applications.

Plants generally require more nitrogen than any of the other minerals because it is necessary for vegetative growth. Too much readily available nitrogen causes the plants to grow faster than normal and develop weak stems. Nitrogen moves through soil quickly so it becomes unavailable as it leaches down beyond the reach of roots. Phosphorus and potassium, required in far smaller quantities, move through soils much slower. Since the plant doesn't take up as much of these two elements, excess builds up in the soil, becoming an issue. Where I live, phosphorus has been banned because excess leaching into water supplies has created contamination issues. This is one reason to avoid what are referred to as "balanced ratios," equal ratios of all three elements such as a 10-10-10 or 15-15-15. It sounds logical to apply equal amounts of each element but plants do not require or take up each proportionately.

Most gardeners do not have deep, porous, friable soils ideal for root growth; garden soil depth may be 6 in. deep or less. If a gardener continually applies water-soluble fertilizers with immediately available nutrients, plants have no "incentive" to send out deep roots. It's easy for the plant to concentrate roots in a shallow zone containing readily accessed nutrition with little exertion of energy. Perennial plants evolved to draw nutrition from organic matter. They adapted to send roots out far and wide to maximize their access to any source of fertility. Holding back fertility forces plants to send roots deep to find it on their own. Supplemental fertilization will benefit newly transplanted plants as they establish roots. The first year, I provide a timed-release fertilizer to encourage development of strong, fibrous root systems. Slow release of nutrients through the first season assists the plant in developing extensive root systems to survive the first summer and winter. I never fertilize that plant again unless I identify a problem. Plants spend each subsequent year sending roots further, seeking life-enhancing nutrients. Forcing them to do it over time results in slower growth, shorter cell elongation, and stronger stems. More importantly, they have established deep roots to withstand drought, freezing temperatures, and spring heaving.

The same philosophy is true for watering. Few people water correctly, primarily because they don't check to see how deep water penetrates soil. One commonly touted and overly simplistic watering rule is "an inch per week." Really? This ignores variables such as time of year, type of soil, shade versus sun, tree roots, and individual plant requirements, among other factors. One inch could be excessive one time of year and nowhere near enough another time, or excessive in one area of the yard and not enough in another.

Take as example a typical sultry summer day of 95 degrees F. Conscientious gardeners water the entire garden by moving watering systems around through the day. The next day is a scorcher and they water with the same method. Day number three, another wickedly hot day, the garden is dry . . . you get the picture. Each day they water the entire garden, they are likely only wetting the upper few inches in the process; it takes amazingly large amounts of water to thoroughly moisten soil down to a root-deep level. Much of it evaporates that same day. Like fertilizer, these gardeners are providing plants their water needs in the shallow uppermost layer, and plants have no incentive to force deep roots.

Believe it or not, some wilting is not a bad thing. Permanent wilting point is the water content of soil when plants wilt and fail to recover upon rewetting and die; we want to avoid this. But most plants withstand fair amounts of wilt before getting to

that point. When a plant wilts, the stress triggers hormonal mechanisms that warn the plant it is in danger of dying and stimulate root development. Each time a plant experiences wilt, it expands root systems seeking new sources of moisture. Letting a plant wilt between soakings strengthens it over time. Combine frequently applied and easily accessed fertilizer with equally available moisture, and you have plants with shallow root systems—and higher risk for damage and death.

You should keep records of every distinct bed or area of your yard. Each time you water, find a spot in every bed where you can dig a hole to physically determine how far water penetrated (thoroughly

Many times, we can't avoid overhead watering due to time and labor limitations, but it's important to understand the true depth of watering regardless of system.

soaked to full root depth). Gardeners are amazed at how many hours of solid drenching it may require. Repeat the process an entire season, so you are aware of any variability and repeat in years that fluctuate from the norm. It is likely you will discover that some areas require hours of watering and others less. If you don't have time to water each area for true, deep soaks, then alternate days. Allow each area to dry out enough to wilt before soaking thoroughly again. This process scares the novice; it takes some time to watch and understand where wilt is acceptable before it becomes irreversible.

Understanding individual plant requirements helps as well. Group water-thirsty plants together in one bed; cluster water-thrifty plants in another.

Adequate compost retains water without water logging.

I advocate using what I call water-indicator plants. Some plants evolved in areas with consistently moist soils and will exhibit wilt in the heat of the day, even though water is available. This is a natural defense mechanism to keep them from unnecessarily losing water. As soon as the sun recedes and temperatures drop, they regain turgor. Hydrangeas are notable examples; they can stress out beginning gardeners until it becomes clear that the shrub isn't dying when it wilts in heat. I use durable perennials that do the same thing, including *Ligularia*, *Rodgersia*, and *Kirengeshoma*. It is startling when foliage droops practically flat to the ground, but wilt in these plants

Ligularia dentata 'Othello' is an excellent water-indicator plant.

indicates to me that within several days the other plants will reach wilting point. Forewarned is forearmed; you can watch for stress before it is too late. Once you understand the area's water idiosyncrasies, you no longer need the indicator plant and can move it to a bed for plants with continually moist root systems (it will adore you for that!).

The tree taproot misconception

In recent years, new research has changed how we understand and care for trees. I began gardening with the understanding that tree root extent ended at the canopy drip line. We also alleged that trees extended roots to great depths supporting their great size. We believed trees such as oaks, hickories, and walnuts developed deep taproots. In reality, those trees develop a taproot only while establishing as seedlings. They send out that one primary root to find a reliable source of water; it might be 1 ft. away, it might be 6. Then the water-seeking root stops growing and the tree begins developing an all-important fibrous root system extending horizontally. Once a solid fibrous system develops the taproot disappears.

Most Midwest ornamental trees generate over 90 percent of their root system very close to the surface, within the top 12 to 18 in. of the soil. Roughly 75 percent of the roots are within 6 in. of the surface. Let that sink in! This is where oxygen, fertility, and soil moisture are most available. It is especially true in cultivated landscapes where soils are dense due to compaction, and root penetration is difficult. Additionally, we've discovered those roots may extend five to six times the diameter of the tree's drip line. This is why compaction has become such an issue. We used to believe that as long as we avoided roots directly under the canopy we were protecting tree health. Now we realize how vulnerable a significant portion of tree roots are,

with only about 6 in. of soil depth as protection.

This deep root misconception damages trees more than any other plant. Because we feel mature trees have deep roots, they are the last plants we water during drought stress. Another little known fact is that turf (lawn) is the heaviest water consumer in landscapes. If shallow tree roots extend under lawn, non-native turfgrasses rob essential moisture from shallow tree roots. Because trees are

TOP Volcano mulching serves no purpose in protecting tree roots that extend wide from the tree, only to rot away bark, exposing the critical cambium tissue. ABOVE Mulch as wide as possible under trees to maximize their health.

so much larger than other plants and are extremely durable, they take longer to show damage; recovery may be too late by the time you notice.

Understand plant biology and how trees grow. A tree's life system is not deeply interior, but immediately under the bark, in a thin layer called the cambium. The essential, circulatory xylem system transports water and nutrients upward where the digestive phloem transports food downward. Damage to bark exposes this thin, delicate layer to air, disease, and system blockage, eventually killing the tree. Although professionals and homeowners alike understand that mulching tree roots is beneficial to moisture and nutrient retention, I often see a travesty called volcano mulching: massing the bulk of the mulch up against and around the trunk. Of what value is this if most of the roots are extending a vast width away from the tree? Any wood that contacts the trunk holds moisture, eventually rotting protective bark and exposing the cambium to damage. Mulch trees with moderate layers extending outward, without touching the trunk. Several inches a year will be beneficial to long-lived healthy trees.

The Problem with Soilless Mixtures

Some fertility and watering issues are a consequence of contemporary growing media. Soil used to be one of the ingredients in potting and growing mixes, but disease, weight, and watering issues made it beneficial for commercial horticulture to convert to soilless mixes because they were porous and sterile; they prevented waterlogging, disease, and insect contamination. Most potting mixes for containers and soil amendments today are 100 percent soilless. Ingredients include vermiculite, perlite, bark, sand, gravel, compost, oyster shell lime, gypsum, bone meal, and other inert ingredients.

This is where some chemistry basics come into the picture. In a nutshell, every molecule has a negative, positive, or neutral (inert) charge. Positively charged molecules (cations) and negative molecules (ions) are attracted to one another and bind tightly together in different percentages depending on the type of charge. In terms of soil particles, sand is largely neutral or has minimal charge; silt may have a small negative charge; and clay can have a substantial negative charge. Compost also may contain ingredients with negative charges. Most fertilizer minerals have positive charges such as nitrogen as ammonium (NH_4+), calcium (Ca_2+), magnesium (Mg_2+), potassium ($K+$), phosphorus (P_5+), and hydrogen ($H+$). These nutrients are attracted to and held by negative soil particles, thus balancing the charge. But because soilless mix ingredients are predominantly inert materials, components have no charge to attract and hold fertilizer minerals.

Recall too that clay (absent in soilless mixtures) retains water. Even though clay has a bad reputation in gardening, it has its beneficial properties. Loam is 20 percent clay; if clay was all bad, it wouldn't be part of ideal soil. Depending on soil porosity, you lose a large amount of watering effort to gravity. Roots need to access water particles as media dries, so enough capillary water (moisture trapped in small pores or forming as film around particles) must be retained that the roots can continue to utilize it until the next watering.

Imagine watering a hanging basket planted with soilless mix. Most of the water will flow through the pot and out the bottom. The soluble fertilizer flows through with the water, because there are no components attracting charged mineral molecules. The soilless mix has bound no extra water or fertilizer for the plants to use later. You have wasted water and fertilizer, leaching excess fertilizer into the groundwater. You may need to water again the next day and even twice a day in summer. Many annuals start failing by midsummer due to overcrowded containers, extremes of constant wetting with quick drying, and poor nutrition due to leaching fertilizer. If you ask uninformed garden center employees about remedial action, the standard response is generally to increase fertilization. I just established that fertilizer is doing no good because it is leaching through media too quickly, so additional fertilization adds to the problem!

I blend my own potting mixes and repot pre-planted containers. I add compost and roughly 10 percent soil (bagged to minimize weeds and disease) to soilless ingredients that already provide macro and micro pores in order to attract and hold minerals and water. I include timed-release fertilizer to minimize the need for soluble fertilizers. I don't water as often and the fertilizer I use is reduced and more effective.

Culture is an extensive topic, and I have broached only the most basic facts to assist your gardening efforts. I encourage you to continue learning about soils, plant biology, and culture for gardening success. All gardeners learn from experience, but minimize the heartbreaking ones in order to celebrate the triumphs!

LOW-IMPACT GARDENING

The term low-impact gardening generally references horticultural practices that conserve, improve, and preserve the quality of a site's ecosystem. Rain, xeriscape, bioswale, rooftop, and native plant gardens are all examples of low-impact gardens that I will discuss under a broad banner of sustainability. Low impact also refers to practices and systems that lessen physical exertion and time stress. I am part of the largest group of gardeners, Baby Boomers, who are aging and downsizing lifestyles. This has inspired a plethora of new ergonomic tools. Home landscapes have decreased in size, stimulating development of limited-space gardening techniques and accessories that are less intense in scope.

Some of the following systems were originally designed for edible plants (vegetables, fruits, and herbs) but can be used for ornamental gardens as well. They offer the same benefits of adaptation to small landscapes, low environmental impact, and less physical exertion.

Raised and Elevated Beds

In the modern edible garden we place plants closer together than we did in traditional kitchen gardens. Most of my gardening career I owned large plots for vegetable gardening because agrarian row cropping dictated kitchen garden design. I created the same wide-spaced rows, especially if using rototillers to weed. Limited-space gardening has taught us that rich, composted growing media allows plants to perform well close together. We no longer waste space formerly relegated to row spacing. Good mulching between plants eliminates the need for rototilling.

Early raised bed philosophy was that the deeper the growing media, the better, so raised beds were constructed upward to 4 ft. high. The higher the bed, the easier it was to work, reducing the need for bending—but it required far more growing media than necessary and rendered it fairly immobile due to size and weight. Mel Bartholomew's square-foot gardening technique revolutionized raised bed gardening. I admit that I was skeptical that a 4-ft.-by-4-ft. simple frame only 6 in. high would work as well as my colossal deep boxes, but I learned his method was inexpensive, easy to construct, compact, and successful.

Elevated tables or benches follow the same premise but are supported on legs to make them more accessible to gardeners (and less accessible to pests such as rabbits and rodents). They take

Square-foot gardening beds at Allen Centennial Gardens, based on Mel Bartholomew's book on the technique.

more material to construct and must be solid so they do not collapse under the weight of media and plants. Prefabricated forms are a (pricey) option if you aren't carpentry savvy. Be aware that prices increase dramatically when freight is added! One cedar raised bed I purchased cost more to ship than the purchase price. Elevated table forms dry out faster than ground-level beds.

Across the many growing-medium recipes for raised beds, the common denominator is a large percentage of organic matter. Bartholomew uses peat moss, vermiculite, and blended compost in equal quantities. My gardening friend and author Doreen Howard offers a recipe you can find in her gardening blog on the Farmers' Almanac website. It utilizes peat moss, vermiculite or perlite, screened compost or composted cow manure, sand, pelleted timed-release fertilizer, and lime. Because peat moss is a non-renewable, non-sustainable resource, I recommend replacing it in garden mix recipes with compost (my first choice), composted leaves, coconut coir, or other composted materials.

An inexpensively built elevated bed raises produce above rodent access and provides accessibility.

Vertical Gardening

Vertical gardening is effective for plants that traditionally take up more than their fair share of space in gardens, such as vining crops like vegetable cucurbits or ornamentals such as clematis, ivies, and roses. Vertical supports range from a totally vertical 90 degrees to those angled around 45 degrees, either as a single panel or joined to create an A-frame. Single-sided trellises increase growing space by drawing vines upward, while providing additional space beneath for shading vegetable leaf crops and brassicas, or ornamentals such as *Heuchera*, *Pulmonaria*, and *Dicentra*, that otherwise fizzle in summer heat. Some plants are space efficient simply by growth form; for instance, choose pole beans over bush and climbing hydrangea over shrub forms. Other plants can be trained to narrow, vertical growth or constrained and forced upward by staking. Many types of caging structures elevate vegetables, simultaneously saving space and preventing rot and varmint thievery by holding fruits/vegetables into the air. Likewise, they elevate floppy perennials whose

Vertical lattice supports allow vining plants to grow in limited space at the Minnesota Landscape Arboretum.

flowers dissipate quickly when dropped into surrounding vegetation or ground level.

Living roofs and walls are complex forms of vertical gardening. Most efforts have utilized perennials, but edible plants are used in some situations. Enormous amounts of research and plant trialing are determining the best plants to adapt to such unique growing conditions. Some rooftops are constructed to be planted; others make use of containers. Regardless, rooftop gardens need to be designed or augmented to withstand weight, with adequate water removal. Transporting materials can

Ornamental Edibles

Many ornamental gardeners start their gardening experience growing vegetables. Edible plants are relatively easy to grow and offer a high success rate with a less-intense knowledge requirement. Generally, the growing medium is closely managed and anticipation of harvest inspires attention to detail. Edibles are predominantly annuals, so in general, they require more labor, water, fertilizer, and pest control than perennials. Yield is highly dependent on these factors as well.

Edibles can be ornamental as well as functional. This is called an ornamental edibles garden or foodscaping. In 2009, I did an ornamental edibles theme at the public garden and visitors delighted in how many plants had edible parts but weren't traditional kitchen garden standards. They were intrigued by cardoon (*Cynara cardunculus*), Malabar spinach (*Basella alba*), and purple okra (*Abelmoschus esculentus*). They reveled in new uses and even had a hard time identifying some varieties outside the context of row-based vegetable gardening. I used red (purple) cabbage as accents throughout display beds, and some visitors asked the name of the exotic round purple globes! I use the beguilingly wrinkled savoy cabbage every year and some of my favorite fall annuals are 'Bright Lights' Swiss chard, kales, rosemary and lavender, ornamental peppers, and parsley. They persist longer than garden mums and color intensifies the colder it gets. Many edibles offer a high nutrient content along with their good looks, such as antioxidant-rich chokeberry (*Aronia melanocarpa*), kale, goji berries, Haskap honeyberries, and dandelion.

Part of the 2009 Ornamental Edibles (now termed foodscaping) display at Allen Centennial Gardens.

With the right plant choices, living walls can be dramatic elements.

be challenging and heat, cold, and wind are amplified. Living walls are also challenging. Plants are being asked to set roots in limited soil depths and grow horizontally, which most do not do in nature. Plants low on the wall may become overwatered and upper plants dry out quickly. Living walls are directly exposed to elements; rooftop gardens are easier to protect with windbreaks and shade cloth. If the living wall is the side of a building, labor increases with difficult watering, replacing dead plants and maintenance of pruning, dividing, and pest and disease control.

I applaud efforts that employ both strategies. I believe much advancement will come over time to make these systems successful with less effort.

At this point, they aren't particularly applicable to home gardens so I advise starting small and simple. I have seen many fun rooftop gardens on outbuildings that would be fairly easy to manage. If you are considering building roofs and walls with any degree of complexity, seek professional guidance to make sure your attempts don't damage structures and to maximize plant survival. These forms of gardening will be far more successful in areas with less severe winters, such as the Lower Midwest, and will be far more challenging for climes with severe winter cold such as South of the Boreal or the drying and chilling winds of the Plains. It can be done, but attention to hardy plant selection and protective siting may be necessary.

Living screens may be more practical applications of live walls for the homeowner. Mounting them on wheels provides mobility and they can be placed side by side to create changeable garden walls.

Portable living screens are smaller versions of living walls scaled to home landscapes. They are versions of stacked or tiered window boxes, or they might be created from a wide assortment of fabric planters attached to vertical support. An inexpensive version utilizes cast-off wooden pallets. Screens have the same challenges of exposure to elements, inconsistent watering top to bottom,

and sub-optimal growth media, just on a smaller scale. Wheels or durable casters allow them to be rotated when one side isn't getting enough sun or the site becomes too harsh. Mobility also allows using them as changeable screens dividing outdoor living spaces. Structures mimicking window boxes are more successful than those where plants are inserted horizontally. These mobile living screens will be more practical than living walls for all areas of the Midwest since they are portable and can be moved if in adverse sites.

Grow Bags

An increasing number of different grow bags, which are essentially containers constructed of some form of fabric or fabric-like material, are available to purchase. Grow bags are lightweight, flatten for storage, and provide more water and oxygen permeability than traditional planters. Experimentation may be necessary to achieve the best growing medium to provide adequate drainage while retaining moisture. The first grow bags I tried were vinyl mesh and I never felt I achieved that drainage-moisture balance. Even though it was woven vinyl, water and air movement didn't differ much from traditional pots, and drainage holes were too small to be effective. I tried them for two years and they were always either too dry or too wet.

The newest versions, which the nursery industry has used successfully for years, are made of landscape fabric. Water and air movement through this fabric is improved and they are sold in a wide selection of sizes. I truly appreciated their versatility after visiting the Maison de Lauberivière rooftop garden in Quebec, where they were harvesting tons of produce from hundreds of these bags.

Currently, most of the lightweight, practical, inexpensive containers offered are being used predominantly for vegetables, where black or green color is not detracting. I fully expect their use for ornamentals will be soon appreciated and companies will develop more decorative colors and forms for annuals and perennials.

Water Systems

Limited space gardens are still forms of container gardening, which is controlled, portable, and space efficient. But it is also the most labor-intensive form of gardening, with watering as the prevailing culprit. Slow drip systems are efficient and, if timed/watched properly, soak containers without excess. As a result, irrigation systems are increasing in availability and have become heavily marketed to homeowners.

Many irrigation systems are scaled for home use and are excellent tools for successful gardening. Research systems thoroughly and use skepticism if claims are too good to be true. Irrigation systems can be pricey, programming electrical components will be necessary, and the process of splitting lines to different zones can be complex. Like any intricate system, they need to be managed, maintained, and repaired. It will take time and experimentation to determine the correct amount of water for each irrigated area and to tweak timers, zones, and regulators. Ask businesses for references of clients who have used their system long enough to share experiences.

SUSTAINABILITY

Sustainability is becoming a commonplace term because it is such a broad concept, covering everything from an individual's energy use to global biodiversity. The definition of sustainability varies considerably depending upon intent of the source, but I think the United States Environmental Protection Agency defines it best: "Everything that we need for our survival and well-being depends, either directly or indirectly, on our natural environment.

Fabric pots provide a cheap, lightweight, easy-to-store alternative to traditional containers.

Sustainability creates and maintains the conditions under which humans and nature can exist in productive harmony, that permit fulfilling the social, economic and other requirements of present and future generations. Sustainability is important to making sure that we have and will continue to have, the water, materials, and resources to protect human health and our environment." The short version: we need to leave global resources as good as or better than we found them for the well-being of future generations.

Sustainability may be considered a trend but I believe future generations will consider it a way of life out of necessity. It is hard to deny that many human activities are negatively impacting the ecosystem and gardening is no exception since it incorporates management practices utilizing pesticides, monocultures, turf, inorganic fertilizers, genetic manipulation, and tillage. We are experiencing adverse effects that include ground-water contamination, an increase in invasive species, a decline in genetic diversity, the demise of species, and amplified human, animal, and soil toxicities. Because gardening is directly tied to natural systems, it is subject to a large number of conscientious garden movements.

Organic Lawns

Organic lawns are safe lawns. I converted both major turf areas of the public garden I direct to 100 percent organic and it was surprisingly effortless and ultimately cheaper. Here are some simple processes:

Add compost annually. If compost supports essential microorganisms, adds soil quality, and is nature's fertility, why would it be different for turf? I acknowledge controversy over efficacy of compost teas and will let the debate reach its final conclusion with further research, but I pay for four applications a year in addition to annual compost application. This is equivalent to the number of applications of toxic pesticides and inorganic fertilizer by chemical companies. Thick, healthy, robust grass eliminates opportunities and space for weeds to germinate.

Mow high. This is the hardest concept to get across to the homeowner who wants his lawn to look as manicured as a golf course. However, weeds that homeowners battle regularly cannot establish if grass is too dense for germination and tall enough to shade seedlings. Short-cropped grasses cannot outcompete weeds, so lawn care becomes a vicious circle of never-ending frustration. The lawn is mowed short, creating opportunity for weeds to establish; the homeowner sprays chemicals to kill them, creating new open spaces. Turfgrasses deter weed growth if they are cut at 5 to 6 in. I mow at the maximum height of a push mower. When I started

this process our lawns had weeds that two years later were eliminated by doing nothing more than high mowing.

Aerate. Compacted soils are as unhealthy to lawns as perennial gardens. Since lawn is generally the most trafficked area it benefits from fall aeration to restore porosity.

Accept summer dormancy. In periods of drought, most municipal homeowners have no choice, watering may be regulated. Turfgrasses can go summer-dormant for roughly 45 days; they will start to die if left unirrigated much longer. If the municipality allows it, you may have to start light irrigation after that. However, organic treatment produces healthy turf that takes longer to go dormant and recovers faster. Preventing any plant from achieving healthy size will always weaken it. It is amazing we never make that connection with turf. Continuous shearing to near ground level doesn't allow robust root development and reserves, making lawn extremely prone to drought, insect, and pest damage.

Prairie-Style Gardens

Quite possibly one of the most tragic failed garden trends was convincing Midwest gardeners to convert portions of their home landscapes into prairie plantings. The reasoning was superficially sound; prairie is indigenous to a large share of the Midwest, so plants would be resilient to the region's unique climatic conditions, soils, and pests. However, proponents sold it to the public as "no maintenance" based on the premise that prairies are self-sustaining Midwest ecosystems with long-lived, issue-free plants outcompeting weeds. Many homeowners embraced the movement and converted areas of lawn into so-called prairies. They weren't familiar with prairie plants, which take several years to flower, so anything

Turf: The American Tragedy

I give tours that include a history of garden design, using Italian, French, English, Japanese, and similarly inspired gardens as illustration. I'm often asked what will be considered the American garden, our contribution to design history. Sadly, it will be non-native turf lawn. It is the one garden element that practically every American homeowner feels is necessary, regardless of the resources required to sustain it. From the fascinating book *Edible Estates: Attack on the Front Lawn*, here are just a few alarming statistics that the fanaticism for manicured lawns has created:

- Lawns cover more than 30 million acres of the United States.
- Lawns use more equipment, labor, fuel, and agricultural toxins than traditional farming, making them the country's largest agricultural sector.
- Lawns consume around 270 billion gallons of water per week, enough to water 80 million acres of food one season.
- Of the 30 commonly used lawn pesticides, 13 are probable carcinogens; 14 are linked with birth defects, 18 with reproductive disorders, 20 with liver or kidney damage, and 18 with neurotoxicity; and 28 are irritants.
- Homeowners use up to 10 times more chemical pesticides on their lawns than farmers use on crops.

There are equally compelling arguments against turf that aren't as obvious. For example, the number of non-migratory Canada geese that spend their winters in the Midwest has increased enormously. One of their primary food sources is the native grasses that die back, providing no nourishment over winter. Turf remains green, providing a food source and thus causing no migration pressure. That's why heavily managed turf areas such as golf courses are covered with them. Unfortunately, geese lose the instinct to migrate in a single generation. The human influence of providing geese with a winter food source is increasing populations of geese that could not migrate if they had to.

I don't advocate complete elimination of lawn. I do promote alternatives for areas of the yard where turf isn't necessary. I support the concept of converting traditionally non-utilitarian front lawn into gardens, meadows, edible landscapes, or other low-impact alternatives, and encourage organic management of turf you keep.

Vast expanses of lawn with no real purpose other than a visual aesthetic may be America's regretful tribute to landscape design history.

The spectacular prairie at Rotary Botanical Gardens is still treated as a garden and requires large amounts of labor to maintain.

growing during establishment was considered the result of planted seed. Meanwhile, weed seeds were arriving, establishing, and dominating less-durable prairie seedlings. By the time prairie plants started flowering, the plot might contain as many weeds as desirable plants. These interlopers had already dropped their own seed and established tough rhizomes, making them difficult to permanently eradicate. Additionally, many wildflower and prairie seed mixes contained large quantities of less-desirable plants that multiplied rapidly and became an inordinately large percentage of the population. I learned from personal experience; I bought a prepackaged garden center wildflower mix heavy with the biennial common evening primrose (*Oenothera biennis*), which tried to take over in just a few years.

Home prairie plots visible to neighbors generated hostility, particularly those fearful that weed seeds from these perceived messy plots would invade manicured lawns. Owners became discouraged with the weed issue, so prairie gardens were tilled under and replaced with turf. I attended an environmental conference where a speaker broached prairie restoration. One attendee asked how she could control weeds in her home prairie, which was the area where her front lawn had been, about 50 by 20 ft. Our expert explained that by definition alone, she did not have a prairie; native prairies consist of continuous expanses of hundreds and thousands of acres. Trying to establish a prairie without intensive weed control results in failure, and the small size of home prairies makes them vulnerable to a much larger quantity of invasive weed seeds and plants invading its borders. The take-away message is that in the home landscape, we are establishing prairie-*style* gardens, not prairies. This is an important concept for all native gardens in the home landscape. They are attempts to replicate natural ecosystems on human-impacted properties, with altered soils and transformed cultural factors. Rarely does the homeowner have acreage, funds, or labor to authentically restore property landscapes. Whether prairie garden, rain garden, or woodland garden, it is important to always consider the "garden" portion of the term.

I certainly advocate creating prairie and prairie-style gardens if that is your desire. Here are some suggestions to make sure you are successful in your endeavors:

- Educate yourself. Read, take classes, go to public and private gardens, and talk to the people managing their prairie gardens. The best educators will be those who have already tried it in your area; what works for someone in Illinois is not likely to work for someone else in North Dakota.
- Research the plants. Just because they are native doesn't make them ideal for your situation. I mentioned my experience with evening primrose. Plants need to be durable for your area but they should also not become nuisances.
- If there is a company that specializes in native plant/prairie gardens, utilize them. Paying for expertise will cost less in the long run than mistakes that will create headaches, work, and possibly the expense of removing the garden and replacing it with something else.
- Treat it as a garden. It will need to be nurtured, weeded, and maintained to be successful.
- Enjoy the beauty and satisfaction of creating a prairie-style garden with its own unique sense and look!

Meadow Gardens

Meadow gardens were popular in English garden design and are useful in the United States as lawn alternatives. Meadows are even more grass-focused than prairies; in fact, the intent is to appear grass-like the entire season, possibly with minor bulbs for spring and fall interest. English meadows tend to be approximately waist high, whereas American meadows are shorter, to mimic turf more closely. Native grasses or sedges are used due to hardiness, durability, and minimal mowing, watering, pesticides, or fertilizer. The most common grasses for Midwestern meadow gardens include blends of fine fescues, meadow-like turfgrasses with broadleaf components, native sedges, and buffalo grass.

Fine fescues

Fine fescues are best for conditions where low-maintenance and low-input lawns are desired. Fescues prefer low levels of or no fertilization and can handle shade conditions. They appear similar enough to turfgrass that they transition manicured lawns to grassy areas more natural in appearance. Blends that are 100 percent fine fescue are receiving attention as low-maintenance alternatives, producing fine-textured blades that prefer low nitrogen and have reduced water requirements. Most blends focus on five types of fine fescue: hard fescue, Chewing's fescue, sheep fescue, creeping red fescue, and

The fescue meadow at Olbrich Botanical Gardens is spectacular with early spring bulb bloom.

slender creeping red fescue. Two excellent mixes on the market from Midwest companies include Old's Seed Solutions Care-Free Fine Fescue Mix, a blend of seven fine fescues, and Prairie Nursery's No-Mow Mix blend of six different fescues.

Fine fescues are cool-season grasses, which means they flourish primarily during spring and fall months and may go dormant during summer heat without supplemental irrigation (typical of lawn turfgrass) and remain green through winter. Fine fescues grow well with full sun to shaded conditions, prefer infertile soil, and require little to no irrigation once established. They do not need to be mowed; they can be trimmed to a desired height or left uncut to 6 in. (mature height). Uncut fine fescues

produce a flowing, carpet-like appearance of dark green. One disadvantage is that they do not appreciate heavy foot traffic, but meadows are generally not used as activity areas. Fescues are not likely to work in the Plains states region without excessive watering, defeating part of the purpose.

Meadow-like turfgrass mixes are combinations of turfgrass mixes with forbs. These mature 7 to 9 in. high, so they don't look like typical lawns and don't visually transition as smoothly from turf areas as fine fescues. They provide a meadow feel while maintaining an appearance of low vegetation, intermediate in height between turf and 3- to 6-ft. native meadows or prairie. The broad-leafed component provides an advantage over many cool-season, all-grass mixes by

A delightful oak sedge lawn alternative at Olbrich Botanical Gardens.

containing plants that thrive and flower in the heat of summer, when low-input grasses may go dormant. These grasses recover in areas with moderate foot traffic.

Native sedges

Carex is the sedge genus. It is an enormous group of grassy plants with over 1500 species considered true sedges. They typically have rhizomes, stolons, or short rootstocks, although some species grow in tufts. Because it is such a large group of plants, there are species that thrive in every cultural condition: wet to arid, full sun to shade, infertile soils to rich. I have long recommended native species adapted to dry shade as alternatives to shady lawn mixes

marketed for shaded areas but that end up sparse and scrawny.

Native sedges have many advantages as lawn alternatives. They tolerate some foot traffic, thrive in Midwest climatic extremes, require no water or fertilization after establishment, and do not like to be mowed. Certain species grow turfgrass height and provide soft texture from lovely, fine and flowing dark green foliage. They may be evergreen and emerge lush from winter while turfgrasses are still winter brown. They have no insect or disease issues requiring chemicals and are essentially carefree once established. Here are two examples. Our native oak sedge, *Carex pensylvanica*, is a tough plant with fine-textured spreading habit. It makes an excellent shade ground cover. The fountaining habit gives it a soft appearance and, once established, it is very drought tolerant, making it ideal for dry Midwest shade gardens. Another native, *C. eburnea*, bristle-leaf sedge, is a more sun-tolerant species with 6- to 8-inch-long soft, thread-like foliage. It naturalizes easily with stoloniferous growth that forms sizable colonies in loose, friable soils.

Buffalo grass

Buffalo grass is best for dry, hot climates where water and fertilization are not available or desired and traditional turf or any of the other alternatives will simply not thrive; our neighbors in the Plains are much more likely to use this grass than the rest of the region. As a warm-season grass, it grows during the warmest months of summer, browns out after fall frost, and remains dormant until spring, so the appeal is quite different from cool-season grasses that remain green for most of the year. It is best used for naturalization and stabilization and is not suited for heavy foot traffic or areas of high precipitation.

Rain Gardens and Bioswales

Rain gardens are shallow areas filled with plants, which serve to reduce polluted runoff from entering water systems. They are based on commercial catch basins that manage stormwater runoff flow and quality, recharging groundwater systems. Urbanization and increased commercial and residential development have great impact on local water resources. Impervious surfaces such as roads, rooftops, parking lots, and other hard surfaces do not allow stormwater to soak into the ground, and increase rates of stormwater runoff. This boosts volume of water-carrying pollutants in surface water, with less water soaking into the ground. Urban and suburban development has created additional issues with water that

is effluent from residential contaminants, including settled air pollutants, pet excrement, yard waste, and pesticides and fertilizers. Less water soaking into the ground lowers ground water levels, which can dry up and damage stream ecosystems, reducing the supply of potable well water.

Rain garden plants capture 30 percent more water than lawn, and filter water reentering the soil. Because most excess runoff occurs in late winter and spring, plants that can tolerate saturated roots early and dry conditions in summer are best suited for this unique, man-made situation. Most areas of the Midwest receive so much rainfall in late winter and spring that flooding becomes an issue. However, we generally become extremely dry by summer, so ground depressions that might stay wet all season in other areas of the country become arid for us. Midwest rain gardens utilize mostly prairie-based plants because they have extremely deep roots that can handle dramatic seasonal moisture variations. Interestingly, deep-rooted prairie plants were the choice of East Coast designers who started the rain garden concept. They are used mostly to take care of excess water naturally, especially if your water runoff affects neighbors or floods portions of your property or basement.

This is another garden trend with a sound environmental basis, but it has failed in many cases for much the same reason as prairie gardens. Proponents convinced homeowners that their rain garden would be free of maintenance once established. What were essentially "prairies" were planted in depressions and the weed infestation and problems manifested—the only difference was the contour. Large, gangly plants choked with weeds were not what homeowners signed up for, so they filled in the depressions or turfed them over. This is a shame

A bioswale at Sinnissippi Park in Rockford, Illinois.

Xeriscape gardens are more than cactus and agave; they can be deliciously ornamental.

because rain gardens are excellent ways to improve residential water issues using natural systems. Once again, the "garden" part of the terminology was ignored. It seems that when native plants are encouraged, the often inaccurate impression is that the planting becomes carefree. I encourage a mix of natives and ornamentals, creating an ornate impression, and thus the realization that it has to be treated as a garden.

Bioswale can be used interchangeably with rain garden but is more generally referencing curving, swaled drainage ditches with gently sloped sides. A bioswale can be designed to remove silt and pollution, directing runoff to a destination which could be a rain garden, retention pond, storm sewer, or even watershed. Properly built and planted, successful bioswales can filter runoff to the point that the runoff is clean by the time it reaches its destination. A common application is around parking lots, where substantial automotive pollution and contaminants are collected by the paving and flushed by rain to surrounding soils.

A fine example of a complete, biological, mediated runoff system is the parking lot of the Morton Arboretum in Lisle, Illinois. The arboretum's main parking lot is surfaced in permeable, interlocking concrete pavers atop 4 ft. of gravel that filters stormwater, slowing progress through groundwater systems. Effluence moves into bioswales bordering parking lot aisles, which additionally filter water contaminants. The water empties into nearby Meadow Lake and eventually the DuPage River as uncontaminated and clean.

Bioswales and rain gardens are easily incorporated into small landscapes and are effective natural filtration systems at a time when groundwater contamination is increasing at alarming rates. They do require a certain amount of engineering to ensure correct water movement and some knowledge of soil structure and permeability. They aren't as simple as digging a basin in your backyard, but with research and professional advice, they can serve as sound ecological practices as well as new garden spaces.

Xeriscape Gardening

In an era when fresh, clean, potable water is nationally becoming a concern, every gardener should be familiar with the term "xeriscape." Xeriscape doesn't mean desert gardening. It is a process based on choosing plants appropriate to their site (right plant, right place again) and creating landscapes utilizing minimal or no supplemental watering. Xeriscaping was termed in the 1970s in Denver to define waterwise or water-efficient landscaping. It doesn't just have a low impact on the environment; it is low impact in time and labor as well. Xeriscape plants usually require deep porosity and superb drainage, which is generally provided by gravel and coarse sand rather than soil.

Most of the Midwest is fortunate that water in general isn't a serious issue. We see occasional summer drought and, even though those periods can be seasonally severe, overall water is still fairly abundant. A large portion of the region adjoins the Great Lakes, the largest bodies of fresh water in the world. Folks in the Plains states experience more water deficiencies than the rest of us, but many gardeners in the center of the country might ask why they should try xeriscape gardening. The obvious answer is that there is only a finite amount of water and, in drought years, even less. The basic philosophy of water conservation is to group plants according

to water needs, use mulch to reduce evaporation, and select drought-tolerant plants. A benefit to those of us in water-available ranges is healthier gardens, since most Midwest diseases tend to be moisture-stimulated fungal issues. Less water use also means gardeners contribute less as nonpoint sources of groundwater pollution.

I created a xeriscape garden as a segment of a larger Sustainability Garden at Allen Centennial Gardens. It is so colorful and interesting in texture and form, visitors rave about it as something novel and fascinating. Plants will vary somewhat according to respective geographical, environmental, and cultural variations, but here are some of the genera represented in my garden, which should work in many of yours: *Armeria* (thrift), *Coreopsis*, *Yucca* (Adam's needle), *Dianthus* (dianthus), *Asclepias* (milkweed), *Callirhoe* (poppy mallow), *Sedum*, *Gaillardia* (blanket flower), *Penstemon* (beardtongue), *Centranthus* (Jupiter's beard), and *Gypsophila* (baby's breath). Many of these would not survive in the standard Wisconsin perennial bed due to heavy soils, but thrive in the xeriscape garden because of the sharp drainage.

Gravel Gardens

In this system, garden plants have the advantage of contact with the soil to set establishing roots, but a surrounding 4- to 6-inch layer of gravel prevents weed seeds from germinating. Several garden schemes make use of gravel, including xeriscape and rock gardens, but the gravel gardening system I am referencing, which originated in Germany, is not widespread in the United States. However, it has been successfully implemented in Wisconsin at Northwind Perennial Farm, Olbrich Botanical Gardens, and the Epic System's campus. I have used the philosophy as a base layer to a new Sustainability Garden at Allen Centennial Gardens, with rain, xeriscape, and meadow components.

Xeriscape gardening should not be limited to arid regions and thrive in the Midwest. I created this one for Allen Centennial Gardens in Wisconsin.

The initial site should start with good quality, well-drained soils; if it does not, you will have to work at developing a correct base first. The gravel needs to be a sizable stone that will not degrade over time; those of us here have used ¾-inch quartzite. It must be thoroughly washed clean of any fines with no small particles that will compact and restrict water or air flow. The gravel is spread evenly at a depth of 4 to 6 in., depending on the pot size of plants you are using. The reason for this depth is that the bottom of the plant root ball needs to make contact with underlying soil whereas the sides are surrounded by gravel. My advice is to remove the plants from their pots, place them, and then add the gravel around them; if you place the gravel first, it is not easy to dig holes that maintain integrity in 6 in. of heavy gravel.

Gravel gardens are relatively low maintenance, but be aware that you will need to exert some effort two times a year. The reason weeds cannot establish is because they are trapped in air space. However, if plant materials die and dropped vegetation accumulates, it creates organic matter which fills pores and becomes a prime growing medium for weed growth. So in late fall and spring, all plant material must be cut and removed completely.

For the Fauna

Finally, as you increase low impact for the benefit of environment, time, and labor, consider landscaping

Olbrich Botanical Garden's gravel garden demonstrates that gravel does not prevent lush appearance.

for benefit of fauna. Human intervention continues to disrupt, destroy, and damage habitats and food sources for insects and animals. Unfortunately, it is the opportunistic pests that raze our gardens, giving wildlife a bad name; creatures such as deer, rabbits, rodents, and deleterious insects. Most resources concentrate on insects as garden beneficials but I can't remember the last time I saw a garter snake or weasel in the garden. Be mindful of all fauna that need assistance and protection. As you garden, consider the following:

Eliminate or reduce chemicals. This should be a no-brainer. Toxic pesticides indiscriminately sprayed around plants are often toxic to other living organisms. In the six years I have been at Allen Centennial Garden, I have achieved roughly 95 percent organic control. We have seen a tremendous increase in quantity and diversity of insect populations. It is a sad statement that many of our visitors notice this and say, "There are a lot of bugs in this garden!" They think it is a bad thing. I like to smile and say, "That's a sign of a healthy ecosystem." The insect populations also increase bird life; people forget how many birds dine on insects. Unfortunately, the mentality that all bugs (at least the unpretty ones) are bad is far more prevalent than understanding how many insects are beneficial to humans. I hope it isn't the demise of honeybees that brings the message home, because there are many insects necessary to human well-being—and the honeybee isn't even native to the United States! Chemicals that eliminate unwanted pests also eliminate large numbers of beneficials; that loss may outweigh damage from the nuisance.

Plant selections. Make plant selections that provide beauty and utility while also offering sustenance and habitat for advantageous birds, animals, and insects. Monarch butterfly larvae, which need *Asclepias* (milkweed) species as a food source, and swallow-tail butterfly larvae that are dependent on plants in the family Apiaceae are famous examples of plant/insect dependencies, but others are much more complex and integrated among many species. Many resources are available to help you select plants based on wildlife interactions. Realize it may require a combination of plants to attract fauna. If you are serious about creating sustainable gardens attractive to wildlife, consult with professionals. Natural systems are based on intricate and complex balances that they have studied.

Encourage fauna including the small, less-obvious garden denizens such as this red eft.

Create habitats. Include bird and bat houses in your garden and water features such as birdbaths or fountains. Bees, wasps, and butterflies utilize water but need a place to land; placing a flat rock in a birdbath works well. Use recirculating pumps to move water and create sound; birds are attracted to the sound of water before any other sensory cue. Small reptiles and amphibians like cool, shaded areas near the ground and close to water. By placing groupings of rocks, overturned pots, and other items, you'll provide crevices for toads and snakes to hide in.

SCOURGES OF THE GARDEN

I categorize scourges of the garden as pests (animals and insects), diseases, and weeds. Entire books are written on each topic and every region has very unique issues so a gardening guide can only provide generalized information about control. I highly advocate Cooperative Extension and associated diagnostic labs as your primary source for specific issues. Good gardening practices are always the first line of defense.

Animal Pests

Rodents, birds, and other critters can cause damage in gardens, but generally the major culprits are deer and rabbits. The damage inflicted by these two species can amount to hundreds or even thousands of dollars in damage, depending on property size. This issue is escalating as both continue to urbanize.

Deer

One would think that deer would be a rural issue, but population densities have increased to the point where individuals and herds have moved into suburban and urban areas. They do extensive garden damage because they have less fear than their country cousins, and food sources are condensed from expansive farm fields to parks and home properties.

This has motivated plant merchandisers to label plants as deer-proof or, more accurately, deer-resistant. In truth, deer have traditionally avoided some plants due to flavor, access, and noxious or toxic components, but the list grows smaller and smaller. Many plants appeared on such lists simply because they either weren't available in natural settings or there were plenty of tastier alternatives. I no longer will declare any plant as deer-resistant. If I do in large audiences, invariably someone raises a hand and announces, "But they ate mine!" When someone reported that deer had eaten his western red cedar (which I had thought immune because it has a distasteful chemical component), I knew we had to become more careful calling plants "deer-resistant." Certainly if you have issues, concentrating on plants labeled as resistant helps, but do not expect that all will remain deer-proof.

The most common deer deterrents, such as fences, dogs, and hunting, are difficult for the urban gardener. Fences need to be 10 ft. high to be effective and deer can jump even that height if they have clearance to charge it with speed. Nurseries have found electric fencing effective but this only works for large rural properties. Not all dogs scare other animals and are often indoors at night when deer tend to feed. Hunting is restricted and objectionable to some people. Other deterrents include hanging bars of soap or bags of human hair on branches; various forms of "cannons" randomly shooting water or making noise; draping plants in netting or surrounding them in wire cages; tree wraps; and urine from coyote, fox, and wolves. But deer are fairly intelligent and learn tricks quickly, and some deterrents are offensive to more than the culprit. I used coyote urine pellets on my Main Street garden to deter rabbits and the overpowering, repulsive stench deterred the community from walking by on the sidewalk! Physical barriers will be most effective, but fences, cages, netting, and chicken wire are unattractive and detract from the beauty of the garden. Physical barriers are most often used in winter because grazing occurs when the food supply is limited, so you need to put them up in the fall and remove in spring.

The most effective non-obtrusive deterrents are sprays of various forms. However, they must be reapplied on a regular basis. Rain washes ingredients off in spite of claims otherwise. More importantly, plants continually produce new growth all season. Any new flush of growth has no applied spray and this is the tenderest, most delectable portion of the plant. Sprays add up significantly in cost and labor, especially since most of these products are sold in handheld spray bottles. I met a gardener near Milwaukee whose property adjoined woodland; he experienced massive plant damage annually from both deer and rabbits. He turned me on to a home recipe that replicates purchased products using cheap ingredients and the ability to use a backpack sprayer; see Homemade Deterrent Sprays, which follows.

Give the nod to deer-resistant plants if you have issues, but realize few plants are likely 100 percent deer-proof.

As deer urbanize and the young are faced with new dietary options, urban grazing will continue to be an issue.

Rabbits

Rabbits are a constant challenge in my home garden and the public garden. Most female rabbits will produce one litter every twenty-eight days, and urban rabbit populations don't ebb and flow as they do in the country, because they have plenty of food and are free of predators. We rejoice over sightings of hawks, foxes, and other predators in town, but we can't rely on them. The presence of cats deters rabbit nesting but the issue of feral cats and the demise of songbirds have allowed laws where cats can be destroyed if they wander off your property. I've utilized discreetly spread used cat litter, but it is messy and not enjoyable when maintaining the garden. Physical barriers are effective, although rabbits' smaller size requires finer mesh, absolutely no holes, and a buried base, because the creatures will burrow or squeeze under. Light weight allows rabbits to walk on top of snow, so any fence deterrent or tree wrap must accommodate snow height as well as reach. The deeper the snow, the harder it is for rabbits to dig for food and they will chew off perennials, trees, and shrubs above snow level.

Rabbits are extremely difficult to live trap although it can be done. It is most effective in winter when food options are limited. Fresh apples are a good lure and the trap needs to be covered or disguised. I found Milorganite, a Milwaukee-produced fertilizer, effective as a repellent for deer, rabbits, and rodents. It is a by-product of human waste from the Milwaukee Metropolitan Sewerage District, so the deterring factor is obvious. It does have a fairly strong odor, but it is not fecal in nature. It contains a 6-2-0 N-P-K analysis and is 4 percent iron so it is beneficial to plant growth. Although Milorganite's

Homemade Deterrent Sprays

Since many products on the market are pricey and you may require large quantities, you may opt for a homemade solution. The beauty of this recipe is that it is based on hot peppers, and generally deer and rabbits never get used to its taste. In 4 gallons of water, add one 32-ounce carton of Egg Beaters (this is the surfactant, which makes the solution stick to the foliage) and several tablespoons of hot pepper sauce (through a strainer; some sauces clump and clog the nozzle). The amount of hot pepper sauce depends on the degree of heat in the product. Be careful of the quantity; too high a concentration can burn plant foliage and may irritate your eyes. You can find a number of similar recipes online; here is one designed for watering cans: 5 egg whites (whole egg for deer), 1 tablespoon powdered cayenne pepper, 1 tablespoon black pepper; mix well and dilute with 4 parts water.

Rabbits are extremely difficult to trap. I managed to catch a few oblivious innocents initially, but the savvy bunnies eluded me the rest of the winter.

TOP Insects such as Japanese beetles plague gardeners annually.
ABOVE Consider encouraging predatory insects such as the braconid wasp as biological control. It deposits its eggs on tomato hornworms and the emerging larvae digest the caterpillar.

manufacturer does not claim repellence because it would have to be registered as a pesticide, university research confirms anecdotal evidence of its success. I find that it is relatively low cost, easy to apply, and lasts through several rains. The homemade deterrent spray is extremely effective at reducing rabbit browsing.

Remember that for most deterrents, if the plant is desirable enough or the animal hungry enough, they will subjugate themselves to some levels of unpleasantness in taste, odor, or effort.

Insect Pests

Insect damage is difficult to control. Their small size and ability to fly, if they are winged, makes them difficult to detect until they have done irreparable damage and plants are on their way to demise. The advent of invasive species that lay waste to huge areas and populations with no controlling predators has increased concern. Some, like Asian ladybeetles and boxelder bugs, are a greater nuisance to living conditions than they are damaging to gardens. Others, such as emerald ash borer and Asian longhorn beetles have the ability to eliminate entire plant species before we find control. In the Midwest, we anxiously await and fear encroachment from damaging pests that have changed the contours of other regional landscapes, such as woolly adelgids on the East coast and western pine beetles on the West coast. Some insects arrive and traumatize us until populations settle down, such as Japanese beetles that entered our area around 2007. Some, such as the gypsy moth, become so firmly established that millions of dollars are spent annually on control.

Every range within the Midwest will have some insect pests universal to the entire region; some will have insects specific to their area and may overlap into other U.S. regions. All of us will experience new insects entering our areas and becoming pests where they never existed before. This is when you should work with experts in entomology, organizations such as Cooperative Extension, professional arborists, universities, and public gardens. Together, you can identify your pest, make a plan for the best action, and find out what options exist for control, as well as any repercussions from that control. In some cases, minimal damage will not warrant action, in others it might require plant removal and changes in garden composition, and in extreme cases it may demand expensive professional treatment.

We do not seem to learn that monocultures promote insect infestations. Dutch elm disease decimated entire populations of stately American elms because we lined them out in rows, allowing easy access from tree to tree for disease-carrying elm bark beetles. I read recently that the introduction of Dutch elm disease (DED) in Europe and North America is the most significant event in the history of urban forestry. That event occurred from the 1930s through 1950s, and yet today Wisconsin is struggling with how to deal with the encroachment of emerald ash borers—because we lined our streets with ash species whose numbers are estimated at 834 million, combined urban and woodland. It will be yet another example of massive species loss because we avoided diversity and continued to promote monocultural plantings. Insecticidal treatments to prevent infection, mostly systemic, are available, but the homeowner has to deal with added cost, remembering to apply very early in the spring on an annual basis. Plus, they will only work on healthy trees, not those already infested.

As a gardener, you have the option of creating plant communities with diversity rather than mass plantings with limited species. Wider spacing between similar species makes it more difficult for insects and pests to travel plant to plant. Adequate air circulation reduces habitat and hiding spaces. Some plants deter insects when planted next to others to which the bugs are attracted. Choose plants that have no known serious insect pests. If you choose to grow plants with known issues, then you need to be prepared to deal with stress, damage, cost, and the labor of management and control. Cultural control, plant selection, and diversity are your best defenses against insect damage.

Another option is the biological control of insects, from releasing ladybugs and praying mantises into the garden, to large-scale release of sterile screwworm males into the general population. Information and classes on this topic are available; be aware that releases generally need to be controlled in some way or your beneficial bugs may take off to other sites. One of the best things you can do to encourage beneficial predation is to limit or eliminate the use of pesticides, since they kill the desired insects as much as the injurious.

Generally, professional help is highly recommended when dealing with identification, control, and eradication. I recommend starting with your local extension office.

Disease

Some diseases are easy to identify, with distinct symptoms, and others are harder to differentiate from problems with similar symptoms. Some have no effective cure once infestation begins, such as verticillium and oak wilts. Others require regular preventive treatment such as Dutch elm disease. Many are seasonal and, if left alone, will not return the following year under different cultural conditions. Homeowners are constantly forced to address disease issues, and decide whether curative or preventive measures are worth trying or whether to replace the plant with something more tolerant of the conditions. Major infestations will likely require professional consultation.

The most common nonlethal diseases in the Midwest tend to be fungal. Fungi thrive in moist, warm conditions, so issues are apt to be seasonal and weather connected. Anthracnose and tar spot on maples cause very common foliar blackening that eventually creates holes in wet, warm seasons. Gardeners will panic, only to not see it occur again until the next moist, warm season. Scab, powdery and downy mildews, leaf blotch, and soots are common fungal diseases. One can apply fungicides but keep in mind, fungicides are used to prevent more infestation; they are not curative. They need to be applied every seven to ten days. The best recourse is to find a way to dry out the conditions if they aren't totally weather dependent. Avoid overhead watering that moistens foliage. If you do overhead water, do not water in the early evening because moisture will sit on the foliage until morning. Water early in the day, so the sun will dry foliage quickly. Closely packed plants will retain moisture. Allow good air circulation between plants. Grow plants in as ideal cultural conditions as possible; healthy, robust plants deflect disease and are more likely to recover.

Fungi are spread by spores, some so minuscule in size that they can travel windborne for hundreds of miles. The spores can survive years in dormancy until they experience ideal conditions. It is wise to clean up any infected foliage, such as fallen leaves or infected plant parts, and dispose of it, since the spores do not simply go away when conditions improve.

If the disease is diagnosed as viral or bacterial in nature, the plant will have to be removed from the garden. These diseases are vectored by insects

TOP **Leaf blotch is a common non-lethal fungal disease affecting chestnuts to varying degrees depending on species.**
ABOVE **Aster yellows is a virus that causes flower and foliar distortion. Plants must be removed to reduce the spread.**

that travel from plant to plant, spreading infection. They have no cure. Aster yellows, canna virus, fire blight, and viburnum bacterial blight are common examples. If a disease has "wilt" or "rot" in its name, it is generally lethal over time, and sometimes death comes within days. It is always recommended to replace any plants subject to these diseases with something resistant to the disease.

Many plants prone to a particular disease have resistant cultivars. A lot of plant-breeding efforts are focused on developing plants more tolerant of diseases, especially those that are fungal. Flowering crabs have been bred so heavily for apple scab resistance, it has come at the expense of fragrance and flowering. Garden phlox, bee balm, common lilac, and peonies are selected for powdery mildew resistance. Rose breeders became fanatical about black spot.

Remember, the word is "resistant," not "immune." Resistant cultivars have genetics that, under normal conditions, should deflect fungal disorders, but they can still become infected if conditions are overly conducive. Generally symptoms of fungal disorders won't be as severe. Also, fungi are living organisms that rapidly mutate and adapt. So over time, a resistant cultivar not showing susceptibility to disease for years may eventually succumb to a new strain. That's why plant breeders continue to work on disease resistance as a never-ending process.

As with insect infestations, seek professional assistance with severe disease issues and those you cannot easily identify. Plant diagnostic labs are the best place to start. It can be very hard to diagnose issues without a sample of the plant and causal agent (disease or insect) so radio experts and call lines may not be accurate. If the plant is of value, or an issue looks like it might spread and become a larger concern, there is tremendous value in working with a plant diagnostic lab for quick, accurate diagnosis, so that the remedy can be initiated as soon as possible.

Weeds

A weed is a plant out of place. There are many versions of this old chestnut but the spirit is that all plants evolved and adapted with some purpose. Take as example the dandelion, a plant so universally considered a weed that it has generated pure lust for its demise in lawns and garden beds. However, dandelions provide an important source of nectar and pollen for bees, and provide food for the larvae of some species of butterflies and moths. The seeds are an important food source for certain birds, and its nectar is used by the pearl-bordered fritillary. As part of the natural ecosystem, the taproot brings up nutrients for shallower-rooting plants and adds minerals and nitrogen to soil. Dandelion has long been used for a wide range of medicinal properties; in fact, the scientific name *Taraxacum officinale* means "official remedy for disorders." Finally, all parts are edible and it is now sold in grocery stores for its high antioxidant content.

Obviously, not every plant identified as a weed conceals so many valuable properties but all plants generally have some value in the context of the larger ecosystem. Some that we berate now may produce benefits we haven't yet discovered. Kudzu, the Southeast's weed pariah, has high concentrations of the same sugar and starches found in livestock feed, used for making fuel-grade ethanol, and is being researched as a fuel alternative. A

Powdery mildew, a common fungal disease, does not cause death but is unsightly.

plant becomes a weed when it grows where it is not wanted and especially when it competes with native and cultivated plants.

I advocate a number of gardening practices for controlling and eliminating weeds that don't involve the use of chemicals. Hand weeding is still one of the most effective forms of control, especially if done when weeds are young and easy to remove. Mulching helps prevent weed seed emergence and, to some degree, encroachment by plants; it also makes it easier to hand weed young seedlings. If a plant becomes infested with a weed that I feel cannot be effectively removed, I will eliminate and replace the ornamental rather than risking further infestation. For large areas of weed patches, covering the area with black plastic or landscape fabric until the weeds die is an effective method, but never leave black plastic in place for more than two years because the heat generated will effectively kill all organisms, beneficial as well as harmful. Unfortunately, many of the home remedies such as vinegar do not effectively kill weeds. Generally they kill the vegetative portion, but the roots regenerate an even more robust plant as part of future survival.

This may seem repetitive, but it is important enough to repeat. Whether you're battling pests or diseases, utilize companies and organizations such as Cooperative Extension, professional arborists, universities, and public gardens to identify and diagnose the problem, and determine your best course of action. I am asked to serve as a horticultural expert on the radio, and enjoy helping gardeners with their issues. However, if I can't identify their problem 100 percent based on descriptions, I will always avoid dispensing advice, and encourage them to seek help from professionals. Capture the insect for visual inspection and accurate identification, take a sample of the diseased plant in for diagnostic evaluation, give a healthy sample of the weed to a professional for expert eradication advice. If you can't provide the plant, disease, or pest, take a number of clear, in-focus shots, both close-up and wide. In the long run, the time, energy, and any expense will be worth correcting your problems before they escalate. Learn to identify issues quickly and take action immediately. Your garden will be healthier and you will be less stressed as a result.

PESTICIDES

In a perfect world, we would eliminate all pesticide use. I have been involved in two careers, agriculture and horticulture, that both utilize pesticides. I have handled far more than I care to acknowledge today and like many people have become disillusioned with claims of product safety. Over time I have watched nearly every pesticide labeled as "safe" taken off the market as toxic and harmful to environmental, human, and animal health. As a teenager on the family farm, I remember a chemical salesman declaring Atrazine was so safe you could drink it—and he demonstrated by downing a glass in front of us! I suspect what appears to be an increase in new or increased human health issues and birth defects will be traced to contaminated ground water. Widespread use of these chemicals has been the demise of species and the outcry against their use is escalating.

Many adverse effects can be attributed to misuse. Agriculture is, in my estimation, unfairly attached to the highest percentage of blame. Of course, agricultural pesticides are contributing factors, but the average property owner should not be too quick to point fingers, particularly if they manage turf-based lawns. Farm operators are more likely to follow directions for proper application because their livelihoods depend on it, whereas homeowners are far less likely to read directions and discern the selectivity of products. They often proceed with the

Pesticide Definitions

- **Pesticides** are substances meant for preventing, destroying, or mitigating any pest so the term includes both herbicides and insecticides, but also includes biological agents such as viruses, bacteria, antimicrobial agents, or disinfectants that deter, incapacitate, kill, or repel pests.
- **Herbicides** are chemicals that kill plants. Some kill everything within contact range, whereas selective herbicides kill specific targets leaving desired plants (relatively) unharmed. Some act by interfering with the growth of the weed and may synthetically mimic natural plant hormones.
- **Insecticides** are chemicals that selectively kill insects. They include ovicides and larvicides used against eggs and larvae of insects.
- **Systemic pesticides** are translocated through the plant, either from foliar application down to the roots, or from soil application upward to the leaves. Systemic insecticide–treated plants kill pests that ingest the toxin while feeding on the plants; systemic herbicides kill treated plants slowly but are ultimately more effective than contact herbicides.
- **Contact pesticides** are toxic to plants/insects directly touched. Effectiveness is directly tied to proper application.
- **Natural pesticides** such as nicotine, pyrethrum, and neem extracts are produced by plants as natural defense. Natural, however, does not mean non-toxic or human or environmentally safe.
- **Plant-incorporated protectants** (PIPs) are insecticidal substances produced by plants after genetic modification. For instance, a gene that codes for a specific *Bacillus thuringiensis* (BT) biocide protein is introduced into a crop plant's genetic material. The plant is stimulated to manufacture the protein which is incorporated into the plant.
- **Inorganic insecticides** are solutions of metals such as arsenates, copper compounds, fluorine compounds, and sulfur. Sulfur is the only one still commonly used.
- **Organic insecticides** are synthetic chemicals that replaced inorganic solutions and make up the largest percentage of pesticides used today, accounting for about 70 percent of all agricultural pesticide use. They are considered the most toxic. According to the Stockholm Convention on Persistent Organic Pollutants, nine of the twelve most dangerous and persistent organic chemicals are pesticides.
- **Mode of action** is how the pesticide kills or inactivates a pest and is important in predicting whether an insecticide will be toxic to unrelated species, such as fish, birds, and mammals.
- **Repellents** deter pests rather than killing them. Most are non-toxic but not always safe.

mindset that if the recommended rate is effective, then increasing the rate is even better. There is a false sense of security in safety claims from marketing departments of major chemical companies. I cringe every time I see a homeowner on their front lawn enthusiastically and randomly spraying pesticides clad in shorts, T-shirt, and no protective gloves or eyewear. Worse yet is when a commercial for a chemical manufacturer irresponsibly shows a homeowner shooting chemicals great distances from power wands, lauding the process as maverick and manly. If the manufacturer doesn't represent safe application methods, then how can we blame the homeowner for negligence?

I encourage you to see where you can eliminate pesticides from your gardening efforts. However, I am a realist and know that pesticides will be used regardless of best intentions. Many invasive plants are nearly impossible to eradicate without selective chemical interference. We are struggling with control of some noxious weeds such as garlic mustard, purple loosestrife, and common buckthorn as well as pests such as emerald ash borer, mountain pine beetles, and woolly adelgid. As a result, if you must use pesticides, I encourage you to follow these guidelines to minimize negative impact:

Use the product formulated for the problem. This is especially relevant since glyphosate-based products, of which Roundup is the most recognized, have become the ubiquitous chemicals for all weed issues. Roundup is a broad-spectrum, systemic herbicide used to kill weeds such as annual broadleaf weeds and grasses, but that doesn't necessarily make it the most effective product for every situation. Some plants will require multiple applications, which may be effective, but another product might be just as effective in one. Research your problem and follow guidelines for specific products recommended for treatment.

Use the rates specified in the instructions. If a higher rate is more effective, then the company would post it because it would increase sales. A lot of research goes into ideal effective concentrations; not just to achieve the goal, but to limit environmental impact. Whether it's fertilizers, pesticides, or other landscape chemicals, the "more is better" philosophy has contributed massively to environmental contamination issues. Over-concentrated solutions of herbicides often "burn" the aboveground portion

so quickly that the chemical cannot translocate to the roots. To add insult to injury, the plant retaliates by developing even more shoots, to insure it survives the next adversity, and develops resistance to the offending killing agent.

Try a "safer" product before one with toxicity. Many soap-based repellents and eradicators are available either as premixed products or recipes. They generally take repeat applications to be fully effective but multiple doses won't contain toxins. Don't make the mistake of equating "natural" or "organic" with safe or toxin-free. A number of pesticides are produced from plants and other natural materials. Rotenone and pyrethrin are two common organic pesticides derived from plants that are toxic to fish; pyrethrin has been identified as a suspected carcinogen.

Avoid spraying whenever possible. It is difficult to focus sprays to thoroughly cover only the offending plant without drift to other plants and the environment. A spray nozzle creates many fine droplets and nonvisible overspray can damage contiguous desired plants, as well as making its way into water and other natural systems. I use a process that starts by mixing solution to a specified concentration in a non-spill container. I wear heavy-duty rubber or durable vinyl gloves on both hands and add a soft cloth glove on my application hand. I dip the double-gloved hand in the solution and clench my fist to squeeze out any excess solution that might drip. The rubber glove prevents skin contact with the chemical while the soft glove absorbs it. This allows me to grasp the offending plant at the base and run my clasped fist up it, lightly coating the foliage to the top. You still need to properly cover exposed skin and eyes; just because there isn't spray does not mean that other parts of the body won't be subject to possible contamination. Other suggested methods include covering surrounding plants with newspaper to avoid spray and soil contamination, using a milk jug or similar device to cover only the offending plant and then spraying through the opening, and creating cardboard funnels around the selected weed (however, excess fluid may drip into the soil).

Read instructions carefully and acknowledge restrictions. This applies to more than just concentration. Every chemical solution has minimum and maximum temperature restrictions that affect efficacy. Using the chemical outside that range minimizes success or restricts the product from working at all. It should be mandatory to read instructions when working with pesticides.

Use good gardening practices. Understanding environmental and cultural factors and using good gardening practices such as right plant–right place, good air circulation, proper soil condition, limiting plants that attract problems, embracing those that thrive in your region, and other factors I have discussed will produce healthy plants and conditions less conducive to disease, insects, weeds, and pests.

Acknowledge that small amounts of damage are not issues. Part of my career was spent managing a garden center greenhouse where we grew many seasonal plants such as poinsettia, potted azaleas, and other plants that attracted insects and were prone to disease under mass-planted greenhouse conditions. I learned that the consumer was unaccepting of any imperfections to flower or foliage; even a few minute holes could render a plant unsellable. As a result, greenhouses have traditionally used massive amounts of fungicides, pesticides, inorganic fertilizers, and other chemicals to make sure every plant is perfect. Plants in their natural settings have evolved to withstand a certain amount of damage and that injury is part of a necessary process of adapting to adverse conditions. In studies of human health, we learn that raising children in overly sanitized conditions with no exposure to bacteria, viruses, and other microbes makes them much more susceptible as adults, because their bodies develop no resistance. This is true of plants. There is a balance, obviously. One must watch and make sure that damage doesn't escalate to the point where it adversely affects plant health, but there is also no value to applying chemicals every time we see non-life-threatening issues. Accept that nature is full of imperfections and you will be doing your plants a favor.

Read *Silent Spring*. Before the next growing season make time to read (or reread) Rachel Carson's groundbreaking book. There are many resources warning about adverse effects of manmade chemicals. However, reading a book that was published in 1962 which warns about problems that progressed as foretold, and are more relevant than ever, keeps us focused on the fact that our home landscapes are part of a much larger ecosystem. I keep a copy as the most conspicuous book in my library. It serves as a daily reminder that we are stewards of the earth, and of the importance of that role. If you don't have the time to read it, at least understand the relevancy of the E. B. White quote used to preface the book: "I am pessimistic about the human race because it is too ingenious for its own good. Our approach to nature is to beat it into submission. We would stand a better chance of survival if we accommodated ourselves to this planet and viewed it appreciatively instead of skeptically and dictatorially." This is truer now than ever.

Household Pesticide Alternative Recipes

Note: Always test a solution on a single plant first. You are creating contact insecticides with ingredients that may still burn plant cells. Spray top and bottom sides of leaves for thorough coverage without excess drip. Cover the surface of the growing medium so the solution does not drench the roots.

- From the USDA: One teaspoon of liquid dishwashing detergent to one cup of vegetable oil. Shake forcefully to fully blend and add to a quart of tap water. Use at seven- to ten-day intervals as an all-purpose spray for white flies, spider mites, aphids, and various insects on vegetables and perennials.
- Liquid detergent-alcohol spray: One teaspoon of liquid dishwashing detergent to one cup of rubbing alcohol in one quart of water. Repeat in seven days.
- Liquid detergent-hot pepper spray: Steep six tablespoons of dry, crushed hot pepper in one cup hot water for at least thirty minutes. Strain out the particles of peppers, then mix solution with the liquid detergent formula. You can substitute hot Tabasco sauce or other hot pepper sauces, but experimentation may be required for proper measurement since they vary in heat.

Silent Spring occupies a highly visible spot in my work space as a constant reminder that we are stewards of the earth.

Repeating elements, gently winding paths, and the intrigue of a view beyond differentiate a garden and a designed garden.

MORE THAN PRAIRIE GARDENS

Innovative Garden Design

WHEN I FIRST BECAME FASCINATED with ornamental plants, I was overwhelmed by how many appealed to me. I had to have one of everything. I didn't realize it at the time but I was a plant collector, not a garden designer. Many people start gardens that way and some spend their entire lives adding plants to their gardens without worrying about any particular design style. These collections are a treat to those of us who love and appreciate plant diversity, fascinated by the novel and unusual, but as I visited public and private gardens that pulled plants together into show-stopping designs, it caused heart palpitations. I wanted to go home and start my garden all over again!

Over time I realized I was impressed by gardens created with intentional design—some subtle, some flagrant, some exquisite. I especially appreciated those that unified elements of the landscape into a pleasing whole, but still allowed individual plants to shine. The first noticeable difference in these gardens was the repeating or massing of similar plants. Later I would learn how the eye could be "led"

Exquisitely designed gardens provide a visually appealing flow for the eye.

through a garden, stopped by a focal point, intrigued by a curve leading to the unknown, delighted by echoing colors, fascinated by garden accessories, and lulled into a particular mood. I was ready to take my garden to the next level and I delved into the nuances of garden design.

I'm eager to share with you what I came to understand (and continue to learn) about key elements of design. Before jumping in, though, I want to take you through a few planning considerations.

DEVELOP A PLAN

I always encourage new gardeners to take time to develop a realistic plan of what they might ultimately want, then budget it over a five- or ten-year time period. Creating home landscapes and gardens can be time consuming and expensive. I have watched people try to develop too much too fast, then become discouraged when they realize how much time, money, and energy goes into a livable and inspirational landscape.

When I was involved in nursery and garden retail careers, it amazed me how many customers invested

My original garden idea files contained slides; today everything is digitally stored on a computer.

hundreds of thousands of dollars in homes, then came to me with a landscape budget of only hundreds or a few thousand dollars. They might spend $60,000 on a kitchen, but be horrified to learn an outdoor living area could cost $20,000 to $40,000. Few people think of their yard as an extension of their home. Landscapes and gardens don't have to be costly but they generally require more funds than expected.

Gather Inspiration

Don't bog yourself down in specifics as you begin the planning process. I suggest creating an idea file. When I first started teaching design, that meant a manila file folder, but today it could certainly be computer files. I used to tell garden design students that the two most important tools to bring on public and private garden visits were a camera (to take pictures of plants and ideas you love and want to incorporate into your own garden) and a notebook (for notes; the most important of which will likely be plant names). Today smartphones are replacing the need for both camera and notebook.

Regardless of how you do it, take images that can be stored in some type of file and utilize tools to identify content and context of the image. Collect exciting plants and garden ideas you find in catalogs, magazines, and other published resources, as well as on the Internet. Take advantage of gardening classes and save lecture handouts. When it is time to flesh out your garden plan, you will have a file of plants and ideas that specifically captured your attention.

As both plant fanatic and instructor, I had a strong tendency to photograph plants close-up. This is useful for plant identification, but once you get the desired close-up, move back and take another shot of the plant including its setting. This shows the context. Part of what initially makes a particular plant desirable is its surroundings. Maybe it was

an accent plant; perhaps massing was what made it noticeable. Did the colors, textures, and forms of the surrounding plants make a difference? Was it growing in shade, sun, or variable lighting? Was it a foreground or background plant? A number of factors may have contributed to original visual interest. You might use the same plant in your garden and be disappointed with the result, not realizing that replicating factors in the original site could have made the difference.

Map it Out

Start with a properly scaled map of the property. I used to recommend using the plat map that is generally part of the paperwork you get with your deed or can be obtained from county governmental

LEFT *Pennisetum* 'Fireworks' is dramatic when photographed up close. BELOW This is the border where *Pennisetum* 'Fireworks' and a number of others are overwhelmed in the drama of larger plants.

agencies, but today you can also obtain scaled property maps through Google Earth. Good landscape plans start with concepts that are no more than bubbles and geometric forms representing shapes of desired hardscape, plants, and accessories. You don't have to be an artist or use a fancy computer program. If you know what your symbols mean, that is all that is necessary. Then pull out your idea file and start replacing shapes and forms with specifics.

Attempting to insert every plant, path, garden feature, and ornament in detail, particularly those that will evolve over time, can produce a cluttered plan, so I use tracing paper to create layers. Use a scaled line drawing of house and property as the base on a bright white sheet of paper. Add a layer of tracing paper and draw in the concept shapes and bubbles. Use another sheet to lay out hardscape details both present and future. Include a third sheet to insert the to-scale plant materials. Use as many sheets as needed to keep your plan both clear and flexible over time. Add color with colored pencils or markers. Multiple layers of tracing paper also allow you to create several versions easily.

If you are computer savvy, there are many landscape design programs that range in complexity. My one word of warning is to be careful not to use installed plant databases exclusively. One of the best parts of gardening and horticulture is the huge range—hundreds of thousands—of plant species and variations in cultivars. I have never seen a program that will provide every option and you may limit your plant palette as a result. In addition, the program may not make selections based on your region or important cultural factors specific to your site. By creating and utilizing the idea file, your design is more likely to incorporate what you've already found visually stimulating and inspirational.

You may find it helpful to hire a professional landscape architect or garden designer to develop your plan. Often the fee for the plan will be dropped if you use their services. Landscape architects are particularly qualified for properly constructing the hardscape (sidewalks, paths, steps, decks, terraces, lighting, irrigation, water features, and a multitude of other garden features), and it is well worth the investment to insure correct and durable construction. Garden designers tend to be more plant focused (the softscape) and their forte is developing plant-based combinations for visual appeal. If you go the professional route, it is possible to find individuals or firms who combine both effectively, but it isn't the general rule. I have found that the best firms give landscape projects to teams that include at least one hardscape expert and one plant expert.

Consider Your Foundation Plants

Plants provide as much structure to gardens as hardscapes. Consideration of that structure starts with the largest and most permanent elements: trees and shrubs. These are the foundation plants

Foster Creativity

Professional designs can make the process easier. However, use a designer who provides you freedom to add features of your own. Landscape architects and garden designers have favorite plants and their own design aesthetic. Whether it is a professionally developed design or your own, utilize it as a guide, not as a non-deviational blueprint. Gardening should always be fluid and transitional, so give yourself permission to make changes over time.

Start placing trees and shrubs early in the process, before planting, and determine how they affect views.

I'm referencing, not the term sometimes used to describe plants crammed up against a house's literal foundation.

Horticulturalists love to tell gardeners that the beauty of plants is that they can always be moved if you don't like their placement or they aren't thriving. However, it saves time, energy, and money to make wise siting decisions initially. Keep in mind that perennials are relatively easy to relocate but trees and shrubs are either difficult or impossible to move as they mature. Interestingly, many homeowners feel trees are something to be accepted and worked around, essentially ignored as part of the design plan. But trees can block views, their shade can affect plant selections, and their growth and expansion can change the context of the garden over time. So it is critical to consider them as important elements and not just as fixtures to work around.

When adding new trees and shrubs to the landscape, I place them potted where I imagine they should fit into my design, but then I spend a week or more viewing them at different vantage points

This front entrance that looks like Charleston, South Carolina, is actually in Wisconsin.

from both house and garden. Invariably, I find myself changing their positions—sometimes a little, sometimes significantly—if I realize preliminary placement creates initially unperceived issues. This will save you aggravation, because it is easier to make adjustments at planting than after they develop to maturity. I use the same process with perennials even though I know they will be easier to relocate if I miss the mark.

Acknowledge That You Live in the Midwest

Many people assume that a true Midwest garden revolves around prairie plants. But although large parts of the Midwest were indeed prairie, even larger portions of the region were not. Understanding the geographical, environmental, and cultural idiosyncrasies of your range, locality, and microclimate is what I mean by acknowledging that you live in the Midwest. It has little to do with a preconceived look and everything to do with using plants that will thrive in Midwest conditions.

You can use plants such as bananas and non-hardy succulents to create unique and inspiring displays. But know plant limitations. No matter how hard we try, gardeners in my highly alkaline area will never boast rhododendrons that can come even close to rivaling those on the east coast. Pushing parameters

is part of the fun of gardening, but attempting it for most of your plantings will lead to disappointment. Learn your site limitations and assets. Embrace plant materials that excel under your specific conditions. Acknowledge that four defined seasons exist and utilize plant materials that will shine and provide ornamental interest during each time of year.

A strong native plant movement advocates using only plants indigenous to a range or region. There are many admirable merits in doing so and many resources to assist you if that is your goal. It is likely, then, that your garden will reflect your region. But I am still an ornamental horticulturalist and believe ornamental plants have merits if used judiciously,

Midwest gardening means using plants that that will thrive in our unique conditions—but add statements of your creativity, such as this banana that punches up an otherwise traditional border.

and should be removed if they are discovered to cause issues with the local landscape. In the best Midwest gardens I have visited, no one would say, "This is a great garden that represents the Midwest." Rather, they would say "This is a gorgeous, inspirational garden that has embraced and succeeded in Midwest conditions."

If you live in rural or similar areas where the regional landscape plays into your gardening efforts and designs, you have the advantage of utilizing that greater perspective to your advantage. South of the Boreal gardeners are more likely to utilize the relaxing shade of surrounding forests and lighten those areas with the white accents of paperbark birch, soften the feel with fine-textured ferns, and celebrate spring with woodland ephemerals. Great Lakes residents lucky enough to border the water can borrow spectacular aquatic views. Those more inland will take advantage of the deciduous forest much like South of the Boreal residents, but with an expanded plant palette. Our Prairie inhabitants may embrace the large tracts of flat land and replicate prairie style gardens, or may opt for adding vertical accents to break up the vastness of space. Gardeners in the Plains have the ability to use large trees for silhouettes and scale, tall waving grasses, and undulating masses of large-scale perennials. Those in the latter regions will likely add trees for shade and

I don't believe that at first glance you would identify my garden as Midwest. The Midwest aspect is my acknowledgment of climatic, environmental, and geographic limitations that allow my plants to flourish regardless of design style.

relaxation, whereas the first two regions are more likely to call for the removal of trees to create sunny areas. Finally, our neighbors in the Lower Midwest will embrace their advantage of longer growing season, but design their gardens to minimize heat and humidity.

Those of us in more urban conditions will work harder to stylize our gardens without benefit of our region's borrowed views. It will be easier to create nontraditional looks, because we are transitioning into buildings, parking lots, and streets; it will be harder for us to embrace the regionality aspect without adjoining woods, prairies, mountains, and bodies of water into which our gardens might transition. This can be a bane if you want to look extremely regional; a boon if you want to create a nonstereotypical look.

Planting with acknowledgment to the Midwest is not a design style; it is recognition of the uniqueness of your region, range, locality, and home landscape. Just as English, French, Italian, and Japanese garden designations imply specific images of what we think defines their look, no style should be completely stereotyped. If you were to mention Midwest gardens to other areas of the country, it is likely they would immediately envision prairie style gardening or beds dominated by purple coneflowers. Every gardener, regardless of where they live, should feel free to incorporate any style of gardening into their landscapes. Midwest gardening should be an acknowledgment and embracing of the climatic, cultural, and geographic conditions, but should not deter you from using tropical plants, sculptural topiaries, weathered cedar, plant materials, and other elements that might be associated with other regions or design styles.

THE DESIGN ELEMENTS

Good garden designs avoid the static. Many tricks we use in design encourage the eye to move through a landscape and land on particular points. Intrigue happens when a piece of landscape is hidden from view but there is a hint of something to be revealed. Tiny landscapes can appear larger; artifices can make vast landscapes appear more intimate. Plants can stand out as specimens; borders can appear melded into a unified palette. It is even possible to develop multiple spaces with different purposes that retain a visual connection.

Every design class talks about elements of design that are often referred to as "rules of design." With the acknowledgment that there are others, I use eight basic elements:

- Balance
- Repetition and rhythm
- Focal point
- Proportion and scale
- Contrast
- Domination and subordination
- Transition
- Unity

Don't be intimidated by the terminology; the catchphrases make perfect sense once they are defined and explained. Let's discard the notion that these are rules and call them guidelines. I can't emphasize enough that it is ultimately *your* garden, 365 days a year. Following some simple design guidelines will make it visually appealing but ultimately it should be an expression of *your* personality and a space *you* enjoy.

Balance

Balance refers primarily to visual weight. Features that are large, whether plants or structures, command more visual attention than the small or diminutive. For instance, if a large tree in the right corner of your property overshadows small perennials on the left side, then the scene is visually imbalanced, drawing the eye to the overpowering object. There are two forms of balance: formal (symmetric) and informal (asymmetric) balance. Formal balance has been used heavily in classical garden design but the modern garden tends more toward informal.

Formal balance

The first European landscaped gardens were developed as extensions of living space at Roman villas, as advances in the newly developed sense of civilization. Beyond city walls prowled dangerous animals, marauders, disease, and other hardships. The "wild,"

as it was called, was random and unkempt, and the natural landscape unruly. Civilization was defined by newly emerging science and math, so using such things as geometry in early gardens stressed man's civilized hand over the undesirable natural. Gardens were laid out in very deliberate geometric grids; whatever was placed on one side of an axis was duplicated exactly on the other side and could be further divided into quadrants. The more the property was geometric and balanced, the more evidence of civilization. Few acts seemed more human influenced than the process of severely shearing trees and shrubs into topiaries, hedges, knot gardens, and parterres. Throughout garden design history, most

Knot gardens are an example of highly manicured, geometrically perfect gardens, a constant reminder of the influence of man and civilization.

subsequent societies (especially the wealthy class), would utilize balanced landscapes as defined by the formal garden.

Symmetrical balance is used today to complement a formally balanced house or to replicate the grand elegance of periods of wealth and opulence. It can be used with informal house styles, but generally looks out of place. In these situations it is more likely to be used to define a smaller section of the larger landscape, such as an herb garden, garden room, or area focused on a water feature or sculpture.

Informal balance

Whereas formal balance is easy to recognize, most people don't realize there is such a thing as informal balance; in fact, the antithesis of symmetric balance might logically seem to be no balance at all. But our eyes and brains find a lack of balance unsettling. Informal balance stipulates that visual weight in one plane of the landscape must be balanced with equal visual weight in an adjoining plane—it just doesn't have to be accomplished as a mirror image. If an object with mass such as a shade tree dominates one side of the view, it can be informally balanced by combining a small tree flanked by a grouping of shrubs that add up to equal or similar mass. Evaluating balance in informal situations is more difficult and may require more finessing over time than assessing formal balance. Color is a distraction to gauging mass, and even shadows and shade create greater

The dark green mass on the right is informally balanced with the colorful zinnias on the left. Both forms of balance can be utilized.

This mostly informal landscape gives a nod to formality with the geometrically placed boxwood balls.

visual mass than sunlight. To evaluate informal balance, photocopy an image of the scene in black and white, or convert it to grayscale in a computer program. The black will define and demonstrate where you have mass and you can determine where it overpowers white. Either reduce elements that create the black or increase mass in the white areas.

Repetition and Rhythm

Our brains welcome repeating elements as visually pleasing and our vision tends to follow where they lead. If your goal is to direct the view through a garden space to a focal point or destination, then repeating color, texture, lines, and form will "draw" the eye where you intend. Rhythm is a result of repetition. Because grasses move in the breeze they are a great plant group to demonstrate this concept. View ornamental grasses planted in repeated units swaying in the breeze and you will understand rhythm in the garden. But physical movement is not essential. Simply repeating elements can conjure the feeling of rhythm, which in turn suggests movement.

Repeating elements, colors, and forms creates the repetition and rhythm that lead your eye on a path through the landscape.

When you design your garden, determine where you wish to lead the eye to focus on highlighted accents. Straight-line views are rarely interesting. It is more pleasing to view garden space in a relaxed and unhurried manner; winding sightlines decelerate the process. As a result, more of the garden is taken in and appreciated visually. Select several

Color echo garden accessories as well as plants, to maximize effect.

Once you determine the sight line, end it with an ultimate destination. The focal point here is represented by the distant statue on the other side of the swimming pool.

plant genera that work together and repeat them in gentle sweeps in the direction you want to move the view. Once you create directional view with repetition and rhythm, you can interplant with other shapes and forms, and the repeating elements will continue to direct the eye.

Color echoing

I loved the term "color echoing" the first time I heard it. This simple yet useful concept works well as a form of repetition and rhythm and contributes to balance and unity. Repetition of color pleases the eye especially if some restraint is used; the effect is intended to be subtle. Blatant use of large quantities of the same color isn't as appealing as utilizing analogous colors selectively, possibly expressed through the flowers of a few plants and the foliage of others. This is different from monochromatic schemes: monochromatic plantings maximize analogous color, whereas color echoing is a subtler weaving of analogous colors delicately through the combination. Echoing may include the garden accessories, ornaments, building accents, and other hard items integrated with plants.

Focal Point

Repetition and rhythm lead the eye through space, but a destination is needed—something to arrest and intrigue the eye. The most effective focal points for the Midwest are garden ornaments (benches, fountains, sculptures, and arbors) because they are unchangeable all year. They are also an opportunity to add four-season interest to the vista.

Plants can also be used as focal points. Trees and shrubs are structural but are most effective if they possess multi-seasonal interest such as interesting bark or form. Conifers provide four-season interest but it is best to use those that are not dark green in color so they don't blend into the background. Large perennials can be used as accents but the effect is lost in winter if plants are crushed by heavy winter snows, and the impact is nonexistent in spring until plants gain height.

If you have a landscape large enough to subdivide into separate and distinct areas, it is useful to have a focal point for each. Some of the most interesting gardens are those that have enough space to create paths or sight lines that lead to one focal point, then turn a corner to a new view highlighted by another focal point, and so on. Dividing garden space allows incorporation of diverse compositions, impressions, and sensations without compromising harmony and unity. Creating visual corridors leading to enclosed garden rooms provides gardeners the opportunity to create different moods in each area. A focal point at the end of each corridor provides the allure of destination.

If you don't have a large property, you can still achieve this intimacy on a small scale. Garden rooms don't have to be large; the smallest I have seen was an arbor garden swing covered in vines, which made it a private enclave of its own. It is an added benefit when these rooms have function, but part of the goal is to make the garden more visually interesting with curving lines, providing the sense that there is

A garden room can be as small as the space created with this swing.

more to see beyond a single view, and adding curious desire to see what is hidden. The difference between large and small properties is that you have the ability to utilize a number of rooms in the former, but may be limited to one or two in the latter.

Proportion and Scale

Proportion and scale describe the size relationship between the landscape and its individual components as well as of individual elements to each other. In the simplest terms, one would not plant a massive burr oak in a small urban garden. It would take up the entire space and look out of place. In the same respect, if you populated a 5-acre backyard vista with alpine plants, the individual plants would be unidentifiable and the space would lack intimacy.

Because most gardens are created as outdoor living areas, proportion and scale affect movement and human interaction within the space as well. The trend toward outdoor living, with massive outdoor grills, stone fireplaces, and full-sized furniture may

dominate a small yard leaving no room for plants. If you scale down such fixtures you'll have more opportunity for gardening and the hardscape will seem less imposing or ostentatious. Additionally, a terrace that barely provides enough room for a table and chairs set in a large unsegmented yard will feel lost and overwhelmed by space.

Proportion and scale became challenging during a trend of building massive homes on small lots. If a new home takes up most of the lot, there is no room for plants large enough to provide appropriate visual scale and the house becomes disproportionate to the property. It works in reverse as well. Planting a tree that ultimately gets 70 ft. tall near a bungalow home on a small lot will make the house look tiny and lost in the landscape.

An exception is to avoid restricting small lots to entirely small plants and garden ornaments. If all of the components of a small garden are minimized to fit the scale, our brains subconsciously tell us that it is an undersized space. However, if one or several oversized items are selectively placed, then our brains believe the space must be larger in order to contain them.

Perspective

Artists use manipulation of perspective to fool the eye and this technique also works in garden design. It is called foreshortening, and it creates a sense of depth, especially with paths. For example, when building a path from the house, use smaller and smaller paving stones as you get farther away to fool the eye into thinking the far side of the garden is even farther from the house than it really is. You can accomplish this visual perspective with plants as well. To give a small garden more depth, place smaller plants in the background rather than the foreground; reverse this to make a large space appear more intimate.

The massive Norway spruce overwhelms the small bungalow home, making it appear even tinier.

ABOVE **The large, arching scale of the banana makes this small yard appear visually larger.** LEFT **Using an oversized urn in this small area gives the appearance of more space.**

Vertical plants and garden ornaments lead the eye visually upward and this is another mind trick that suggests larger space. Vertical structures provide more growing area for small spaces and bring plants up into more light in areas with limited sun. They provide multiple season interest and rise majestically out of snow. The verticality helps balance the horizontal nature of terraces, walks, beds, and other landscape features.

Contrast

Contrast accentuates the difference between a plant or garden ornament and its surroundings. Using contrast is the best way to avoid predictability in a garden and adds a pleasing sense of tension

It is the contrast of coarse texture with fine that makes this such a visually pleasing combination.

between elements. I discern the range in contrast as visually boring (too little), visually stimulating (just right), and visually agonizing (too much).

Too little contrast causes all of the elements to blend together in a visual fusion and makes the composition mundane. Too much contrast affronts the eye, an overstimulation of the senses, because it lacks no harmony. Ideal is a balance that will vary according to the mood you are trying to achieve. Increasing contrast incites excitement and stimulation. Reducing contrast creates relaxation, respite, and calm. The ability to segment your garden allows you to have some spaces provoking energy and others lending an atmosphere of relaxation. Contrast can be achieved by juxtaposing differences in color, form, light, and texture. The best designs make use

Bring the excitement to eye level!

of all these elements. If you view a garden setting and something subconsciously does not quite feel right about the mood created, the culprit is generally contrast.

Rarely does contrast work effectively pairing plants one-on-one. It is a common mistake. When we go to the garden center to purchase plants that we intend to plant as multiples, it seems logical to purchase each in equal quantity. But one plant's contrasting element may dominate the other. It is just as important to equalize visual weight with contrast as it is with balance.

Textural contrast
One common technique used to achieve contrast is combining plants with fine and bold textures. Fine texture is easily overwhelmed by bold and you may lose the effect if you don't increase the quantity

of fine-textured plants to a single bold form. For instance, to contrast a hosta with a fine-textured fern, you must group multiple ferns to the single hosta. Start the structural foundation of a new garden with the coarsest and finest representatives you plan to incorporate. Determine the visual path you hope to create and place multiples of both together to form that route. Remember to use more fine-to-bold plants to maintain the contrast. Contrast is such a bold statement that the eye will always be attracted to and follow it; you can then add all of the other plant materials of various forms, and your built-in foundation of visual "pull" is incorporated so subtly that the visitor won't even realize you've compelled their view!

Color contrast

Color is the most commonly used contrast element. Strongest color contrast is accomplished by pairing the complementary colors directly across the color wheel from one another. Blue contrasts most dramatically with orange, yellow with purple, red with green, and so on. To minimize contrast, one uses analogous colors, those that are adjacent to each other on the color wheel. So blue combined with blue-green and blue-violet would be an analogous combination. It is easy to see how similar colors blend; in fact this type of color combination is termed monochromatic. Analogous colors harmonize, but keep in mind that if a color scheme is too monochromatic, it may be monotonous.

Pairing complementary colors one-on-one will not necessarily create a balanced and pleasing

TOP These two plants are positioned close together, but the cool blue of the background larkspur contrasting with the bright foreground color of the lily gives the appearance of depth and separation. MIDDLE Vivid, in-your-face contrast. BOTTOM Colorful, stylish contrast.

Dull, boring contrast.

Soft, subtle contrast.

contrast. Every color has specific qualities including hue, value, and saturation. Here is one example using value. All colors (hues) have a relative weight in brightness or darkness, called value. Each hue has a value but not all hues have the same value. Yellow has the highest value, purple the lowest. This means

that yellow will dominate and subordinate purple if pairing a bright yellow plant with one that's purple. In order to balance the composition, you might need three or four purples to equalize the bright yellow. The farther apart in value, the more plants of lower value are needed to balance, whereas similar values, such as blue and green, can be paired more equally.

Lastly, here's another color concept that's useful for garden design. Warm, bright colors like yellow, hot pink, orange, and red leap out, making plants appear closer than they really are. Cool colors like blue and purple appear to recede into the background creating the illusion of more space. If you are trying to make a smaller garden appear larger, place the warm colors in front and the cool colors in back; to make a larger garden seem more intimate, reverse that planting.

Domination and Subordination

This is perhaps the hardest design element to define. It is similar to proportion and scale, so it isn't always described as an element. The natural world is oriented to dominance and submission. In the animal kingdom, predators dominate prey; in nature, some plants dominate others. Consider the forest. The natural structure of woodland consists of four layers: ground, shrub, understory, and canopy. The canopy becomes the dominant layer, towering over the others and impacting their survival. Understory

Bold, relaxing contrast.

trees dominate shrubs and ground layers but are subordinate to the canopy. You see the pattern. Both domination and subordination occur in natural settings and it is subconsciously disconcerting when it doesn't exist.

The key to successfully mimicking nature is to use this property in balance. Subordinates should outnumber dominants. Subordinated doesn't mean weak; it is a description of where something fits in the overall natural or garden scheme. For instance, in a small yard with one canopy tree, there might be three understory trees, nine shrubs, and fifty perennials. Quantities of each depend on mature sizes.

Transition

All plant features, including color, size, form, texture, and contrast, need to demonstrate pleasing transition from plant to plant that makes sense visually and creates an uninterrupted flow for the eye. Height should be considered as well. Arranging plants in rigid rows that stair-step from shortest in front to tallest in the rear is generally unimaginative and rigid; transition should be smooth and imperceptible. When segmenting garden areas into rooms or distinctly different uses, smooth transitions between them are more appealing than distinctly hard divisions.

One of the best examples in nature is the fact that the forest canopy dominates the understory and woodland floor. Gardeners need to replicate that, without losing the impact of the subordinate features.

How the garden fits into the larger landscape is also part of transition. Balancing the garden foreground with the borrowed view background is key to success. Imagine a home in the countryside surrounded by meadows and distant forest. If the borders of the property are defined with contiguous perennial beds or hedges, it makes the home landscape look contrived and plopped into a surrounding natural landscape. Using plants that transition gently between ornamental beds and the adjoining meadow provides a visual connection; one or more openings allow vistas into that meadow. Too much borrowed view may overwhelm the intimacy of the garden, so glimpses of the landscape beyond the garden is more intriguing. Low hedges, fences, walls, and other barriers carved with simulated windows and doors can effectively provide glimpses of the borrowed view. The goal is to maximize the sense of space without allowing the exterior landscape to overwhelm the intimacy of the garden.

If you are surrounded by lovely views, rejoice, since those of us with urban yards rarely have such opportunities unless we adjoin parks or golf courses. Our views tend to be unnatural and blocked with buildings, walls, fences, and hedges, or they are already obstructed for us by neighboring structures

A beautiful transition from lawn to woodland.

we can't change. In these cases, effective transitioning within the garden itself to capture the eye and soften the effect of barrier will be the goal.

Unity

Unity is the last design element we'll discuss because it is the culmination of the other seven concepts and also the most intangible. If done well, the result is a unified view of individual plants, garden sections, and the garden as a whole. The gardens you visit where every turn makes you catch your breath with perceived perfection demonstrate unity. Nothing is grating to the eye; no subconscious discord is felt. Plants, hardscape, and garden ornamentation are appropriate to design theme. All parts are

connected and harmonious, but still offer accents and contrast. The gardens that make you want to return home and start over are the gardens from which you should borrow ideas. The gardeners who attain unity in their garden are always reevaluating their designs and making annual adjustments. It takes time to achieve desired effects and you should enjoy the journey.

One way that I achieve unity in my garden is to weave with repetition and rhythm. I have gardens both in front of the house and behind. I want to pull the viewer's eye through each, while providing a subconscious visual connection between both. You can achieve this by using one plant or plant form that winds in repetition through both areas. My weaver

Unity should be subtle. Using the design elements effectively means they meld and don't stand out as individual components.

of choice consists of cultivars of Japanese forest grass (*Hakonechloa macra*), because it is an additional contrasting architectural form to the already placed bold and coarse elements. This lovely arching grass weeps gracefully to provide a soft connection between my contrasting textural structure and the rest of my garden plants. Its repetition weaves disparate plants together. Additionally, by using the same weaver in front and rear gardens, visitors can walk from one garden to the other and still feel they are tied to each other. Many other plants can be used to achieve a weaving effect. Some designers use white, silver, or silver-blue plants, because neutral tones pull individual plantings together without adding additional complexity.

ADDITIONAL HINTS, TRICKS, AND GUIDING PRINCIPLES

Here are a few additional techniques that don't fall under the category of design elements. Many of these have been passed along, in some form or another, from fellow gardeners. One of the great values of visiting with other gardeners is that you will learn some interesting discoveries they have made that add to overall design.

Plant in Odd Numbers

Nature isn't geometric, so unequal numbers tend to look less forced. Often a grouping of three plants makes more impact than one and the effect escalates as you increase numbers. Massing plants provides

I used units of three in this section of my backyard, but there are also singles and pairs.

drama and allows otherwise inconspicuous plants to stand out if they are unnoticed alone. Often touted as a design rule, planting in odd numbers should be a guideline, not an ultimatum. If you think planting in even numbers is more visually appealing in situations within your space, follow your instincts and go for it. You can always add another plant later. And formal landscapes require that everything be equally balanced, so this rule may not apply in those situations.

Design from Inside the House

My mother was a big offender of this principle. A blue Colorado spruce in front of the living room picture window, a sugar maple outside the kitchen window, a Norway maple fronting one bedroom window, and a clump of sycamore maples blocking two other bedroom window views! Now don't laugh at her mistake, it is not that uncommon. Novice gardeners view the exterior of the home as separate and distinct from the interior. They create gardens and landscapes considering only external space, and it isn't until plants mature that they realize the placement wasn't ideal from indoors.

Design for the exterior view.

For much of the Midwest, half of our year is either brown or white. If you don't believe me, count the months on your fingers. If for half of the year we can expect sporadically inclement weather, no prospect of outdoor gardening, and dull landscapes, then we need to be designing gardens we can enjoy from inside as well as during the off-season. Make sure that the views through your windows maximize garden space. I encourage you to determine the indoor room and outside views you will be enjoying the most before you even start the garden plan.

Also consider where you locate activity areas and focal points traditionally placed at a distance from the house. In another home, I decided I wanted a backyard pond, and my original idea was to create a garden room along the distant back fence line, where I could relax and enjoy the water feature. Before I started the project, the city of Madison experienced a 100-year flood and my backyard was under several feet of water for over a month. The only place I still had lawn was an 8-ft.-by-20-ft. square directly off the back kitchen door. It wasn't what I had envisioned, but I built my pond in this spot and discovered that I ended up enjoying the water feature far more than if I had relegated it to the back. It was viewed on a daily basis because I used the kitchen door and looked out the kitchen window all winter. We love convenience and need to acknowledge that. In my current home, I have a garden room seating area on the back border of my yard but I spend most of my time on the wraparound porch. You can bet it is surrounded by garden!

Container Gardening

This topic deserves an entire chapter of its own. With the advent of fiberglass, resin, and composite containers, gardeners are no longer relegated to traditional terra-cotta, concrete, cast iron,

TOP Arranging containers in straight lines with all of the plants at the same height does not allow the plants to make a statement.

BOTTOM Notice how something as simple as pulling the line into a triangle makes an arrangement more visually appealing.

These large containers are not making the impact they could because the plants blend into one unit.

ceramics, and plastics. These newer containers are lighter weight, winter resilient, less costly, more readily available, colorful, and are hard to discern from time-honored materials. Modern containers include nontraditional raised and elevated beds, living walls, and collapsible bags made from vinyl or landscape fabric. Selection and use is limited only by your imagination.

Although containers may appear to be the simplest form of gardening, in truth they can be the most difficult and labor intensive. Some of the biggest issues already discussed are related to the growing media, fertilization, and watering. Containers should be easy to access for watering and care. Consider their size, weight, and material if you need

them to be portable. Know if they will endure winter freezing and thawing or need to be stored indoors.

Here are some container gardening design considerations:

Avoid the straight line syndrome. Container plantings rarely look visually interesting lined out in rigid rows, even though it may seem intuitive when you place them. Vary heights of plants to create more visual interest and treat each container as part of a whole. Cluster containers and vary their size.

Vary plant materials in the containers. This certainly helps with height issues and is more interesting than similar shapes, forms, and colors repeated in

multiple containers. Mixed usage is very popular and produces fascinating combinations. Modern containers make use of combinations of perennials, tropical, succulents, and even trees and shrubs. When using mixed plants in a container, make sure they all have similar cultural requirements such as water, light, and fertility.

Minimize the number of plants per container but maximize containers. The most common reason for failure is overloading containers with too many plants. In overcrowded conditions, some plants will dominate and overpower those that are less robust. Or the entire container may fail because all plants submit to competition and root binding. It is common to see magazines offering competitions for best container combinations. I advocate that the true test of such contests is a submission of the same container at the end of the season to see how the mix survived overcrowding, competition, and summer heat! Many plant breeders are now acknowledging this truth by selling predetermined annual combinations that have been proved by research to play well together.

If you have ever had to pull a declining plant out of a mixed container you know it is difficult to do so without damaging the other plants. It also changes the overall look. But if you grow fewer plants in each container it will be easier to replace a bad plant, move one of the containers to better conditions if it is performing poorly, or change the overall composition by moving individual containers around. As

TOP Separating the pots and varying the content provides uniformity and individuality. MIDDLE Everybody likes a crammed container, but by summer it lacks elegance and by late summer many of the plants may decline due to competition. BOTTOM More containers with fewer plants are easier to care for and more chic.

plants mature, you cannot give them more space in a crammed container but you can increase space by moving containers farther apart in an arrangement.

Neutralize Your Elephants

I don't remember when I first heard this phrase but I never forgot the concept. Most homes have cumbersome objects that command visual space and detract from the garden, such as fuel tanks, recycling areas, and air conditioning units. Paint large structures or outbuildings in neutral colors to downplay them, or transform the look of the building into something that better fits a garden theme. Selective plants can hide eyesores and decorative fencing may give the illusion that what it hides is more garden space. Adding sizable, weather-resilient mirrors to broad expanses of walls and fences reflects the garden back to the viewer and makes it appear larger. Attaching cast-off doors, windows, and steps gives the impression that something is on the other side, even if there are no tangible openings. Living roofs,

shelves, and window boxes help meld structures into garden space and suggest a more organic purpose. Lattice and other vertical structures for vines cover unappealing expanses of wall and add more growing space.

Add Visual Appeal

Paint is perhaps the easiest and least expensive way to add visual appeal to a garden and allows you to change focus without purchasing new accessories every season. Paint freshens a timeworn look, adds new looks to traditional objects, provides winter color, emphasizes focal points, and forces mundane items to pop. It can be used to dull, hide, or mitigate offensive items. Contemporary spray paints effectively cover any surface quickly and easily. They richen cheap materials such as plastic and provide colors otherwise unavailable in certain materials. They brighten shade where flowers won't flourish and provide color echoing.

I also highly encourage gardeners to support artists and original art. There is unique art in every price range. Art and nature complement one another. You can augment your garden with mass-produced garden ornamentation but handcrafted pieces will garner more compliments, further personalize your space, and support artists. Art also helps define mood and theme. The art you choose can identify a space as classic, contemporary, fun, energetic, natural, or any number of impressions. My custom-built dragon arbor is an expression of my love of gardening, fantasy, and art.

Another way to add interest to your garden is with found and reclaimed ornaments. This trend has exploded due to interest in recycling and minimizing negative impacts on the environment. You can add reclaimed materials to the garden in many creative ways. Old columns, broken pottery, building foundation stone, cast-off furniture, crumbling statues,

I love how the homeowners incorporated the chicken coop as a garden element.

and other items are popular. They are generally used to create the look of ruins or the sense of age. There is a fine line between adding cast-offs to the garden with panache and giving the appearance of debris. Allow restraint to reign and consider placement carefully. Integrating plant materials into the reclaimed object is critical to make it look part of the garden, not something left behind or plopped in with no sense of purpose.

Consider use and materials well. I have seen creative steps and paths built from nontraditional reclaimed materials, but some of those have been slippery, uneven, difficult to navigate, and even dangerous. Crumbling concrete leaches and raises

pH. Terra-cotta has a short life and disintegrates, leaving shards behind. Glass doesn't hold up well to harsh winters and frost heaving. Cast-offs might be short-lived but there are creative ways to extend use when utilized with careful consideration. Lastly, remember that what may be creative in your mind's eye may look like clutter or garbage to others no matter how cleverly you use it. Don't restrict your creative energy, but also try to envision the scene from the point of view of others.

Cheap Styrofoam pots jazzed up with a coat of red paint at Rotary Botanical Gardens.

Judiciously placed, reclaimed items impart the sense of age to garden spaces.

Peeks and Smiles

Sometimes I develop terminology of my own based on reaction to an experience. I apply "peeks" to subtly placed objects that inspire double takes. Gardens should be places to spend time casually, maximizing enjoyment and unexpected discovery. If all the garden elements are highly visible it doesn't take much time for the viewer to believe they have seen all there is to see. But gardens have many layers, and one should be encouraged to stop, possibly kneel, and get closer looks at enticing revelations. Curving paths, hidden views, and garden rooms assist in decelerating a walk. Utilizing strategically placed ornaments where only a hint is obvious is also extremely effective.

I also love carefully placed pieces that make me smile. I'm not especially drawn to the cute or tawdry, so I don't own any bunny sculptures or garden gnomes. If you enjoy those things, go for it; the garden is your space and should be a reflection of your personality. But I do appreciate whimsy, and smiles link nicely with peeks because usually the

whimsical object isn't brashly obvious and it might take a second look to fully comprehend the humor. Some humor is geared toward other gardeners and they appreciate it in a way others would not. This is another area where restraint may be in order, but I think one can always appreciate understated humor and whimsy.

Evoke Memories

A garden can provide pleasant memories and reminders of people we love or care about. A straightforward method of cultivating warm memories is sharing plants. A number of plants in my garden were given to me by other gardeners whom I love or respect, or who may have mentored my gardening. I can't view any of these plants without smiling as I remember the people who gave them to me.

I visited one gardener whose father had carved him a garden gate out of western yew as a gift. The father is now deceased but his son remembers him every time he uses the gate. Another garden friend knew his wife adored sand hill cranes so he had a pair sculpted for a fiftieth anniversary gift, as a constant reminder of his love and their years together. Additions don't have to be expensive; they just need to evoke memories and provide a deeper connection to the garden space.

This subtly placed leaf sculpture causes a double take and slows down visitors rushing uphill on a long path, with Chanticleer's famed Ruins Garden as the ultimate destination.

Create a Sensory Garden Experience

I have gardened in shade for twenty years and one of the best pieces of advice I got was to brighten my paths to make them more inviting to the visitor. This isn't something we think about in our gardens, since we are already intimate with the space. However, many people are subconsciously trepidatious of dark areas. Your garden visitor may enter a dark area and never fully relax to enjoy the experience. Paths made of light-reflective materials such as

TOP The owners of this garden invited friends and family to help create a mosaic wall, a timeless reminder of loved ones.

ABOVE My side path lights up my shade garden.

Stimulate the ears and attract birds at the same time with a water feature.

light-colored mulch, stone or pavers, gravel, or similar materials help alleviate subliminal anxiety and are more inviting.

A garden setting should stimulate multiple senses. Gardens should never be stagnant and movement in the garden adds visual interest and stimulation. Ornamental grasses or cleverly crafted sculptures can capture breezes and provide motion. Sound, from the delicate ranges of wind chimes to the soothing flow of moving water, stimulates the ear. Fountains with moving water attract birds and help abate urban noise. Find plants that provide pleasing fragrance that attracts both you and wildlife.

Use the K.I.S.S. Principle

Keep It Simple, Stupid is one of those timeworn phrases that works well in garden design. The principle maintains that most systems work best if they are kept simple; therefore unnecessary complexity should be avoided and simplicity should govern design. Novice gardeners should start the design process with basic concepts that work and add levels of complexity as confidence builds. If color combinations confuse you, start with simple concepts such as complementary, analogous, and monochromatic color schemes. Instead of trying to make dozens of plants appear unified in texture, shape, and color, use fewer species in multiples. Begin with plants that are durable and likely to thrive under adverse conditions before delving into those with fussy requirements. As you develop confidence in uncomplicated design and growing skills, you can experiment with more complex concepts and plant materials. Nothing boosts confidence like success and rarely can you go wrong with simplicity and restraint.

There can be elegance in simplicity!

A Midwest Plant Palette

A REGION AS LARGE AS THE MIDWEST has a nearly inexhaustible number of appropriate and interesting plant choices. In this section, my goal is to provide enough material for a solid garden foundation, with the idea that you will continue to explore additional options on an annual basis.

Keep some things in mind. Many plants are adaptable to a wide range of environmental, geographical, and cultural conditions; some are very specific. I group plants by conditions that will maximize robust growth and durability, even if the plant tolerates less desirable conditions. In gardening, tolerating situations is not the same as thriving in them. A shade-tolerant plant, for instance, may survive and grow passably but that doesn't ensure it will reach ideal size, shape, or form.

Taxonomists are redefining species and plant names on a continual basis but I make every effort to use the most current and commonly used plant terminology. Plant names and marketing have become complex issues, so for the sake of clarity for purchasing plants I have used the most commonly marketed name—either cultivar or trademark, but not both—in single quotes.

A note on plant sourcing: today an Internet search will provide extensive lists of local nurseries and garden centers as well as mail-order sources. If you have any difficulty, most areas have excellent organizations for helping gardeners with searches and issues; check out your local extension service, your state Master Gardener program, and plant societies. I highly encourage you to meet and visit local gardeners, as they are your single best source of advice for plants, issues, and gardening under your specific conditions. One of the best parts of the gardening community is that gardeners love to share!

Using the Plant Chapter

The critical cultural information for ideal garden placement appears in sidebars, where plants with similar requirements are grouped together. My advice is to first look for sidebars that fit your situation, then locate individual plants in the alphabetical listing.

Eryngium planum and *Silphium terebinthinaceum* make a simple yet dramatic statement.

Symbols

✿ **Full sun:** Six or more hours of sunlight, which can be broken into different parts of the day; the hours do not have to be contiguous.

◐ **Part sun:** Three to six hours of sunlight with more emphasis on the minimum sun requirements; generally afternoon sun.

☼ **Part shade:** Three to six hours of sunlight, with protection from the hottest afternoon sun; generally refers to morning sun.

◗ **Full shade:** Less than three hours of sunlight. All garden plants require sunlight for photosynthesis so most full shade plants are ephemeral.

❂ **Native:** This term is wide-ranging and native plant advocates differ on what they consider native. In the broadest sense, native means indigenous to North America although most designations refer to specific areas of the country. For our purposes, native refers to the Midwest region with the understanding that individual species may be native to smaller ranges within the region and I include cultivars.

Other Terminology

Hardiness: When a zone is listed in parentheses, such as (5)6–9, it indicates either that there is discrepancy between information sources or the plant is likely to survive in the colder climate under ideal growing conditions and microclimate conditions.

Size: Listed as height × width. Some plants may range widely due to cultivar differences. For instance *Heliopsis helianthoides* (oxeye) can reach 6 ft. × 4 ft. but the cultivar 'Summer Nights' reaches 3–4 ft. × 2–3 ft. so the listing for oxeye will be 3–6 ft. × 2–4 ft. Geographical, environmental, and cultural conditions also affect size.

Bloom period: Provided simply as spring, summer, or fall for generalized reference, because spring in St. Louis, Missouri, for example, arrives months ahead of spring in International Falls, Minnesota. You can research what month(s) that means to you.

Non-flowering: All plants within (with the exception of the conifers) are angiosperms, and thus flower in some form. Non-flowering is designated where flowers are not the significant garden feature.

Annual: A plant that under normal Midwest conditions will live only one season.

Perennial: A plant that under normal Midwest conditions will survive six years or more.

Short-lived perennial: A plant that under normal Midwest conditions will survive six years or less.

Shrub: A woody perennial that is smaller than a tree with one to several main stems arising at or near the ground.

Tree: A woody perennial typically having a single stem or trunk (but not always), growing taller than shrubs, and bearing lateral branches above the ground.

Vine: An annual or perennial that derives its support from climbing or twining but may also become a ground cover without vertical support.

Grass: An ornamental annual or perennial used primarily for foliar texture, form, and color.

Weak or lacks vigor: The plant may be hardy, but even in ideal conditions it struggles and never achieves adequate size, scale, or strength.

Fussy: May require more time and attention and does not handle competition well.

Robust: The plant thrives in the area it is planted without becoming a nuisance; it requires no fussing, is durable, and achieves desirable size, scale, and strength.

Aggressive: Robust to the point that it attempts to take more than its allotted space; not so bad as to be considered invasive but it requires attention to keep in check.

Thug: These plants are the ultimate in aggressive without being invasive. Thugs will push less aggressive plants out of existence in the garden.

Invasive: Aggressive to the point that their spread by seed, root systems, or other methods displaces other plants so that the invasive plant becomes the dominant population. Many states have legal definitions and lists; I use the term more generally.

Naturalized: Often confused with native, this is an originally non-native plant that was introduced to an area where it established over time and developed permanent populations.

Tolerant: The plant tolerates the described conditions but they are not ideal.

Resistant: Some tolerance to adverse conditions such as disease or pest damage, but do not mistake the term for immunity. Over time, disease organisms mutate and pests change their habits to overcome resistance.

Drought tolerant: Plants that will survive in the typical or somewhat less-than-typical amount of rainfall in your region with little or no irrigation. Plants tolerant of the Lower Midwest's driest summers, for example, may not necessarily be tolerant of drought in the Plains states.

Exotic: Non-native plants.

Ornamental: Describes cultivars with pleasing genetic variations, propagated for their decorative value from both native and exotic plants. The term is often incorrectly used interchangeably with exotic.

Abelia ×*grandiflora*

Glossy abelia

FORM: Shrub

HARDINESS: Zones (5)6–9

BLOOM PERIOD: Spring, summer, fall

SIZE: 3–6 ft. × 3–6 ft.

✿ ◊ ☼

We all experience zone envy and I drooled when I saw *Abelia* ×*grandiflora* 'Kaleidoscope', adorned with bright golden-yellow variegation on medium green leaves and brilliant red stems, changing color through the season. Glossy abelia is a hybrid, semi-evergreen shrub with rounded, spreading, or gracefully arching branches to 6 ft. tall and 6 ft. wide. Its glossy, dark leaves handle shearing well. It attracts butterflies and has a number of cultivars of various sizes with white to pink flowers. In the colder areas of its hardiness range, all growth will die back to the ground in a hard winter and the subsequent year emerge entirely as new growth. This is fine since it blooms on new wood, not old. Other variegated cultivars include 'Confetti', 'Mardi Gras', and 'Silver Anniversary'; 'Edward Goucher' and 'Little Richard' are compact to dwarf forms.

Abelia ×*grandiflora* 'Kaleidoscope' has a delightful mix of three colors giving it four-season interest.

Fir

FORM: **Tree**

HARDINESS: **Varies within zones 3–6**

SIZE: **Varies by species**

Firs are among the most elegant of the conifers with their short, soft needles and mostly symmetrical pyramidal form. However, they are not as durable in as wide a range of the Midwest as spruces and pines because they require moist, well-drained, acidic soils; high atmospheric moisture (no winds); cool temperatures; and full sun to very light shade. Good drainage and excellent air circulation are essential and they fail over time in heavy soils. The novice may find them hard to differentiate from spruces; key differentiating features include prominent resin blisters on bark, terminal and subterminal buds clustered at twig tip with no needles in between, cones that are held erect versus downward hanging, and needles that are very flat and flexible (versus angular, rigid, and sharp-pointed). Their cones also shatter after seed drop, unlike spruces and pines whose cones remain intact when they drop to the ground. They are generally fairly slow growing and are not urban tolerant. Species common in the Midwest include *balsamea*, *concolor*, *fraseri*, *homolepis*, *koreana*, and *lasiocarpa*. The group includes many cultivars such as *Abies koreana* 'Horstmann's Silberlocke', with curved needles that show off a silver underside.

Abies koreana 'Horstmann's Silberlocke'.

Acanthus mollis; *A. spinosus*

Bear's breeches; spiny bear's breeches

FORM: **Perennial**

HARDINESS: **Zones (5)6–10**

BLOOM PERIOD: **Summer**

SIZE: **3–5 ft. × 2–3 ft.**

❀ ◗ ☼

Both species boast similar spiked flowers but spiny bear's breeches has foliage that is more deeply cut and sharply pointed at lobe tips. The leaves form a glossy mound and are the source of the Corinthian motif used in classical Greek and Roman cultures. Flowers look like large, coarse cream-white snapdragons with hoods and spiny purple bracts. *Acanthus mollis* 'Tasmanian Angel' is a unique form with dramatic white variegation. Novel to us in the north, both species may spread aggressively in warmer climates. It is zone identified to no hardier than 6, yet many people overwinter it in zone 5 in deep, well-drained soils.

ABOVE *Acanthus mollis* 'Tasmanian Angel'.
BELOW *Acanthus mollis* as a grouping.

Maple

FORM: Tree

HARDINESS: Varies within zones 3–9

BLOOM PERIOD: Non-flowering

SIZE: 40–80 ft. × 30–70 ft.

❁ ❁ ☼ ☀

Maples may be the most ubiquitous of American garden trees. Many natives are canopy trees: *Acer saccharinum* (silver) is not suited to home landscapes due to weak wood and shallow root systems; *A. rubrum* (red) gets its name from spectacular red fall color but doesn't like dry, high-lime soils; and *A. saccharum* (sugar), revered for fall interest, prefers deep, rich soils. A few columnar ('Monumentale', 'Newton Sentry') and smaller cultivars ('Barrett Cole', 'Sugar Cone') of sugar maple exist. Understory maples tolerate sun and are usually better options for the small yard. These include *A. pensylvanicum* (moosewood), *A. pseudosieboldianum* (Korean), *A. shirasawanum* (full-moon), *A. tataricum* (Tatarian), *A. triflorum* (three-flower), and *A. griseum* (paperbark), depending on your geographical and environmental conditions.

This planting of *Acer rubrum* demonstrates the variability in fall color among cultivars.

Japanese maple

FORM: **Tree**
HARDINESS: **Zones 5–8**
SIZE: **3–25 ft. × 5–25 ft.**

I confess, I am far too in love with and own too many Japanese maples and related species that are simply not durable in most of the Midwest. They are listed as hardy to zone 5 but any zone 5 can experience zone 4 conditions and you can expect to see losses as a result. Fortunately, cost has come down considerably in recent years but losing a lovely specimen is still heartbreaking. Japanese maples adore the more moderate summers and winters of the Pacific Northwest and Mid-Atlantic; they languish in hot, humid summer heat and the foliage burns with intense sun. Winter cold damages or kills them and they detest wild swings in spring. Warming up dramatically during the day only to drop to freezing temperatures at night "blasts" xylem tissue and buds. Gardeners who think they lost their maple to winter cold often have lost them to winter/spring thaws. There is little you can do to prevent this other than acknowledge that growing Japanese maples may mean loss in harsh years. The cold-hardiest cultivars for the Midwest are 'Emperor I' and 'Bloodgood'.

Acer palmatum 'Emperor I'.

Acer pseudosieboldianum; A. sieboldianum

Korean maple; Siebold maple

FORM: **Tree**

HARDINESS: **Zones 4–8**

SIZE: **12–15 ft. × 12–15 ft.**

Both species require the same culture as Japanese maple but tolerate colder winters. They are green-foliaged forms but display fabulous fall color. Spring leaf emergence is soft chartreuse on red petioles, hardening to summer dark green, which converts to a wide range of autumn purple, scarlet, and orange. *Acer sieboldianum* is slightly taller with smaller leaves; 'Sode No Uchi' grows slowly to 10 ft. and is perfect for small gardens. The "northern" Japanese maple may come from new hybrids between Japanese and Korean maple. 'Northern Glow' and 'Northwind' are currently on the market; expect to see more releases.

Acer sieboldianum 'Sode No Uchi' is the perfect maple for limited-space gardens.

Acer pseudosieboldianum starting its fall show at the University of Wisconsin Longenecker Gardens, which can experience zone 4 winters.

Most Korean maples are seed propagated and can vary widely in range of fall color.

Acer shirasawanum 'Aureum' (syn. A. japonicum)

Golden full-moon maple

FORM: Tree

HARDINESS: Zones 5–8

SIZE: 10–20 ft. × 10–20 ft.

This slow-growing, small-scale, gorgeous gold-foliaged maple requires the same cultural conditions as Japanese maple; however, I have seen specimens survive -25 degrees F with no or minimal damage. This is my "go-to" tree to literally glow in fairly dense shade. I find cultivar 'Autumn Moon' far less winter durable and am trialing several new releases, including yellow-gold 'Jordan' and red-foliaged 'Red Dawn'.

Acer shirasawanum 'Aureum' shines in dark spaces in brilliant gold.

Achillea millefolium; A. hybrids

Yarrow

FORM: Perennial

HARDINESS: Zones 3–8

BLOOM PERIOD: Summer, fall

SIZE: 2.5–3 ft. × 1.5–2 ft.

Robust or thug, yarrow is a plant that laughs at drought, dry soils, and high pH, as long as it has drainage. It has been a dependable garden plant for many years, varying in size from floppy, deeply dissected, ferny foliaged *Achillea millefolium* to coarser, upright hybrids such as 'Coronation Gold', 'Paprika', 'Pomegranate', 'Moonshine', and the new Seduction Series. All have silvery, aromatic foliage and wide, flat flower corymbs. Flower colors range from pastel to bright, including every hue except blue.

Achillea 'Pomegranate'.

Monkshood, wolfsbane

FORM: **Perennial**

HARDINESS: **Zones 3–7**

BLOOM PERIOD: **Summer, fall**

SIZE: **2–3 ft. × 1.5–2.5 ft.**

In Madison, the enchanting delphiniums that grace English gardens simply fail to survive more than a few years due to heavy, dry soils and hot, humid summers. For similar tall spires of blues, purples, and purple-white bicolor I recommend monkshood. Combining species will extend bloom from summer into late fall starting with *Aconitum napellus* and ending with *A. carmichaelii*. All parts of the plant are poisonous; however, the common name wolfsbane refers to yellow-flowering *A. lycoctonum*, not blue-flowering garden varieties. Commonly found cultivars include tall fall *A. carmichaelii* 'Arendsii', 'Barker's Variety', and 'Kelmscott Variety'; *A. napellus* is often sold just as the species with rich purple-blue flowers, but 'Carneum' has untypical pink flowers. Hybrid *A. ×cammarum* has produced blue-and-white 'Bicolor' and a further cross of this hybrid with *A. henryi* produced 'Sparks Variety'.

Aconitum 'Spark's Variety' shows clearly where the name monkshood originated.

Doll's-eyes; red baneberry

FORM: **Perennial**

HARDINESS: **Zones 3–8**

BLOOM PERIOD: **Spring**

SIZE: **1–2 ft. × 2–3 ft.**

Actaea are grown primarily for their attractive large fruit in either deep red (baneberry) or white, with a purple spot (doll's-eyes), but it is difficult to find them in public settings because the fruit is highly toxic and horticulturalists worry about children finding them appealing. The flowers are relatively insignificant, although the stems turn red in summer. Moisture and shade are critical, especially in the south, or the astilbe-like foliage will crisp and die. Under ideal conditions they self-seed. Native plant enthusiasts generally grow the species, although Mt. Cuba Center has selected one cultivar of doll's-eyes, 'Misty Blue', for soft, bluish-green foliage.

Actaea pachypoda has lovely doll's-eye fruit but gardeners should be aware it is toxic to ingest.

Actaea racemosa
(syn. Cimicifuga racemosa)

Black cohosh, fairy candles

FORM: Perennial
HARDINESS: Zones 3–8
BLOOM PERIOD: Summer, fall
SIZE: 3–8 ft. × 2–3 ft.

The biggest mistake gardeners make growing black cohosh and bugbane (*Actaea simplex*) is dry soil. The plants look fine in moist spring weather but foliage burns to a crisp in summer heat without moist roots. This upright perennial typically grows to 4 to 6 ft. but under ideal conditions it can reach 8 ft. tall. It sports numerous small, creamy white, fragrant flowers late summer to early fall in long, terminal racemes rising well above the foliage on wiry stems, giving it another common name, fairy candles. Black cohosh has a number of herbal uses. It has no cultivars and is generally grown by native plant aficionados but has merit in the ornamental garden.

The flowers of *Actaea racemosa* shine as fairy candles in the shade.

Actaea simplex
(syn. *Cimicifuga simplex*)

Bugbane

FORM: **Perennial**

HARDINESS: **Zones 4–8**

BLOOM PERIOD: **Summer, fall**

SIZE: **3–6 ft. × 2–3 ft.**

Bugbane has identical cultural requirements as black cohosh. Typically growing to 4 to 5 ft. tall with lacy foliage, it makes an effective accent throughout the growing season. Numerous small, creamy white, bottlebrush-shaped, strongly fragrant flowers appear in late summer to early fall in long, terminal racemes resembling fluffy spires on upright, wiry stems. This species has become enormously popular with cultivars selected from its Atropurpurea Group, for deeply cut purple foliage, black stems, and purplish pink–tinted flowers, including 'Black Negligee', 'Hillside Black Beauty', and 'Chocoholic'. There have been new releases since 'Brunette' was introduced but I still favor it as one of the most durable.

Actaea simplex 'Brunette'.

Aesculus parviflora

Bottlebrush buckeye

FORM: **Shrub**

HARDINESS: **Zones 4–8**

BLOOM PERIOD: **Summer**

SIZE: **8–12 ft. × 8–15 ft.**

Bottlebrush buckeye is a sprawling, multi-stemmed, deciduous shrub known for spectacular bright-white, lightly fragrant flower spikes with red anthers and pink filaments. It is shade tolerant; has a mounding, spreading, suckering habit; grows wider than tall (give this one room!); and attracts a variety of insects. The leaves are medium to dark green in summer and turn yellow-green in the fall. 'Rogers' is the only notable cultivar and originates from *Aesculus parviflora* var. *serotina*, a variant that grows to about 20 ft. tall and produces flowers close to 3 ft. long around three weeks later than the species.

Aesculus parviflora colonizes and takes up considerable space, so is most appropriate for larger landscapes.

Aesculus pavia

Chestnut, red buckeye

FORM: **Tree**

HARDINESS: **Zones 4–8**

BLOOM PERIOD: **Spring**

SIZE: **12–15 ft. × 12–15 ft.**

Chestnuts are important native trees but most canopy species develop foliar leaf blotch that make them very unattractive. The red-flowering forms are more resistant to foliar issues and are smaller scale to fit home landscapes. They are extremely slow growing so it is worth the investment to purchase the largest B & B specimens possible to maximize early flowering. Large, bronze-green buds start spring emergence with almost metallic new foliage. Showy, erect, 4- to 10-inch long panicles of bright-red, tubular flowers appear on the ends of branches above attractive, large, deeply lobed, palmate leaves. Fall color is insignificant. *Aesculus ×carnea* is a hybrid that achieves greater height (30–40 ft. × 25–30 ft.) and has numerous cultivars, including the most common 'Briotii', 'Fort McNair', and a rarer weeping form 'Pendula'. Another red-flowering hybrid, *A. ×arnoldiana* 'Autumn Splendor', is reputed to have significant fall color, something lacking in most chestnuts.

The rich red flowers of *Aesculus pavia* are attractive to many insects.

Ornamental onion

FORM: Perennial, bulb

HARDINESS: Zones 4–9

BLOOM PERIOD: Spring, summer, fall

SIZE: Varies by species

Alliums are ornamental onions varying in height from the diminutive pink rock garden favorite *Allium oreophilum* to A. 'Globemaster', with 6- to 8-inch round purple flowers topping 4-ft. flower stalks. They are extremely durable and relatively resistant to deer, voles, chipmunks, and rabbits, making excellent cut or dried flowers. Puff-ball-on-a-stick globe alliums such as purple 'Gladiator' and white 'Mount Everest', fall-blooming lavender *A. thunbergii* 'Ozawa' (Japanese onion), rose-purple spidery *A. schubertii* (Schubert's allium), summer-blooming dark purple naturalizer *A. sphaerocephalon* (drumstick allium), azure blue summer *A. caeruleum*, edible *A. schoenoprasum* (garden chives), tiny yellow-flowering *A. moly* (Moly allium), and star-shaped pink *A. cristophii* (Christoph's allium) are only a few of the options demonstrating enormous diversity.

ABOVE An *allium* flower in full bloom with dried flower heads in the background.

BELOW Many people find *Allium schubertii* more fascinating dried than at peak bloom.

Elephant ear; taro

FORM: **Annual**

HARDINESS: **Some hardy to zones (6)7**

BLOOM PERIOD: **Non-flowering**

SIZE: **3–15 ft. × 2–5 ft.**

Both are large temperennials (non-hardy plants usually treated as annuals) used for oversized foliage that may be ruffled, variegated, or colored. Elephant ear is uprightly rigid, often vase shaped with deeply veined, arrow-shaped leaves sometimes marked with black, dark purple, or bronze. It can reach 15 ft. tall. Taro is a large, showy, marginal aquatic plant with heart-shaped leaves reaching 5 ft., with thinner foliage and less-rigid stems. The tubers of both can be lifted and stored over winter.

Both have many exciting cultivars. I am fond of *Colocasia esculenta* 'Black Ruffles' for its rich, purple-black, ruffled foliage; unique 'Diamond Head' for chocolate-colored, ruffled foliage that is thick and glossy like that of elephant ear; and 'Thai Giant' for its massive size. 'Lime Zinger' is a gold-foliaged form I would not be without in the shade; it has been moved to the related genus *Xanthosoma*. Good selections of *Alocasia* that display the ribbed, leathery surface are 'Stingray' for its whipcord foliage end, 'Calidora' for massive 6-ft.-long leaves, and 'Purple Cloak' with rich purple foliage.

Colocasia esculenta 'Diamond Head'.

Amelanchier ×grandiflora

Apple serviceberry

FORM: Shrub, tree

HARDINESS: Zones 4–9

BLOOM PERIOD: Spring, summer, fall

SIZE: 12–25 ft. × 12–25 ft.

Amelanchier ×grandiflora is a cross between two native species of serviceberry: *A. arborea* (downy) and *A. laevis* (Allegheny). All of the native species are relatively small and provide delicious fruit for wildlife and humans—my grandmother's shadberry (*A. canadensis*) pie was to die for! The hybrid crosses boast heavy (improved) white flower bloom in spring and striking fall color. It did not change the tree's durability, so it has become a standard in the landscaping industry. Look for small-scale cultivars such as 'Autumn Brilliance', 'Princess Diana', or 'Ballerina'.

Amelanchier alnifolia 'Regent' (left) and *A.* ×*grandiflora* provide bright white spring color that results in edible fruit.

Amsonia hubrichtii; A. tabernaemontana

Arkansas bluestar; willow bluestar

FORM: Perennial
HARDINESS: Zones 5–8
BLOOM PERIOD: Spring
SIZE: 2–3 ft. × 2–3 ft.

The native bluestars all have clusters of clear blue, star-shaped flowers, which are lovely, but foliage texture and fall color has skyrocketed this genus to adulation as a garden ornamental. Both species appear more shrub-like than perennial. By late summer they turn shining gold, glowing when mixed with other perennials. Arkansas bluestar has a very fine feathery foliage, whereas willow has wider, willow-like leaves. The short spreading form 'Blue Ice' (12 to 15 in. × 2 ft.) is marketed as a sport of *Amsonia tabernaemontana* but some non-native *A. orientalis* parentage is in question.

ABOVE *Amsonia hubrichtii* in spring, covered in light blue, star-shaped flowers.
BELOW *Amsonia hubrichtii* in summer, reaching its zenith late-season color.

Big bluestem, turkeyfoot grass

FORM: Perennial, grass
HARDINESS: Zones 4–9
BLOOM PERIOD: Fall
SIZE: 4–6 ft. × 2–3 ft.

Big bluestem was once the formidable component of the tallgrass prairie, towering over most plants with foliage that emerges bluish green, gradually adds red tones, and puts on finishing touches of bronze and purple in the fall. It is called turkeyfoot grass because the flowers are parted into three toe-like clusters. Even though primary interest in it has been as a tough native, it serves as a striking specimen in ornamental gardens.

Andropogon gerardii is often overlooked in a planting until it shows off its fall clothes.

Japanese anemone

FORM: Perennial
HARDINESS: Zones 4–8
BLOOM PERIOD: Summer, fall
SIZE: 1.5–2.5 ft. × 1–1.5 ft.

Anemones are reliable late summer to fall bloomers with swaying florific masses of light pink, white, rose, or lavender rounded flowers on thin stems. It is a valuable source of nourishment for late-season insects. Renowned plantsman Roy Diblik from Northwind Perennial Farm calls plants like this one "too easy"—it is so durable, robust, and trouble-free that it can become a thug as it marches outward, displacing weaker competitors. 'Honorine Jobert' is a longtime standard, tall with bright white flowers. 'Whirlwind' has semi-double white flowers and is only 25 to 30 in. tall. Popular 'Pamina' has deep pink, semi-double flowers on deep red stems. 'Party Dress' is a taller selection featuring exceptionally large and fluffy bright pink flowers with double petals surrounding a green eye.

Japanese anemone is robust to the point where it could be considered aggressive, but produces masses of late-season bloom.

Anemone acutiloba
(syn. *Hepatica nobilis* var. *acuta*, *H. acutiloba*); *A. americana* (syn. *H. nobilis* var. *obtusa*, *H. americana*)

Sharp-leaf hepatica; round-leaf hepatica

FORM: Perennial

HARDINESS: Zones 3–8

BLOOM PERIOD: Spring

SIZE: 6–8 in. × 6–8 in.

Hepaticas lie in wait, ready to bloom as soon as I uncover my beds in spring. Flowering begins before leaf emergence, so they put on a pretty display before the leaves cover the delicate blooms. Flowers may be white, pink, blue, or purple and solitary on a silky-haired stalk with multiple stalks per plant. Bloom is followed by thick, leathery basal leaves with three rounded or pointed lobes that may be mottled. The native range for both species overlaps almost completely; the major difference is whether their lobes are rounded or pointed.

Anemone acutiloba may be diminutive and ephemeral but it delights in spring.

Anemone canadensis

Windflower

FORM: Perennial

HARDINESS: Zones 3–9

BLOOM PERIOD: Spring

SIZE: 12–24 in. × 24–30 in.

Windflowers are cheerful, bright white, yellow-centered, poppy-like flowers that mass readily, spread by rhizome, and self-seed. Windflowers work better in large embankments and woodland edges rather than organized perennial beds, where they may become overly aggressive.

Anemone canadensis.

Anemonella thalictroides (syn. *Thalictrum thalictroides*)

Rue anemone

FORM: **Perennial**

HARDINESS: **Zones 4–8**

BLOOM PERIOD: **Spring**

SIZE: **6–8 in. × 6–8 in.**

This much-loved woodland flower arrives early, heralding spring, and is a joy to see. Rue anemone's delicate flowers are generally white but sometimes pink or green-yellow or with accents. It is relatively easy to grow in woodland or rock gardens. Spectacular cultivars with double flowers such as 'Green Hurricane', 'Shoaf's Double Pink', and 'Cameo' look like extremely miniature peonies.

Anemonella thalictroides.

Angelonia angustifolia

Summer snapdragon

FORM: **Annual**

HARDINESS: **Not hardy**

BLOOM PERIOD: **Spring, summer, fall**

SIZE: **1–2 ft. × 8–10 in.**

A fine addition to a standard line-up of annuals, angelonia is a shining star. It has salvia-like flower spires that reach 1 to 2 ft. and are covered with captivating snapdragon-like blooms in stunning purple, white, or pink. This tough annual laughs off heat stress all summer with continuous bloom—Lower Midwest gardeners, this annual won't "melt" in your summer heat. It is still not common, so visitors continue to ask what it is when they see it in my public garden. A large number of cultivars are sold in series with new ones annually, such as the vibrantly colored Archangel Series and the Selena Series in pastel tones.

Angelonia angustifolia 'Archangel Raspberry Improved'.

Aralia racemosa

American spikenard

FORM: **Perennial**

HARDINESS: **Zones 3–8**

BLOOM PERIOD: **Summer**

SIZE: **3–5 ft. × 3–5 ft.**

It is easy to mistake this large herbaceous perennial for a shrub with very large compound leaves. It can spread en masse to appear much like a shrub copse. Flowers are intriguing, with blooms on very long stalks, floating high overhead like circular white fireworks. Late summer, they turn into inedible (except for birds), hanging black berries. A relatively new cultivar of non-native *Aralia cordata* (Japanese spikenard) called 'Sun King' becomes a 6- to 8-ft. monster of gold; it is reputedly hardy to zone 4.

Aralia racemosa does not provide splashy flowers but offers foliar interest to the native garden.

Arisaema Asian species

Cobra lily

FORM: **Perennial**

HARDINESS: **Zones 5 to 8**

BLOOM PERIOD: **Spring**

SIZE: **1–2 ft. × 1–2.5 ft.**

I have become enamored with cobra lilies. Interesting variations in form and size abound and the timing of emergence creates surprise. *Arisaema sikokianum* is going dormant around early July, when my *A. consanguineum* 'Perfect Wave' is just emerging. *A. urashima* is short, delicate, and requires kneeling for true appreciation; *A. ringens* produces massive, glossy foliage that can be seen from a distance. Cobra lilies are pricier and require richer, moister soils than native species but are easily grown once established.

It doesn't get more exotic in the ornamental garden than *Arisaema urashima*.

Green dragon; jack-in-the-pulpit

FORM: **Perennial**

HARDINESS: **Zones 4–9**

BLOOM PERIOD: **Spring**

SIZE: **12–24 in. × 12–18 in.**

As a child I was fascinated by jack-in-the-pulpit when my folks explained Jack was represented by the spadex hidden in the spathe under the hood flap. I still appreciate this woodland oddity for resilience and interesting green-and-white or green-and-purple stripes. Foliage is exotic, with two large compound leaves; a cluster of bright red fruit adds color. I am aware of two cultivars of *Arisaema triphyllum*. Highly prized 'Black Jack' has shiny black foliage and a few green veins and is available from Plant Delights Nursery. And a personal favorite, 'Starburst', recently more available through mail-order nurseries, is striking with all of the plant's venation outlined in gold. Regardless of cultivars, a large amount of natural variation exists in color patterns. *A. dracontium* has a single long compound leaf that forms a spiral and a less-prominent green spathe and spadex. It achieves greater height and width than *A. triphyllum* and spreads readily. In spite of its alien look, it is easy to grow, self-seeds, and has no cultivars.

ABOVE *Arisaema triphyllum* 'Starburst'.
BELOW *Arisaema dracontium*.

Aristolochia macrophylla

Dutchman's pipe

FORM: Vine

HARDINESS: Zones 4–8

BLOOM PERIOD: Spring

SIZE: 15–30 ft. × 15–20 ft.

This vine is valuable as a native and as food for swallowtail butterflies, but it was so aggressive in the public garden that we took it out. It is a vigorous deciduous vine grown for its bold, almost-10-inch, heart-shaped leaves. Once established it soon smothers walls, fences, and even entire buildings. The only real control for its growth is to site it where its rampant nature does not interfere with other plants. The small purplish-brown flowers look like small saxophones or "Dutchmen's pipes."

Aristolochia macrophylla should be used as a source of swallowtail butterfly larvae food only where it can be controlled.

Aronia melanocarpa

Black chokeberry

FORM: Shrub

HARDINESS: Zones 3–8

BLOOM PERIOD: Spring

SIZE: 3–6 ft. × 3–6 ft.

Historically, black chokeberry was mostly used by commercial landscapers for its tough durability in scorching sun, poor soils, and urban conditions. It has multi-season interest with white flower clusters, purple-black fruit, and purple-red fall color. But recently the native plant movement has brought it more attention as a source of wildlife food, and also because of its high antioxidant content, for which it is becoming an important fruit crop. Cultivars selected for fall color and fruit production include 'Professor Ed', 'Viking', 'Iroquois Beauty', and 'Autumn Magic'.

Aronia melanocarpa fruit is high in antioxidants and is excellent wildlife food.

Aruncus dioicus and related species

Goat's beard

FORM: **Perennial**

HARDINESS: **Zones 4–8**

BLOOM PERIOD: **Spring**

SIZE: **4–6 ft. × 2–4 ft.**

White flowers are often bypassed for vibrant colors but nothing shines in shade like white, and goat's beard fits the bill. It is fairly tall and erect, although I do have to support it in my rich soils. Dark green foliage offsets plumes of creamy white blooms, which last a fairly long time for perennials and provide dried interest right up to winter. 'Zweiwel-tenkind' is a reportedly compact form although I find it almost as large; 'Kneiffii' is a true dwarf form with finely dissected foliage. *Aruncus aethusifolius* is a miniature Korean goat's beard with the same traits, at roughly one-third the size; 'Noble Spirit' is the most noted cultivar. 'Misty Lace' and 'Horatio' are lovely hybrids between both species. They are intermediately sized between the two and tolerate more humidity, making them the better goat's beard choices for the Lower Midwest.

Aruncus dioicus in my garden, thriving in dry shade.

Asarum canadense

Wild ginger

FORM: **Perennial**

HARDINESS: **Zones 4–6**

BLOOM PERIOD: **Spring**

SIZE: **6–12 in. × 12–18 in.**

This easy-to-grow woodland perennial's kidney-shaped, dark green leaves form a pleasing ground cover that spreads slowly by rhizomes and is tolerant of deep shade. Wild ginger prefers rich soils but is highly adaptable; it thrives in sun if roots are evenly moist. It flowers in spring but the blooms are indiscernible at ground level, deep under foliage, where they can be pollinated by beetles. It is worth lying on the ground to discover these odd-looking, cup-shaped, purplish flowers but they are of little ornamental interest.

Asarum canadense is a useful native ground cover with intriguing, nearly indiscernible flowers.

Asclepias incarnata

Swamp milkweed

FORM: **Perennial**

HARDINESS: **Zones 3–6**

BLOOM PERIOD: **Summer**

SIZE: **4–5 ft. × 2–3 ft.**

A beautiful but infrequently used native perennial with willow-like leaves and clusters of large, upturned, rosy pink flowers that exude a light vanilla fragrance. It attracts butterflies and is one of the milkweed food sources for monarchs. It prefers consistently moist soil but performs admirably in average, well-drained gardens. 'Cinderella' is a pink-flowering cultivar; 'Ice Ballet' is white.

Asclepias incarnata works both as a native food source for monarch butterfly larvae and as a lovely ornamental.

Asclepias tuberosa

Butterfly weed

FORM: **Perennial**

HARDINESS: **Zones 3–9**

BLOOM PERIOD: **Summer**

SIZE: **1–2.5 ft. × 1–1.5 ft.**

Butterfly weed is a native perennial with flat-topped orange or yellow flower clusters at terminals of stems or in its leaf axils. It produces late-season clusters of brightly colored flowers, which attract insects, including many butterflies, followed by fruit and long, dry seedpods typical of milkweeds. The fact that it is often found along railroad beds, in dry fields and prairies, and along roadsides indicates how tough it is. 'Hello Yellow' is a bright yellow cultivar.

I've never understood the people who don't want orange in their gardens, especially when *Asclepias tuberosa* does orange so well.

Pawpaw

FORM: Shrub, tree
HARDINESS: Zones 5–9
BLOOM PERIOD: Spring
SIZE: 12–30 ft. × 12–30 ft.

Pawpaw is a small, short-trunked tree or large, multi-stemmed shrub with large, tropical-like leaves. It is hardy to zone 5 and has a large native range into Canada, but the season is not long enough to produce fruit in the northern zones; I love it for texture in the landscape. Thick, bright green, deciduous leaves turn yellow-green to bright yellow in fall. The unusual, small, purple, six-petaled flowers show up individually in leaf axils before foliage emerges. Large, cylindrical, edible fruit follows, with a long enough season.

Asimina triloba is a Midwest durable plant that lends a tropical feel with large, broad foliage.

Astilbe

FORM: **Perennial**

HARDINESS: **Zones 3–8**

BLOOM PERIOD: **Summer**

SIZE: **6 in.–5 ft. × 8–12 in.**

Astilbe produces attractive mounds of glossy, fern-like foliage topped with delicate plumes of colorful flowers. Although it is sold as a readily available plant for shade, astilbe blooms lightly and sporadically in shade with spindly, weak vegetation, especially if dry. However, full sun in dry soils burns vegetation to a crisp. It does best in regions with cool summers, full morning sun with dappled afternoon light, and continuously moist roots. The frothy flowers arrive late spring or early summer in colors such as pink, red, lavender, and white. It grows between 6 in. and 5 ft. tall depending on cultivar. There are a number of species and many cultivars, including the relatively new gold-foliaged hybrid 'Amber Moon'. Some of the timeless good do'ers include the *Astilbe chinensis* Visions Series including 'Visions', 'Little Vision in Pink', and 'Visions in Pink'. A personal favorite is *A.* 'Straussenfeder', part of the *A. thunbergii* hybrid ostrich plume group, with larger, looser, weeping panicles of pink flowers on arching stems, blooming later in the season than other species.

Astilbe chinensis 'Visions' is one of the more brilliant colors available.

TOUGH AS NAILS

The durable plants listed below are generally accepted as "good do'ers" across the entire region of the Midwest, as long as their cultural requirements are met. With attributes that extend their range throughout most of the country and reliable performance over time, they have many cultivars—some hundreds, some thousands. They are robust to aggressive (mostly robust), multiply readily, are easily propagated, and will be reasonably priced.

Perennials	Trees and Shrubs
Calamagrostis ×*acutiflora*	*Acer* native species
Echinacea purpurea	*Amelanchier* ×*grandiflora*
Ferns	*Cornus alternifolia*
Hemerocallis hybrids	*Crataegus* species
Hosta cultivars	*Malus* species
Hydrangea paniculata	*Physocarpus opulifolius*
Hylotelephium hybrids	*Quercus* species
Iris sibirica	*Sambucus* species
Nepeta species	*Spiraea* species
Paeonia lactiflora	*Viburnum carlesii*
Panicum virgatum	*Viburnum* native species
Pennisetum alopecuroides	
Phlox paniculata	
Polygonatum odoratum	
Pulmonaria species	
Rudbeckia fulgida	
Salvia species	
Veronica spicata and hybrids	

Astilboides

FORM: **Perennial**
HARDINESS: **Zones 5–7**
BLOOM PERIOD: **Summer**
SIZE: **3–5 ft. × 2–3 ft.**

Astilboides is more common in the Northeast and Pacific Northwest, due to the moderate summers and moister soils in those areas, but it does very well in the Midwest when given adequate sun and evenly moist to wet soils all season. It is dramatic, with huge, slightly lobed, umbrella-like leaves. The edges are gracefully scalloped, bright green, roundly flat leaves measuring in excess of 2 ft. across. It easily falls into the category of bold- and coarse-foliaged plants. Flowering stems soar aloft to 5 ft., topped by heavy, drooping plumes of star-shaped, creamy white, astilbe-like plumes—but the tropical-looking foliage remains the scene-stealer.

Astilboides tabularis.

Greater masterwort

FORM: Perennial

HARDINESS: Zones 4–7

BLOOM PERIOD: Spring, summer

SIZE: 2.5–3 ft. × 1–1.5 ft.

I consider greater masterwort an underutilized perennial. It thrives in cooler climes (it doesn't appreciate high humidity), providing long bloom with interesting compact umbels of tiny, tightly packed florets surrounded by rosettes of showy, petal-like bracts on erect, branched, wiry stems. Looking like stars or fireworks, the flowers are generally in combinations of white, pink, rose, and purple. Cultivars include 'Abbey Road' with dark violet-purple flowers on black stems, 'Sunningdale Gold' flaunting gold foliage, 'Sunningdale Variegated' with green-and-gold variegation, and bright red 'Ruby Wedding'.

Astrantia major 'Abbey Road'.

Blue false indigo

FORM: Perennial

HARDINESS: Zones 3–9

BLOOM PERIOD: Spring

SIZE: 2–4 ft. × 2–2.5 ft.

You might swear blue false indigo is a shrub. This member of the legume family develops great mass in mounds of trifoliate glaucous foliage, and sets roots so deep you will never enjoy dividing and transplanting it. It tolerates extremely challenging conditions and rewards gardeners with stiff, long racemes of indigo-purple flowers. Recent breeding efforts have produced cultivars with chocolate, cream, apricot, lemon, bi-color, blue, and violet flowers, such as the Prairieblues Series from Chicagoland Grows and the Decadence Series from Walters Gardens. *Baptisia sphaerocarpa* (yellow false indigo) produces bright yellow flowers. *B. leucantha* (white false indigo), and *B. alba* var. *macrophylla* (largeleaf false indigo) are smaller, white-flowering forms native to prairies.

Baptisia australis.

SHADY CHARACTERS

Shade gardening remains one of the hottest topics in gardening. Many people begin gardening in sun-drenched areas of the home landscape, but may eventually be forced into the less desirable real estate: shady areas. Not all shade is equal and you need to determine which you have. People often equate dark with moist, but many Midwest woodlands and forests have significantly dry soils with shallow, fibrous-rooted trees that outcompete herbaceous plants for water. Goliath will defeat David with ease if planting beds are not rich and deep. Most homeowners are working with highly modified soils (due to home construction), rather than soils original to the site; displaced soils tend to be devoid of organic matter. It takes a great deal of modification to increase soil's water-holding capacity, and supplemental irrigation will likely be necessary during the heat of summer. The Lower Midwest may be the exception, but in general most shade gardens will require augmentation before they are ready for shade plants that prefer evenly moist soils.

DRY SHADE

These plants, once established, will tolerate dry soils, competition with shallow tree roots, and infrequent watering. They will require moisture and added fertility the first year or two of establishment and must remain well drained. Adding compost on an annual basis will improve conditions for these plants and start the process of amending the site for more-demanding plants. Some of these prefer moist soils but also become aggressive in those conditions, so their adaptability to dry conditions provides control.

Perennials
Asarum canadense
Deschampsia cespitosa
Dryopteris ferns
Epimedium species
Galium odoratum
Geranium maculatum and related species
Polemonium reptans
Polygonatum biflorum
Polygonatum biflorum var. *commutatum*
Porteranthus trifoliata
Sesleria autumnalis
Sesleria caerulea
Stylophorum diphyllum
Thalictrum aquilegiifolium
Veronicastrum virginicum

Trees and Shrubs
Carpinus caroliniana
Caryopteris divaricata 'Snow Fairy'
Diervilla sessilifolia 'Cool Splash'
Ostrya virginiana
Philadelphus coronarius 'Variegatus'

MOIST SHADE

This group requires deep, porous, well-drained soil rich in organic matter; soil that remains evenly moist through the season and receives regular irrigation in dry periods. However, these plants need excellent drainage during wet seasons. They require regular additions of organic matter and benefit from winter mulch as protection from heaving. They are fussy to robust.

Perennials

Actaea pachypoda
Actaea rubra
Anemone acutiloba
Anemone americana
Aralia racemosa
Aruncus dioicus
Begonia grandis
Bletilla striata
Brunnera macrophylla
Cypripedium parviflorum var. pubescens
Cypripedium reginae
Dicentra eximia
Dicentra hybrids
Hakonechloa macra cultivars
Heuchera hybrids
×Heucherella
Lamprocapnos spectabilis
Molinia caerulea
Mukdenia rossii
Spigelia marilandica
Syneilesis aconitifolia
Syneilesis palmata
Tiarella cordifolia
Tricyrtis species

Trees and Shrubs

Acer pseudosieboldianum
Acer shirasawanun 'Aureum'
Acer sieboldianum
Chionanthus virginicus
Dirca palustris
Microbiota decussata
Tsuga canadensis
Tsuga diversifolia
Weigela florida

Hardy begonia

FORM: Short-lived perennial
HARDINESS: Zones (5)6–7
BLOOM PERIOD: Summer, fall
SIZE: 1.5–2 ft. × 1.5–2 ft.

☼ ◗

Grow hardy begonia just so you can tell your friends that you are such a good gardener you can overwinter begonias! This delicate plant looks like potted begonias and belies its durability. Flowers are either pink or white and one of the appeals is the rich, red-purple foliar underside; plant it where it will be dramatically backlit by sunlight. Protective mulch applied in fall will aid winter survival. Drainage is critical. 'Heronswood Pirouette' and 'Rosea' are pink-flowered cultivars; 'Alba' is white.

Surprise visitors with *Begonia grandis* if you are in a moderate zone 5 or warmer; they won't believe you are overwintering this one in the ground.

Bergenia cordifolia

Pigsqueak

FORM: **Perennial**

HARDINESS: **Zones 3–8**

BLOOM PERIOD: **Spring**

SIZE: **12–18 in. × 12–18 in.**

Rub the thick, waxy foliage between your fingers and hear the pig squeak! Pigsqueak is generally grown as a ground cover in rosettes of thick, glossy, oblong green leaves that are sometimes purplish on the underside. It turns magenta in fall and is evergreen except in extreme cold. Flowers are charming pink to white compact panicles on tall stalks but emerge so early in spring that they are often frost damaged in cold climates. It works best as foliar interest as a result; let the occasional flowers be a pleasing surprise. Cultivars include 'Bressingham Ruby' and 'Eroica' (dark pink flowers), 'Bressingham White' (white flowers), 'Apple Blossom' (pink and white flowers), and 'Winterglut' (gold foliage with pink flowers).

Since flowers are highly susceptible to spring frosts, grow *Bergenia cordifolia* 'Eroica' for foliage first.

Betula papyrifera

Paperbark birch

FORM: **Tree**

HARDINESS: **Zones 2–6**

SIZE: **40–70 ft. × 25–30 ft.**

This commonly used landscape tree is a boreal species which prefers moderately cool air temperatures and cool, moist roots. Unfortunately, homeowners often place this tree in the front yard in dry, compacted soils. I call it the suicide tree because when stressed, it produces chemicals, predominantly rhododendrol—which attracts bronze birch borers to infestation. Keep root systems cool and moist by annual mulching, summer supplemental watering, and afternoon dappled shade. No stress, no chemicals, and no borer attraction! The best resistant cultivars are *Betula populifolia* (gray birch), which looks much the same; 'Whitespire Senior' is most resistant.

Betula papyrifera is a true cool season tree, happiest in the South of the Boreal range.

Bletilla striata

Chinese ground orchid

FORM: Short-lived perennial

HARDINESS: Zones (5)6–9

BLOOM PERIOD: Spring

SIZE: 12–18 in. × 6–12 in.

Terrestrial orchids are worth trying once soils are enriched, and this one is among the easiest. It is so satisfying to show off orchids in your garden! Chinese ground orchids grow from corms, with flowers similar to pink cattleya orchids. If happy they will naturalize. They will likely require protective winter mulch for zone 5. The only cultivar I am aware of is 'Albostriata', with thin, white, foliar marginal variegation.

Bletilla striata is perhaps the easiest terrestrial orchid for home gardeners to grow.

Brugmansia suaveolens

Angel's trumpet

FORM: Annual

HARDINESS: Not hardy

BLOOM PERIOD: Summer, fall

SIZE: 6–9 ft. × 4–5 ft.

It is worth overwintering angel's trumpet in cool basements, on the sun porch, or in similar conditions to develop size; they are small trees where hardy. They flower with huge, foot-long, downward-facing trumpets in pink, white, or yellow. Several have variegated foliage such as 'Peaches and Cream Variegated' and 'Snowbank'. Place them where you relax at twilight, because the fragrance is intoxicating.

Plant sweetly fragrant *Brugmansia suaveolens* near walks and seating areas where you will enjoy it.

Brunnera macrophylla

Siberian bugloss, heart-leaf brunnera

FORM: Perennial

HARDINESS: Zones 3–8

BLOOM PERIOD: Spring

SIZE: 12–18 in. × 18–24 in.

Brunnera is sometimes called false forget-me-not because the flowers are very similar to *Myosotis*. They almost float above thick, dark green, heart-shaped foliage. Many cultivars have been selected for foliar interest, including variegated 'Dawson's White'; silver overlaid 'Jack Frost'; or intriguing silver over white, creamy yellow, and green 'King's Ransom'. 'Mr. Morse' has white flowers with silver-enhanced foliage. Reversions are common. Brunnera foliage can burn in summer heat; new cultivars 'Sea Heart' and 'Silver Heart' are more heat tolerant.

Calamagrostis ×acutiflora

Feather reed grass

FORM: Perennial, grass

HARDINESS: Zones 5–9

BLOOM PERIOD: Spring, summer, fall

SIZE: 3–5 ft. × 1.5–2.5 ft.

This hybrid reed grass is so tolerant of adverse conditions, it has become ubiquitous in commercial landscapes. It emerges early in the spring as a cool-season grass, becoming an extremely erect and rigid, slow-spreading clump with rich, golden-tan fall color. It tolerates clay and dry soils but prefers those that are moist and rich. It is a superb ornamental grass for tough sites; use it ornamentally for its rigid architectural structure. 'Karl Foerster' is the most common cultivar. Variegated forms such as 'Overdam' and 'Avalanche' are also available but not as robust.

Calamagrostis ×acutiflora 'Karl Foerster'.

Brunnera macrophylla 'King's Ransom'.

Calamintha nepeta subsp. nepeta

Calamint

FORM: Perennial

HARDINESS: Zones 5–7

BLOOM PERIOD: Summer, fall

SIZE: 1–1.5 ft. × 1–2 ft.

Tough. Massively florific for a long period of summer. Aromatic. Issue free. Covered with every insect imaginable, especially bees. The attributes of this durable plant are many, and I continue to use it heavily. The small, bright white flowers are mounded on bushy plants giving it a baby's breath impression under conditions *Gypsophila* would never survive. It is a superb performer above zone 7 range, below that it languishes.

Calamintha nepeta subsp. *nepeta*.

Callirhoe involucrata

Poppy mallow

FORM: Perennial

HARDINESS: Zones 4–8

BLOOM PERIOD: Spring, summer

SIZE: 6–12 in. × 6–36 in.

Poppy mallow is a native wildflower that sprawls with a summer-long display of bright neon, dark pink-magenta flowers; long branches spread out across the ground to create colorful mats of flowers and foliage well into fall. Its long taproot makes it difficult to transplant once established, but gives the plant excellent drought tolerance. It may self-seed and can spread. *Callirhoe alcaeoides* 'Logan Calhoun' is a spreading relative with pure white flowers.

Callirhoe involucrata frustrates some gardeners with its spreading habit, but I love its robust nature and rosy, plum-purple flowers.

Campanula species

Bellflower

FORM: Perennial

HARDINESS: Zones 5–7

BLOOM PERIOD: Spring, summer, fall

SIZE: 6–18 in. × 6–12 in.

✿ ◐ ☼

Campanula is a huge genus identified by characteristic bell-shaped flowers that can also be shaped like tubes, stars, cups, or saucers. Flower color varies widely, and plant form covers a wide range—from delicate, filamentous rock garden denizens, to densely clumping with drooping, tubular flowers, to upright, stiffly stemmed with raceme or panicle flower stalks. They are so easy to grow that some will become overly aggressive as evidenced by the rampant nature of some of the luscious *C. punctata* (spotted bellflower) hybrids that include lovely cultivars such as 'Ringsabell Mulberry Rose', 'Sarastro',

'Pink Octopus', and 'Cherry Bells'. They prefer cool evenings and full sun.

Rock garden species include *Campanula poscharskyana* (Serbian bellflower) with cultivars 'Blue Waterfall' and 'White Waterfall'; *C. portenschlagiana* (Dalmatian bellflower) with 'Birch's Double' as a pleasing cultivar; *C. garganica* 'Dickson's Gold' (goldleaf Adriatic bellflower); and *C. carpatica* (Carpathian harebell) with the well-known 'Blaue Clips', 'Weisse Clips', and 'Deep Blue Clips'. Taller perennial border species include *C. glomerata* (clustered bellflower) with the likes of 'Superba' and 'Purple Pixie', the aforementioned spotted bellflowers, and *C. persicifolia* (peachleafed bellflower) including cultivars 'New Giant', 'Takion Blue', and 'Telham Beauty'. Avoid native *C. rotundifolia* at all costs; although it has been used as a cottage garden perennial, it spreads noxiously and is nearly impossible to eradicate, looking much like equally insufferable *Adenophora liliifolia* (lilyleaf ladybells).

Campanula 'Ringsabell Mulberry Rose' is one of many introductions with big, blousy flowers, but watch their rambunctious nature.

Campsis radicans

Trumpet creeper

FORM: Vine

HARDINESS: Zones 4–9

BLOOM PERIOD: Summer

SIZE: 25–40 ft. × 5–10 ft.

Trumpet creeper is another aggressive native climber that appeals to the home gardener—until it overwhelms support. I had one that made it to the top of a telephone pole and linemen had to keep cutting it out of the wires. It will also sucker outward from the base. Its appeal comes from the clusters of trumpet-shaped orange, red, or yellow late-season flowers that turn into interesting, banana-shaped seedpods. It takes several years to flower and draws hummingbirds. The species sports orange-red flowers; cultivars include a redder form called 'Crimson Trumpet' and yellow 'Yellow Trumpet'. Make sure you have strong support.

Campsis radicans 'Flava' growing with *Aristolochia*.

Carpinus caroliniana

Blue beech, musclewood, American hornbeam, ironwood

FORM: Tree

HARDINESS: Zones 3–9

BLOOM PERIOD: Non-flowering

SIZE: 20–35 ft. × 20–35 ft.

This native understory tree adapts to sun and shade, but develops the best canopy in sun. The name musclewood originates from extremely hard, strong, smooth, gray bark appearing sinuous and muscle-like. The canopy is globose to wide spreading, but grows more open and stretched in shade. Flowers are male and female catkins; the female becomes a winged nutlet. The tree demonstrates respectable fall color in yellow, orange, and red but nursery offerings have been seed propagated with variable fall color. Wisconsin propagator Mike Yanny has spent more than thirty years developing cultivars with reliable fall color, including 'Ball O' Fire' and 'Firespire'.

Carpinus caroliniana.

Caryopteris divaricata 'Snow Fairy'

'Snow Fairy' Himalayan caryopteris

FORM: **Perennial, shrub**

HARDINESS: **Zones 5–8**

BLOOM PERIOD: **Summer**

SIZE: **3–5 ft. × 3–5 ft.**

I value variegation in the shade garden because it helps plants stand out in the dark and 'Snow Fairy' fills the bill nicely, with consistent broad bands of white on green. Unlike other caryopteris in the north, it is a dieback shrub that performs more like a herbaceous than woody shrub. New growth emerges quickly and can reach 3 ft. tall and wide by midsummer. It rarely blooms in shade but I am growing it for season-long foliar interest, not flower. Make sure soils are well drained for root depth for winter survival.

Caryopteris divaricata 'Snow Fairy' provides reliable variegation, lighting up my shaded garden.

Cedrus species

Cedar

FORM: **Tree**

HARDINESS: **Most are zones 6–7**

SIZE: **Varies by species**

Cedars are sizable trees with spicy-resinous scented wood and distinctive, thick-ridged or square-cracked bark. There are several conifers with cedar in their common names, such as *Thuja occidentalis* (white-cedar) and *Thuja plicata* (western redcedar), because they have similar attributes such as the scent, but are not true cedars. You can tell because the common name has no space separating the word cedar. True cedar is the least Midwest-hardy of the conifers listed. Broad, level branches display ever-green leaves, which are needle-like and arranged in open spiral patterns on long shoots and in dense spiral clusters on short shoots. The seed cones are barrel-shaped and green, maturing to gray-brown, and disintegrating to release the winged seeds. Cedars prefer deep, acidic, moist but well-drained (intolerant of poorly wet soils) loams in full sun, and are drought tolerant once established. Species common in the Midwest include *atlantica*, *deodara*, and *libani*. They produce large trees but dwarf cultivars such as *Cedrus atlantica* 'Glauca Pendula' fit better in smaller landscapes.

Cedrus atlantica 'Glauca Pendula'.

Celastrus scandens

American bittersweet

FORM: Vine

HARDINESS: Zones 3–8

BLOOM PERIOD: Spring, summer

SIZE: 15–50 ft. × 3–6 ft.

Bittersweet is disappearing from the native landscape due to over-collecting for showy, orange capsules that split open, exposing a crimson aril that dries as everlasting. It is a woody perennial vine that can reach 50 ft. up trees or shrub-like draping over fences. It is dioecious, requiring a male to pollinate females. Cultivar 'Autumn Revolution' (released by Bailey's Nursery) has male and female on the same plant; it is so robust that I have to keep it severely cut back on my fence. It spreads by trailing branches rooting into soil, but it flaunts fruit much larger than the species. Do not plant *Celastrus orbiculatus* (oriental bittersweet), currently choking many parts of the northeastern United States and moving west.

Celastrus scandens.

Cephalanthus occidentalis

Buttonbush

FORM: Shrub

HARDINESS: Zones 5–9

BLOOM PERIOD: Summer

SIZE: 3–15 ft. × 3–8 ft.

Buttonbush reaches 8 to 15 ft. tall, and is often wider than tall, depending on whether it is planted in dry or moist soils, so can be somewhat massive for small landscapes. It may be pruned into small, multi-trunked trees, revealing the curly bark of young stems and punctuated pale spots of older stems. Midsummer blooms look like fuzzy white balls arranged in clusters at the end of each twig, maturing into spherical, golden-brown autumn fruit, persisting into winter and attracting wildlife. Blooms are extremely rich in nectar, attracting butterflies and other insects. New cultivar 'Sugar Shack', touted as only 3 to 4 ft. tall and wide, is a good choice for smaller gardens.

Cephalanthus occidentalis has insignificant flowers but the seedpods garner attention.

Cercidiphyllum japonicum

Katsuratree

FORM: **Tree**

HARDINESS: **Zones 4–8**

BLOOM PERIOD: **Non-flowering**

SIZE: **40–60 ft. × 25–60 ft.; weeping forms are smaller**

Grace defines katsuratree with some of the most attractive foliage among trees. The species is an elegant, medium-sized deciduous tree with paired, heart-shaped leaves that are bronze-tinted when young, turning hues of yellow, orange, and pink in autumn. Some forms like 'Red Fox' are selected for red foliage, but although prominent in spring, the color dulls in summer heat. The fallen leaves are described as smelling like cinnamon or burnt sugar. The species is dioecious with lovely form, but may be too large for many home landscapes. 'Pendula' is a smaller, graceful, weeping form worthy of the finest gardens.

Cercidiphyllum japonicum at Allen Centennial Gardens shows glorious fall color.

Cercidiphyllum japonicum 'Pendula'.

Cercis canadensis

Eastern redbud

FORM: **Tree**

HARDINESS: **Zones (4)5–8**

BLOOM PERIOD: **Spring**

SIZE: **20–30 ft. × 25–35 ft.**

✿ ○ ☼ ☀

Eastern redbud is a moderate grower, noted for numerous tiny purple-pink flowers lining tree branches before leaves emerge. Fall color ranges from dull to bright yellow. It is grown throughout its entire hardiness range, but southern provenance seed sources will not be hardy in northern zones; look for 'Northern Strain' from Minnesota Landscape Arboretum or 'Columbus Strain' from Wisconsin. Cultivars include white-flowered 'Alba' and 'Royal White'; strict weepers 'Lavender Twist' and purple-foliaged 'Ruby Falls'; red-purple 'Forest Pansy'; gold 'Hearts of Gold'; apricot-based tricolor 'The Rising Sun'; and others. Low-forked branch unions may be weak and split.

Cercis canadensis 'Hearts of Gold'.

Chamaecyparis species

Cypress

FORM: **Tree**

HARDINESS: **Varies within zones (4)5–8**

SIZE: **Varies by species**

✿ ○ ☼

Cypress is a medium-sized to large evergreen tree; most species grow from 40 to 80 ft. tall with foliage in very distinctive flat sprays somewhat similar to arborvitae. There are two types of leaves: needle-like juvenile leaves on young seedlings up to a year old and scale-like adult leaves. The cones are globose to oval in shape. In their native habitat they thrive in a cool, moist atmosphere where protected from drying winds; in cultivated situations they require fertile, moist, well-drained soils in full sun. They are moderately shade tolerant, although they open up and lose dense form in heavy shade.

The most damaging force to the survival of *Chamaecyparis* in the Midwest is winter wind; *C. obtusa* and *C. lawsoniana* are especially prone to severe desiccation and damage. They tolerate light shearing and pruning prior to growth in early spring, which keeps them denser in form, although branch removal can be performed any time. They are adaptable trees, easily transplanted from containers or ball-and-burlap wraps about any time of year, making them popular garden plants. Species common in the Midwest include *obtusa*, *pisifera*, *lawsoniana*, *nootkatensis*, and *thyoides*. *C. nootkatensis* 'Pendula' suffers from harsh winter winds but is resplendent where it is happy; *C. pisifera* 'Golden Mops' is a very durable gold threadleaf form commonly sold throughout the United States.

Chamaecyparis nootkatensis 'Pendula'.

Chionanthus virginicus

Fringe tree

FORM: Shrub, tree

HARDINESS: Zones 3–9

BLOOM PERIOD: Spring, summer

SIZE: 12–20 ft. × 12–20 ft.

I would think fringe tree would be more commonly sold after seeing peoples' reactions to one in bloom. The white, slightly fragrant, drooping clusters with fringe-like petals define it in spring. Fringe tree is dioecious; male flowers are showier than the female although I'm not sure they're easily discernable. If a male is present, the female will develop olive-like elongated fruit, turning dark blue in late summer and feeding birds and wildlife. It is urban tolerant and can be purchased as multiple or single stemmed. It is slow growing, carefree, and requires no pruning. 'Emerald Knight' is a male cultivar said to differ from the species with a more tree-like habit and larger, more profuse flowers but I have not seen it in trade.

Chionanthus virginicus attracts admirers, who marvel over the feathery white flowers.

Claytonia virginica

Spring beauty

FORM: Perennial

HARDINESS: Zones 3–8

BLOOM PERIOD: Spring

SIZE: 6–8 in. × 6–8 in.

In my youth, my family always competed to see who could find the first spring beauty, as a harbinger of spring. They are tiny and delicate, featuring clusters of five-petaled white or pink flowers with defined veins and anthers. They naturalize by corm offsets and self-seed; rodents often dig and relocate, adding to their spread.

Small and delicate doesn't mean insignificant: *Claytonia virginica* shines on the woodland floor before other plants emerge and compete for attention.

OPPOSITE Select clematis that bloom at different times and you can have flowers from spring through fall.

Clematis

FORM: Vine

HARDINESS: Zones 4–8

BLOOM PERIOD: Spring, summer, fall by cultivar

SIZE: 6–15 ft. × 3–6 ft.

Ubiquitous and much loved, clematis is one of the most decorative and spectacular of flowering garden vines. In this varied group of mostly woody deciduous vines (and a few herbaceous, shrub-like perennials) you'll find enormous variety in flower form, color, bloom season, foliage effect, and height. They prefer cool, evenly moist roots with sunny tops. Clematis fall into two pruning categories, dependent on bloom time, with a simple explanation: don't prune those that bloom on previous year's growth (spring and early summer) and hard prune those that flower on next year's growth (late summer and fall).

Species commonly found in gardens are *Clematis alpina* (alpine), *C. drummondii*, (Drummond's), *C. durandii* (Durand's), *C. fremontii* (Fremont's), *C. integrifolia* (bush), *C. macropetala* (downy), *C. microphylla* (small leaved), *C. montana* (anemone), *C. recta* (ground), *C. tangutica* (golden), *C. terniflora* (sweet autumn), *C. texensis* (scarlet leather flower), and *C. viticella* (Italian leather flower). In spite of the many species available, the bulk of garden clematis are hybrids that began with *Clematis ×jackmanii*, a garden standby since 1862. Today there are thousands of options. At the top of my list are creamy white 'Guernsey Cream'; robust, downward-turning, purple, bell-flowered 'Rouguchi'; floriferous, time-proven 'Betty Corning'; tulip-shaped, deep pink 'Duchess of Albany'; and large-flowered 'Omoshiro', whose blooms are white with pink edges—but I've never met a clematis I didn't love.

Sweet pepperbush, clethra

FORM: Shrub

HARDINESS: Zones 3–9

BLOOM PERIOD: Summer

SIZE: 3–8 ft. × 4–6 ft.

This upright, suckering shrub exudes late summer fragrance. Its white or pink terminal flower spikes look like bottle brushes and attract butterflies and bees. Leaves turn a pleasant yellow in autumn. It prefers acidic soils; in high limestone areas it will struggle to achieve ideal growth and flower. It colonizes where happy and cultivars range from dwarf 3-ft.ers, such as 'Hummingbird', to specimens up to 8 ft. tall and almost as wide, such as 'Pink Spires'.

Place *Clethra alnifolia* where you like to relax, and enjoy the fragrance.

Coreopsis, tickseed

FORM: Perennial

HARDINESS: Zones 2–11

BLOOM PERIOD: Spring, summer, fall

SIZE: 1–2 ft. × 1–2 ft.

Tickseed adds bright, sunny flowers to the landscape and non-hardy cultivars make excellent container plants. A large number of coreopsis are available, but use caution and research hardiness to your locality. Many recent hybrids of *Coreopsis* ×*grandiflora* hybrids have not been as durable as their hardiness zone designation. All of the coreopsis listed here are native to various parts of the United States, but they are not equally hardy to cold climates. Darryl Probst has been crossing more durable hybrids, including his Big Bang and Permathread Series. If you are in zones 5 and colder, I highly recommend starting with whatever colors you prefer out of either of these series. *C. verticillata* (threadleaf coreopsis) and *C. auriculata* (mouse-ear tickseed) cultivars are much hardier. *C. tinctoria* (plains coreopsis) is an annual that has been used in the hybridization of many of the garden cultivars, so you can see the need to research true hardiness.

Coreopsis 'Mercury Rising'.

Cornus alternifolia

Pagoda dogwood

FORM: Tree

HARDINESS: Zones 3–7

BLOOM PERIOD: Spring

SIZE: 15–25 ft. × 20–30 ft.

Pagoda dogwood made its mark as a shade-tolerant understory tree. "Pagoda" refers to the tiered layering of its branching. Keep in mind that this structure develops in sunny conditions; the deeper the shade, the greater the branch stretches to seek light. The plant can be found as a large, multi-stemmed shrub or small, single-stemmed tree and width can almost match height. It is adaptable to moist or dry soils and provides edible fruit for wildlife. Fall color is modest. Like most dogwoods, it is susceptible to leaf spots, twig blight, canker, and root diseases. Keep the foliage dry and provide good air circulation around the plant. Cultivars include small-leafed, delicate 'Argentea'; medium-sized, solid gold 'Gold Bullion'; and the larger, coarser-foliaged 'Golden Shadows', with green and gold variegation.

Cornus alternifolia 'Golden Shadows'.

Cornus kousa
(syn. *Benthamidia kousa*)

Kousa dogwood

FORM: Tree

HARDINESS: Zones (5)6–8

BLOOM PERIOD: Spring

SIZE: 15–30 ft. × 15–30 ft., colonizes

Kousa dogwood is a small, deciduous, flowering tree or multi-stemmed shrub, with a vase-shaped habit that ages into a more rounded canopy. It flowers late spring to early summer, depending on location. What appear to be flowers are actually four narrow, pointed, petal-like, white or whitish-pink bracts, which surround a cluster of almost obscure, yellowish-green true flowers. The flowers turn into berry-like fruits that mature to a pinkish red in summer and persist into fall, making good bird forage. Kousa dogwood can be confused with *Cornus*

Cornus kousa is a superb small landscape tree with new cultivars continually released.

florida (flowering dogwood), and makes an excellent replacement, since flowering dogwood has been ravaged by anthracnose in its native range. Some C. *kousa* cultivars of note include 'Milky Way' (white), 'Satome' (deep pink), 'Summer Stars' (white), 'Beni Fuji' (pink), 'Heart Throb' (red), and 'Prophet' (white). Some variegated forms are 'Wolf Eyes' (white edges), 'Sunsplash' (yellow edges), 'Summer Fun' (cream and pink edges), 'Trinity Star' (cream, yellow, and pink), and 'Gold Star' (central yellow blotch). 'Lustgarten Weeping' is a weeping form.

Cornus sanguinea; *C. sericea*

Bloodtwig dogwood; redosier dogwood

FORM: Shrub

HARDINESS: Zones 3–8

BLOOM PERIOD: Non-flowering

SIZE: 5–10 ft. × 6–8 ft., colonizes

Redosier dogwood is a common deciduous shrub that has been used extensively for its durability in home and commercial landscapes. Green-red stems turn reddish or purple-red in late summer and fall, brightening in winter; best color is on new growth, so annual renewal pruning is advisable. Green and white variegated forms include 'Elegantissima', 'Silver and Gold', and 'Ivory Halo'; 'Hedgerow's Gold' is green and gold. 'Arctic Fire' and 'Kelseyi' are compact to dwarf forms. Fall foliage color exists in dull red, purple-red, or orange, but a plethora of foliar diseases may make them more tattered and ratty than spectacular. Bloodtwig dogwood reaches 10 ft., is tenderer than redosier, and has more stem color variation. Easy-to-grow 'Midwinter Fire' is one of my favorite shrubs, with brilliant yellow-gold fall foliage and pink-red-yellow stems. 'Arctic Sun' has equally striking fall color with beautiful red-tipped, yellow stems.

Cornus sanguinea 'Midwinter Fire'.

Crataegus species

Hawthorn

FORM: **Tree**
HARDINESS: **Zones 4–7**
BLOOM PERIOD: **Spring**
SIZE: **20–40 ft. × 20–40 ft.**

Hawthorn was once a common Midwest landscape tree, but dropped out of favor for more ornamental species. This durable tree works well for larger properties with challenging site conditions. Avoid *Crataegus mollis* (downy hawthorn), because it develops severe rust in moist summer heat. *C. phaenopyrum* (Washington hawthorn) satisfies native plant enthusiasts with white flowers in spring and bright red wildlife-edible fruit in fall, under conditions too harsh for flowering crabs. *C. viridis* (green hawthorn), in particular 'Winter King', is equally tolerant, about the same size, displays profuse white spring flowers, and has winter-persistent fruit that develop a purplish-red fall color.

Crataegus viridis 'Winter King' has been around a long time but remains a tough, trouble-free Midwest stalwart.

Crocosmia hybrids

Montbretia

FORM: **Bulb**
HARDINESS: **Zones 5–9**
BLOOM PERIOD: **Summer**
SIZE: **2–4 ft. × 1–2 ft.**

Plant montbretia for a vivacious splash of hot late-season color and narrow-bladed foliage that provides gladiola-like architectural accents. Even though it is available in vibrant wands of scarlet, red, orange, and yellow, montbretia has almost become defined by *Crocosmia* 'Lucifer', which flaunts copious attention-grabbing, vivid-red, tubular midsummer flowers atop bold, slightly arching 3-ft. stalks. Tubular blooms attract hummingbirds and seedpods persist, attracting birds in fall. Drainage is key for these bulbs.

Flowers don't get much more in-your-face red than *Crocosmia* 'Lucifer'.

Cynara cardunculus

Cardoon

FORM: Annual

HARDINESS: **Not hardy**

BLOOM PERIOD: **Fall**

SIZE: **4–5 ft. × 3–4 ft.**

You can't beat cardoon's bold architectural structure of foliage that grows from 4-inch pots to massive mounds in a few months. We don't always get flowers in our short season, but when we do the round, purple, thistle-like blooms—combined with large, prickly, almost dagger-shaped gray-green arching leaves—raise eyebrows. It is an annual for us but I've heard reports of overwintering in isolated cases.

I plant 4-inch pots of *Cynara cardunculus* every season and am still amazed at how huge the plant gets in three months' time.

Cypripedium parviflorum var. pubescens; C. reginae

Lady's slipper orchid; showy lady's slipper

FORM: **Short-lived perennial**

HARDINESS: **Zones 3–7**

BLOOM PERIOD: **Spring**

SIZE: **1–3 ft. × 12–18 in.**

Few flowers are as sophisticated as lady slippers. They aren't as difficult as they look, although they aren't a beginner's plant either. They prefer moist, well-drained, organically rich, slightly acidic soil. Cypripedium roots don't grow into the ground. Recommendations are to prepare the soil, bare root the plants, stretch the roots out horizontally on the soil, and cover with natural compost followed by mulch. Because roots are shallow, they can't dry out until the plants are well established.

Cypripedium parviflorum var. *pubescens* is just one of the delicate orchids that has stolen my heart.

Daphne

FORM: Shrub

HARDINESS: Zones 5–9

BLOOM PERIOD: Spring, summer, fall

SIZE: 1–6 ft. × 1–6 ft.

Finicky, persnickety, difficult, magnificent, perfumed, irresistible—all of these qualities have described daphne. Four-lobed flowers range from white and pink to lavender. Once established, they are beautiful, low-maintenance shrubs with intoxicating fragrance, and don't require pruning. Daphnes have the reputation of perishing without warning and mature wood can be severely damaged by the weight of snow. Some popular choices include *Daphne ×burkwoodii* 'Carol Mackie', *D. odora* (winter daphne), *D. cneorum* (rose daphne), *D. mezereum* (mezereon), *D. laureola* (spurge laurel), *D. arbuscula* (shrubby daphne), *D. collina*, and many hybrids.

Daphne arbuscula ×collina 'Lawrence Crocker', like many daphnes, often reblooms several times a season.

Delphinium, tall larkspur

FORM: Short-lived perennial

HARDINESS: Zones 5–7

BLOOM PERIOD: Spring, summer, fall

SIZE: 2–6 ft. × 1–3 ft.

Delphinium is a regal, elegant perennial standard in English cottage gardens. Large spikes of eye-catching, spurred flowers tower over mounds of dark green, glossy foliage. They thrive in regions

Delphinium 'Blue Lace'.

with relatively cool and moist summers, but struggle in hot, dry summers and do not survive winter in heavy (clay-dominant), moist soils. They are available in a range of sizes, from dwarf varieties less than 2 ft. tall to those with towering 6-ft. blooms. Flower colors include red, white, yellow, and (especially desired) rich, clear blue. They bloom late spring to early summer and flowers are suitable for cutting. Delphiniums need rich organic matter in addition to drainage and sun, and generally require staking. The tall Pacific hybrids come in blue, white, pink, and violet, but are short-lived for the entire region; the Magic Fountains Series is a dwarf version of the former with rich colors; *Delphinium ×belladonna* 'Bellamosum' is more multi-branched than the spike forms, possesses more rigid 4-ft. stalks, has deep blue flowers and a long bloom period, thanks to secondary flower stalks that bloom again later in the season.

Deschampsia cespitosa

Tufted hair grass
FORM: **Perennial, grass**
HARDINESS: **Zones 4–9**
BLOOM PERIOD: **Summer, fall**
SIZE: **1–6 ft. × 1–4 ft.**

The grass family by nature is not particularly shade tolerant, but tufted hair grass shines in shade or sun. It is an early-emergent, cool-season, tuft-forming grass ideal for small-scale gardens. It prefers moist soils but is quite tolerant of dry shade once established. Dark green, slightly arching, narrow foliage flushes a dense mass of airy, tiny flowers that look cloud-like floating over the foliage in late summer and turn golden brown in fall. Cultivars vary in size from 1-ft. 'Goldstaub' to 4-ft. 'Schottland'. 'Goldtau' is among the best cultivars of this tough, adaptable grass.

Deschampsia cespitosa 'Goldtau'.

Dutchman's breeches

FORM: Perennial

HARDINESS: Zones 3–7

BLOOM PERIOD: Spring

SIZE: 6–12 in. × 6–12 in.

☼ ◑ ☀

This is the most delicate form of *Dicentra*, with lacy, deeply cut, glaucous-blue foliage creating airy mounds. The waxy, yellow-tipped white flowers form in rows as racemes mimicking upside-down pants (breeches). This plant is far more durable than the delicate form indicates, as long as you provide excellent organic matter content with adequate moisture. It naturalizes under ideal conditions—and that's a good thing!

Dicentra cucullaria can form lovely masses in the woodland garden over time.

Fringed bleeding heart

FORM: Perennial

HARDINESS: Zones 3–9

BLOOM PERIOD: Spring, summer

SIZE: 12–18 in. × 12–18 in.

☼ ☀

Most gardeners are familiar with the old-fashioned bleeding heart, but less familiar with native woodland species. Fringed bleeding heart is an eastern U.S. native with deeply dissected, fernlike, bluish-green foliage and nodding, delicate, pink-to-rose, heart-shaped flowers. In cooler climates flowers may persist into summer; there may be no rebloom until fall. The species has pink flowers, whereas 'Alba' and 'Snowdrift' are white. This species has been used in a series of multiple hybrid crosses to generate some lovely forms of fringed bleeding heart. They have produced reblooming forms such as 'Bountiful', 'Luxuriant', 'King of Hearts', 'Ivory Hearts', 'Silversmith', and 'Burning Hearts'.

Ferny and lacy, *Dicentra eximia* is tougher than the fine foliage suggests.

DISAPPEARING ACTS

Ephemeral plants like those listed below have adapted to deep deciduous shade. These plants take advantage of early season spring sunlight passing through tree branches before foliage emerges. They surface and flower quickly, producing the energy they need to survive and storing it in root systems in short periods of time. They are valued and appreciated as harbingers of spring, but by early to midsummer foliage has dried up and disappeared, with energy stored in roots for the following season. It is important to note their placement in the garden so you don't attempt to fill empty spaces with other plants in summer. Ephemerals do well in woodland settings with adequate compost and obviously don't require supplemental summer watering. They are fussy to robust.

Anemone canadensis
Anemonella thalictroides
Arisaema Asian species
Arisaema dracontium
Arisaema triphyllum
Claytonia virginica
Dicentra cucullaria
Dodecatheon jeffreyi
Dodecatheon meadia
Mertensia virginica
Phlox divaricata
Podophyllum peltatum and Asian hybrids
Sanguinaria canadensis
Trillium species
Uvularia grandiflora

Dicentra hybrids

Bleeding heart
FORM: **Short-lived perennial**
HARDINESS: **Zones 3–8**
BLOOM PERIOD: **Spring, summer, fall**
SIZE: **8–18 in. × 8–18 in.**

Dicentra 'King of Hearts' is a lovely low-mounding bleeding heart with the same unusual dissected blue foliage as *D. eximia* and rich, rose-colored flowers. It may bloom continuously through summer if sited in cool locations and is effective when massed. It is the result of a triple cross between *D. eximia*, the western U.S. native *D. formosa*, and Japanese native *D. peregrina*. Since its release other hybrid variations have emerged, including white 'Ivory Hearts' and deep rose-red 'Burning Hearts'.

The glaucous blue foliage is a unique color for perennial foliage. *Dicentra* 'King of Hearts' may rebloom a time or two.

Diervilla sessilifolia 'Cool Splash'

Bush honeysuckle

FORM: **Shrub**

HARDINESS: **Zones 5–8**

BLOOM PERIOD: **Summer**

SIZE: **3–5 ft. × 3–5 ft.**

Bush honeysuckle is a fairly common landscape shrub in the Lower Midwest and less often seen in northern climes. It is rather unremarkable, sporting long, lanceolate, green foliage on reddish, arching stems and new growth with red highlights. Its small, bright yellow flowers are somewhat reminiscent of potentilla but overall it is just a durable shrub good for embankments and filling space. The spectacularly variegated 'Cool Splash' takes the shrub to a whole new stratosphere, as a garden addition with strong, creamy white, wide leaf margins and excellent durability; I have seen it doing well in Minneapolis.

Diervilla sessilifolia 'Cool Splash' is an excellent recent shrub introduction, elevating an otherwise durable but plain parent with gorgeous variegation.

Dirca palustris

Leatherwood

FORM: **Shrub**

HARDINESS: **Zones 3–9**

BLOOM PERIOD: **Spring**

SIZE: **4–6 ft. × 4–6 ft.**

This tree-shaped deciduous shrub should be more readily available, due to its durability and truly small scale; it grows slowly to only 5 to 6 ft. tall. It is native to the forests of eastern North America but infrequent in most of its range, and even more uncommon in nurseries. The lemon-yellow, bell-shaped flowers with long yellow stamens consistently mass the plant in early spring, before foliage emergence. Excellent yellow fall color with intriguing winter form rounds out four-season interest. The tough, strong bark has a leathery look and feel, with extremely elastic twigs. Worth the search.

Dirca palustris fall color.

BLAZES OF GLORY

Annuals such as the suggestions below provide season-long, consistent color. Whether grown in containers or in the ground, they require porous, friable growing media with regular supplemental fertilization until late summer. Proper balance is essential, as most are not forgiving of even short periods of stress. Maximize growing media quantity and avoid overcrowding. This list covers less common plants instead of traditional, well-known favorites such as petunia, marigold, and zinnia, even though new colors and forms of those stand-bys are released every year. They are fussy to robust.

Alocasia
Angelonia angustifolia
Brugmansia suaveolens
Colocasia esculenta
Cynara cardunculus
Datura stramonium
Ensete
Euphorbia hypericifolia
Furcraea foetida 'Mediopicta'
Gomphocarpus physocarpus
Heliotropium arborescens
Lobularia maritima
Melianthus major
Musa
Nigella damascena
Passiflora incarnata
Salpiglossis sinuata
Salvia 'Wendy's Wish'
Senna didymobotrya
Strobilanthes dyerianus
Succulents
Thunbergia alata
Torenia fournieri

Dodecatheon jeffreyi; *D. meadia*

Jeffrey's shooting star; shooting star
FORM: **Perennial**
HARDINESS: **Zones 4–8**
BLOOM PERIOD: **Spring**
SIZE: **8–18 in. × 8–24 in.**

☀ ◑ ☀

Walk into an area where shooting stars have naturalized and see if you can avoid adding them to your garden. The foliage grows as a basal rosette; each plant generates one to four tall, leafless scapes topped by an umbel of numerous flowers that look like dropping badminton birdies or shooting stars. The petals reflex backward and the yellow stamens pull together into a point, giving the impression of downward acceleration speeding to earth. Jeffrey's shooting star is native to west of our region and has similar attributes in rose-pink flowers.

Dodecatheon meadia is lovely whether in a meadow or ornamental garden.

Echinacea hybrids

Coneflower

FORM: Short-lived perennial
HARDINESS: Zones 4–9
BLOOM PERIOD: Summer, fall
SIZE: 3–4 ft. × 2–3 ft.

Note: I have separated out new coneflower hybrids from our tough-as-nails native *Echinacea purpurea* (purple coneflower). Numerous coneflower hybrids are as robust and durable as the species but many recent releases are the result of crosses of purple coneflower with *E. paradoxa* (native to Missouri, Arkansas, Texas, and Oklahoma) and *E. tennesseensis* (native to a specific location in Tennessee). Both are shorter lived than purple coneflower and hardy to warmer climates, so the amount of each in the background will affect true hardiness. Coneflower also requires a vernalization (exposure to cold) period and most sale plants are sown, grown, and sold in the spring without that process. Many ornamental plants are no longer exposed to extensive trialing before release so it is the homeowners who learn durability the hard way. Eventually the tough sorts from the weak, but realize when purchasing new cultivars that sturdiness due simply to parentage is not assured. If you have not seen any trialing results on new releases, I recommend sampling them in small quantities to measure their durability before mass planting.

Echinacea trial plots at Ball Seed. A few will be great, some will fail.

Purple coneflower

FORM: **Perennial**

HARDINESS: **Zones 3–8**

BLOOM PERIOD: **Summer, fall**

SIZE: **2–5 ft. × 1.5–2 ft.**

Coneflower is a durable native plant with an extensive indigenous range and tolerance to drought, heat, humidity, and poor soil. Colors were limited to purple, magenta, or white before recent extensive hybridization (see *Echinacea* hybrids). Extended late-season bloom makes them popular in the perennial bed, but they shine in prairie and meadow gardens. They will self-seed from a spiny central cone, so dividing may be necessary every four years or so. Seeds make excellent bird food. Prone to some leaf spot issues, aster yellows, and Japanese beetle damage. Some of the more time-tested durable cultivars include 'Pixie Meadowbrite', 'Pica Bella', 'Milkshake', 'Magnus', 'White Swan', 'Marmalade', 'Fatal Attraction', and 'Ruby Star'. 'Cheyenne Spirit' is a seed strain that produces a variety of colors in one planting.

Echinacea purpurea—overused? Not if you evaluate the merits of this time-tested favorite.

Echinops ritro; E. sphaerocephalus

Globe thistle; great globe thistle

FORM: Perennial

HARDINESS: Zones 3–10

BLOOM PERIOD: Summer, fall

SIZE: 2–5 ft. × 1–2 ft.

Globe thistle may not appeal to everyone but I love its unique strongly architectural structure and steel-blue color. A tall, upright perennial with metallic, purple-blue, spherical flowers and spiny leaves; bees love them and they work well fresh cut and dried. *Echinops ritro* is a compact species with cobweb-like, woolly foliage. It matures from stainless blue to late summer bright blue before fading to everlasting brown. *E. sphaerocephalus* forms a bushy, upright mound of gray-green leaves with large, rounded, silver-white flowers that contrast beautifully with sturdy, reddish stems.

The steely blue of *Echinops ritro* complements other colors in the garden.

Enkianthus campanulatus

Redvein enkianthus, furin-tsutsuji

FORM: Shrub

HARDINESS: Zones 4–7

BLOOM PERIOD: Spring, summer

SIZE: 6–15 ft. × 4–6 ft.

Redvein enkianthus is a large, erect, deciduous shrub with small elliptic leaves that turn bright red, orange, and yellow in autumn. Clusters of small, bell-shaped, cream or reddish, flowers adorn the plant from late spring to midsummer. It matures into stately specimens with gracefully tiered branches up to 15 ft. tall. 'Showy Lantern' has distinctly showier, more brilliantly colored blooms and denser branching, making it more compact with an elegant horizontal habit. 'Red Bells' produces luscious cream-colored flowers tipped with red, and exhibits good autumn color. *Enkianthus campanulatus* var. *albiflorus* has white flowers. Harder to find are 'Venus' with large shell-pink flowers, dwarf 'Hollandia' (to 3 ft.) with rosy red flowers, and pink-flowering 'Wallaby'.

Enkianthus campanulatus can boast a real show of flowers when happy.

Banana

FORM: **Annual**

HARDINESS: **Zones (5)6–11**

BLOOM PERIOD: **Non-flowering**

SIZE: **3–15 ft. × 2–6 ft. (depending on single stem or clumps)**

Bananas are fun tropicals for the northern gardener to evoke exotica! *Musa basjoo* claims hardiness to zone 5 and I have friends who have accomplished that successfully, with carefully selected sites and thick, protective winter mulch. But banana plants are reasonably priced and grow quickly so everyone can enjoy their splendor. They may be overwintered in several ways. I dig the plants, shake off soil, place in sealed black garbage bags, and store where they won't freeze. They can also be potted and the stems cut off, then stored in the same conditions. Varieties range from 3- to 4-ft. 'Dwarf Cavendish' to 12- to 15-ft. towering giants such as my personal favorite, *Ensete ventricosum*, the Abyssinian banana.

Bananas are the ultimate in making beds look tropical regardless of where you live, and there are many selections, including *Ensete ventricosum* used in this border.

SUNNY DISPOSITIONS

These plants love it hot, dry, and well drained. They will tolerate compost-deficient soils; adding inorganic fertilizer will make them stretch and develop weak stems. Fertility should be provided by annual applications of organic matter. They are robust to aggressive.

PERENNIALS

Acanthus mollis
Acanthus spinosus
Achillea hybrids
Achillea millefolium
Aconitum species
Allium species
Amsonia hubrichtii
Amsonia tabernaemontana
Andropogon gerardii
Anemone hybrids
Astrantia major
Baptisia alba var. macrophylla
Baptisia australis
Baptisia leucantha
Bergenia cordifolia
Calamintha nepeta subsp. nepeta
Campanula species
Coreopsis hybrids
Echinops ritro
Echinops sphaerocephalus
Eryngium planum
Eryngium yuccifolium
Eurybia divaricate
Helianthus angustifolius
Helianthus ×multiflorus
Helianthus salicifolius
Heliopsis helianthoides hybrids
Leucanthemum hybrids

Liatris spicata
Ratibida columnifera
Ratibida pinnata
Rudbeckia maxima
Sanguisorba obtusa
Schizachyrium scoparium
Silphium integrifolium
Silphium laciniatum
Silphium perfoliatum
Silphium terebinthinaceum
Solidago canadensis
Solidago rigida
Symphyotrichum species
Thalictrum delavayi
Thalictrum rochebrunianum
Vernonia noveboracensis
Yucca filamentosa

TREES AND SHRUBS

Aesculus ×carnea
Aesculus parviflora
Aesculus pavia
Aronia melanocarpa
Cercidiphyllum japonicum
Fagus sylvatica
Ginkgo biloba
Gymnocladus dioicus
Hibiscus syriacus
Lespedeza bicolor
Magnolia species
Syringa meyeri
Syringa reticulata
Syringa reticulata subsp. pekinensis
Syringa vulgaris
Tilia cordata
Tilia heterophylla
Tilia tomentosa

Epimedium species

Barrenwort, epimedium, bishop's hat

FORM: Perennial

HARDINESS: Zones 5–9

BLOOM PERIOD: Spring, summer, fall

SIZE: 6–12 in. × 8–18 in.

When you see the shallow, rhizomatous root systems of barrenwort you may wonder how it can possibly be drought tolerant. But during a recent severe drought when other perennials were drooping or dying, the foliage of this plant looked untouched by stress. I love this genus for tiny, delicate spurred flowers that dance over the foliage in early spring, like ethereal miniature orchids in orange, yellow, red, purple, white, and mixed colors. Lanceolate foliage can display spots, toothed edges, or red to purple coloration and is evergreen in mild climates. It establishes as an excellent ground cover with a medium growth rate. Favorites you will find in my garden include hybrids 'Lilafee', 'Amber Queen', 'Pink Champagne', 'Spine Tingler' (serrated leaves), 'Dark Beauty', 'Pink Elf', 'Yokihi', 'Rubrum', and 'Princess Susan', as well as *Epimedium* ×*warleyense* 'Ellen Willmott' and 'Orange Queen', both with orange flowers.

Epimedium grandiflorum 'Lilafee' is an oldie but goodie.

Giant sea holly; sea holly; small globe thistle

FORM: Perennial

HARDINESS: Zones 5–9

BLOOM PERIOD: Summer, fall

SIZE: 2–4 ft. × 1–3 ft.

The hardy genus *Eryngium* appears as a smaller version of globe thistle, featuring open umbels of prickly, steel-blue flowers that attract butterflies. It is tolerant of hot, dry sites and soils high in salts, and spreads into small patches. *E. giganteum* (giant sea holly) boasts two spectacular ethereally silver forms: 'Miss Willmott's Ghost' and 'Silver Ghost'. Cultivars of *E. planum* (sea holly) include 'Jade Frost' and 'Sunny Jackpot', both with variegated foliage; extra-blue 'Blue Glitter'; silver-flowered 'Silver Salentino'; and dwarf 'Blue Hobbit'.

Eryngium giganteum 'Miss Willmott's Ghost' combines surprising color with dramatic texture.

Eryngium yuccifolium

Rattlesnake master

FORM: Perennial

HARDINESS: Zones 3–8

BLOOM PERIOD: Summer, fall

SIZE: 2–4 ft. × 1–3 ft.

Rattlesnake master is considered a native plant and isn't used extensively in ornamental gardening, but its unique and eye-catching structure should not be overlooked for dry, sunny sites. "Structurally architectural" defines its value and I use it even among ornamentals for visual interest. The slightly spiny leaves are arranged in rosettes resembling yucca. Flower stems shoot skyward in summer and are topped with thistle-like, bluish-silver flowers attracting many insects.

Eryngium yuccifolium adds necessary architectural structure to the garden, native or ornamental.

Euphorbia hypericifolia

Spurge

FORM: **Annual**

HARDINESS: **Not hardy**

BLOOM PERIOD: **Spring, summer, fall**

SIZE: **10–12 in. × 8–10 in.**

Tough as nails! This plant looks like baby's breath but don't be fooled: these wispy, mounding plants have the durability *Gypsophila* lacks. It is drought tolerant and I can use it in areas that miss regular watering with no worries. It grows quickly to white mounds, needs no deadheading or care, and blooms continuously until winter. There are numerous cultivars such as 'Diamond Frost', 'Breathless Blush', and 'Breathless White', but I have a hard time discerning any real differences other than the fact that 'Breathless Blush' has darker stems.

Euphorbia hypericifolia 'Diamond Frost' still amazes me with how hot and dry it can take it and still perform all season long.

Fagus sylvatica

European beech

FORM: **Tree**

HARDINESS: **Zones 4–7**

BLOOM PERIOD: **Non-flowering**

SIZE: **50–60 ft. × 35–50 ft.; smaller cultivars in weeping and fastigiate forms**

European beech is more durable in many areas than native *Fagus grandifolia* (white beech). Beeches feature upright oval forms with shiny, dark green leaves turning yellow to rust-colored in fall. Flowers are insignificant but birds and squirrels favor the small nuts. It is an excellent slow-growing shade tree but massive when mature. Small landscapes favor reduced-sized cultivars, including tall, weeping, purple-foliaged 'Purple Fountain' and small, strict weeping 'Purpurea Pendula'; layered, 35-ft.-tall, tricolor-foliaged 'Roseomarginata'; columnar gold 'Dawykii Gold'; purple 'Dawykii Purple' and red-purple 'Red Obelisk'; contorted, flattened 'Tortuosa' and 'Torulosa Purpurea'; and golden weeping 'Pendula Aurea'.

Fagus sylvatica 'Roseomarginata' is the flashiest of the European beeches.

FORM: **Perennial**

HARDINESS: **Varies**

BLOOM PERIOD: **Non-flowering**

SIZE: **3 in.–5 ft. × 3 in.–5 ft.**

Ferns are popular garden plants and one of the best ornamental plants for exhibiting fine texture in plant design. Hardiness varies according to species, but many are as hardy as zone 3. This group includes many genera and species and hundreds of cultivars. Some of those utilized in the Midwest include *Adiantum, Arachnoides, Asplenium, Athyrium, Blechnum, Botrychium, Cheilanthes, Cyrtomium, Cystopteris, Dryopteris, Matteuccia, Onoclea, Osmunda, Pellaea, Polypodium, Polystichum, Pteridium, Thelypteris*, and *Woodsia*. Most prefer rich, evenly moist soils and dappled light, but some tolerate dry, sunny conditions; some even grow on cliffs.

Native plant enthusiasts can't go wrong with ferns and you'll find forms for every condition, from diminutive rock wall–hugging *Polypodium virginianum* (rock cap fern) to the moisture-loving, stately *Osmunda* (royal, cinnamon, and interrupted ferns) to delicate fine-textured woodland *Adiantum* (maidenhair ferns), and even oddities such as the *Asplenium rhizophyllum* (walking fern). Two natives I suggest you avoid for their aggressive nature are *Dennstaedtia punctilobula* (hay-scented fern, sunny sites) and *Pteridium aquilinum* (bracken fern, shadier sites), unless you want to fill a lot of space quickly. *Matteuccia struthiopteris* (ostrich fern) also gets a bad rap for aggressive spreading but I still love its impressive, stately vase form and ability to thrive in dark sites such as the north side of a house; just give it necessary space and it provides an elegant backdrop to other plants.

Athyrium (lady fern) and *Dryopteris* (wood fern) are currently dominating the ornamental market. Award-winning *A. niponicum* 'Pictum' (painted Japanese lady fern) have become so popular since the early 2000s that a large number of color variants were released, including 'Silver Falls', 'Burgundy

Ferns will flourish in every range of the region, such as this South of the Boreal garden.

Dryopteris marginalis is coarser in texture, more rigidly upright, and often more evergreen than *Athyrium*.

Lace', 'Pewter Lace', and 'Wildwood Twist'. It can be hard to tell many of these apart, as the color variations aren't always distinctively different in garden settings. There are additional variants with unusual foliar mutations such as crested, cruciated, laciniated, congested, and undulating fronds, particularly in *Athyrium*, *Dryopteris*, and *Polystichum* (hollyfern). Japanese lady ferns with these mutations were further selected, such as 'Soulmate' and a personal favorite, 'Applecourt'. These interesting fronds showed up in the common lady fern, *A. filix-femina* and produced beauties such as 'Victoriae', 'Dre's Dagger', 'Frizelliae', and 'Minutissima'. It didn't stop there. *A. niponicum* and *A. filix-femina* were then crossed to create hybrids combining the silver and purple accents of Japanese lady fern with the upright, arching form of lady fern to create such stunners as 'Branford Beauty', Ghost', and 'Ocean's Fury'. The same mutations have created fascinating variations in *Dryopteris* as well, producing the likes of 'Jimmy Dyce', 'Parsley', and 'Linearis'.

The home gardener has a plethora of ferns to select for the fine-textured component of their garden design. It certainly pays to attend a fern lecture to get a true picture of the tremendous selection and variation available to the gardener.

Fothergilla major

Witch alder

FORM: Shrub
HARDINESS: Zones 4–8
BLOOM PERIOD: Spring
SIZE: 4–10 ft. × 4–9 ft.

One of the most pH-tolerant of acid-loving shrubs; I have a lovely specimen in my high-lime garden. It thrives in sun or shade with early, honey-sweet, white bottlebrush blooms; fiery fall foliage; and open, airy habit. Intriguing winter branches need protection from rabbits; it is extremely slow growing, requiring no pruning. Leathery fall foliage turns shades of red, orange, and bright yellow; best color is in sun. Several glaucous blue foliaged forms, such as 'Blue Shadow', are available; best fall color is 'Beaver Creek'. *Fothergilla gardenii* is a supposed dwarf at 3 ft. tall but most seem as large as *F. major*.

The white flowers of *Fothergilla major* light up shady areas in spring.

Furcraea foetida 'Mediopicta'

Variegated Mauritius hemp

FORM: Annual

HARDINESS: Not hardy

BLOOM PERIOD: Non-flowering

SIZE: 3–4 ft. × 3–4 ft., depending on size purchased

I bought variegated Mauritius hemp on a whim and coincidentally the same year saw large specimens in another garden. Since this is a slow-growing succulent, I overwintered it for five years and now have magnificent specimens that provide stunningly elegant architectural form in the center of massive cast iron urns. They tolerate the heat generated by the iron with minimal water and no fertilization.

Furcraea foetida 'Mediopicta' is such an important plant in my annual design schemes at the public garden that I overwinter it every year to keep gaining size.

Gaillardia aristata

Blanket flower

FORM: Short-lived perennial

HARDINESS: Zones 3–8

BLOOM PERIOD: Spring, summer, fall

SIZE: 6–12 in. × 6–12 in.

Described as "sunshine on the western prairie," blanket flower blooms in golden beauty with red-tinted centers (some cultivars have a red ring around the center of the outer petals). The subdued, silvery green leaves vary in shape and stay low growing. There has been a large influx of blanket flower cultivars on the market; unfortunately many are hybrids of hardy *Gaillardia aristata* and *G. pulchella* (Indian blanket flower), which is native, but also an annual that doesn't survive winters and heavy soils. Blanket flower detests heavy soils but will thrive in sandy, well-drained media. If you want blanket flowers as perennials, find *aristata* forms, such as 'Amber Wheels', 'Oranges and Lemons', 'Sunburst Burgundy Silk', and 'Sunburst Tangerine', otherwise treat most cultivars as annuals or short-lived perennials at best.

Planting *Gaillardia aristata* is like inserting brilliant little suns in your garden.

Galium odoratum
(syn. *Asperula odorata*)

Sweet woodruff

FORM: Perennial, ground cover
HARDINESS: Zones 4–8
BLOOM PERIOD: Spring
SIZE: 6–12 in. × 8–18 in.

Sweet woodruff is deceivingly delicate in appearance, with small whorls of emerald-green foliage generally rising no more than 6 in. from the dry woodland floor, holding masses of tiny white spring flowers. It is tougher than it looks and spreads by rhizome and seed to create large mats of soft ground cover. It can become quite aggressive if happy. Dry conditions keep it in check and robust woodland plants will grow up through it. You may recognize the name from herbal uses; foliage is aromatic if cut or crushed.

Galium odoratum looks diminutive at first glance but can form large areas of ground cover in dry shade where other plants fail.

Gentiana andrewsii

Bottle gentian

FORM: Perennial
HARDINESS: Zones 3–7
BLOOM PERIOD: Fall
SIZE: 1–2 ft. × 1–1.5 ft.

I am fond of all gentians for true-blue flowers with forms ranging from ground-hugging alpines to tall, erect perennials. Bottle gentians are slow growing but long lived and require little care once established. Their deep blue flowers never actually open, giving them their bottle-like appearance. Bumblebees are the main pollinators because they are the only insects strong enough to pry open the closed flowers. Bottle gentians bloom late into fall, seemingly impervious to frost. No cultivars exist but natural color can vary greatly, typically blue to purplish, but occasionally pink or white.

A white-flowering form of *Gentiana andrewsii*.

Geranium maculatum and related species

Wild geranium

FORM: Perennial
HARDINESS: Zones 3–8
BLOOM PERIOD: Spring
SIZE: 8–18 in. × 12–18 in.

Wild geraniums that naturalize readily in woodlands provide hardy genetic material for hybridizing many free-flowering cultivars that are durable in sun or shade and adaptive to less-than-ideal soils. White, pink, rose, violet, and multicolored flowers light up the woodland floor, framed by dark green, deeply dissected palmate foliage that may assume rusty red fall tinges. Some variegated forms exist; size varies by cultivar. 'Rozanne' is an outstanding lilac-flowering cultivar garnering much attention. I am particularly attracted to densely mounding, florific hybrids such as *Geranium ×cantabrigiense* 'Karmina'. Selections are wide and appealing.

Geranium ×cantabrigiense 'Karmina' carpets the woodland floor of a garden in Wisconsin.

Geum triflorum

Prairie smoke

FORM: Perennial
HARDINESS: Zones 3–7
BLOOM PERIOD: Spring, summer
SIZE: 6–18 in. × 6–12 in.

This native perennial is called prairie smoke because of the wispy, smokelike seed heads. It is among the earliest prairie bloomers (late spring through early summer), bearing clusters of nodding reddish-pink, maroon, or purple flowers on 1-ft.-high stems. Each stem may have as many as nine flowers, but they generally occur in threes (therefore *triflorum*).

Geum triflorum is a delightful native flower to call our own.

SUNNY TOPS, MOIST FEET

For maximum growth and flowering, this group loves adequate sun, but foliage will burn severely in heat stress with dry roots. In the same regard, the shade that deters foliage burn will limit flowering and cause weak, spindly growth. In areas of the Midwest with intense summer heat, it is best to site these plants with full morning sun, filtered afternoon light, and deep, organically rich soils. Summer supplemental watering will likely be essential in dry periods. They are fussy to robust.

PERENNIALS

Actaea racemosa
Actaea simplex
Asclepias incarnata
Astilbe species
Astilboides tabularis
Gentiana andrewsii
Helenium autumnale
Hibiscus moscheutos
Kirengeshoma palmata
Ligularia dentata
Ligularia stenocephala
Lobelia cardinalis
Petasites japonicus
Primula species
Rodgersia species

TREES AND SHRUBS

Cephalanthus occidentalis
Cornus sanguinea
Cornus sericea
Ilex verticillata
Metasequoia glyptostroboides

Nyssa sylvatica
Salix alba 'Britzensis'
Salix elaeagnos subsp. *angustifolia*
Salix matsudana 'Tortuosa'
Salix sachalinensis 'Golden Sunshine'
Taxodium distichum

SUNNY TOPS, DRY FEET

Typical of the High Plains and alpine areas, the plants below love full sun but abhor excess water around their roots and crowns. They set deep roots that help them survive severe winters in sandy and graveled soils. Also known as xeriscape plants, these perennials are excellent choices for waterwise gardens. They are fussy to robust.

Asclepias tuberosa
Callirhoe involucrata
Crocosmia hybrids
Daphne hybrids
Delphinium hybrids
Gaillardia aristata
Geum triflorum
Kniphofia uvaria
Oenothera lindheimeri
Penstemon hybrids
Pulsatilla vulgaris
Verbascum hybrids

Ginkgo biloba

Maidenhair tree

FORM: Tree

HARDINESS: Zones 3–8

BLOOM PERIOD: Non-flowering

SIZE: 50–80 ft. × 30–40 ft.; numerous dwarf cultivars

The only survivor of a genus 150 million years old, *Ginkgo biloba* is categorized as a deciduous conifer. The distinctive fan-shaped, two-lobe leaf is identifiable from herbal use. Fall color is spectacular yellow to yellow-gold. Species reach 80 ft. but fortunately numerous cultivars with variable growth rates, forms, and leaf shape have been selected for garden use, including weeping 'Pendula', globose 'Chi Chi', short-mounded 'Mariken', and vase-shaped 'Jade Butterflies'. Used as street trees, ginkgoes have exceptional urban tolerance; dropped fruit from female trees produces unbearable odor due to butyric acid content, so only males are sold.

Ginkgo biloba, resplendent in fall apparel at Allen Centennial Gardens.

Gomphocarpus physocarpus

Swan flower

FORM: Annual

HARDINESS: Not hardy

BLOOM PERIOD: Summer, fall

SIZE: 4–5 ft. × 1–2 ft.

Okay, you have to grant me an oddity. We love this one for children in the garden, but have to keep ourselves from using the most apt common name: hairy balls. It is an annual milkweed, supporting butterflies as well as producing milkweed-filamentous floating seed. Rest assured, it will generate conversation and chuckles. It does also reseed.

Gomphocarpus physocarpus.

Giant rhubarb

FORM: Perennial
HARDINESS: Zones 7–10
BLOOM PERIOD: Summer
SIZE: 6–12 ft. × 8–15 ft.

Giant rhubarb is an enormous, striking tropical plant with leaves that can reach 7 ft. or more. It grows well in temperate and subtropical zones as long as it is provided with plenty of water and given proper winter care. A patch can grow to cover a very large area. Tiny red-brown flowers borne in erect panicles to 3 ft. are interesting but not significantly ornamental.

I would love a yard large enough to grow *Gunnera manicata* to the impressive size it can achieve.

Kentucky coffee tree

FORM: Tree
HARDINESS: Zones 3–8
BLOOM PERIOD: Non-flowering
SIZE: 60–80 ft. × 40–50 ft.

Kentucky coffee tree is a large, stately shade tree with delicate, bipinnately compound leaves suited only for large landscapes. It as an excellent native alternative to the overused honeylocust, which has been developing disease issues due to overplanting. It is used in landscaping well beyond its natural range because it transplants easily and tolerates urban conditions. The roasted seeds were once used as a coffee substitute; raw seeds are poisonous. It is a nectar or larval host for several native moths. The foliage develops no appreciable fall color. 'Espresso' and 'Stately Manor' are male selections, therefore seedless, which is an advantage because the pods are large and messy.

Gymnocladus dioicus is a fine native tree that is urban tolerant and resilient.

Hakonechloa macra cultivars

Japanese forest grass

FORM: Perennial, grass

HARDINESS: Zones 5–9

BLOOM PERIOD: Fall

SIZE: 12–18 in. × 12–24 in.

You will find many cultivars of Japanese forest grass winding through my personal garden as weavers that tie other garden plants together. It is shallow rooted and spreads slowly by rhizomes. The species is solid green and two to three times larger than the cultivars. The most popular cultivar is award-winning 'Aureola' (green and gold variegation). Others include 'Sunny Delight' (green and gold); 'Albostriata', 'Stripe It Rich', and 'Fubuki' (green and white variegation); robust 'All Gold' (solid gold); and 'Naomi', 'Nicolas', and 'Beni-Kaze' that darken red in fall. Drainage is key for the elegance provided by this cascading stunner.

Hakonechloa macra 'Aureola' is my garden weaver and favorite ornamental grass.

Hakonechloa macra 'All Gold' in my garden in autumn.

Halesia species

Silverbell

FORM: Tree
HARDINESS: Zone (4)5–8
BLOOM PERIOD: Spring
SIZE: 20–40 ft. × 15–35 ft.

Halesia carolina (syn. *H. tetraptera*) is a small deciduous understory tree with an abundance of petite, pendant, bell-shaped white flowers tracing the branches in spring. The flowers turn to four-winged seed capsules. It can have pleasing yellow fall color but foliage drops fairly quickly. 'UConn Wedding Bells' is purportedly more compact and heavier flowering; 'Rosea' has pink flowers. *H. monticola* (mountain silverbell) is sometimes listed as a variety of *H. carolina* and is similar, except it is larger in growth, flowers, and habit; cultivar 'Arnold Pink' has pink flowers. It is listed hardy by some sources to zone 4 but is rarely seen there. *H. diptera* (two-winged silverbell) is also small, reaching 20 to 30 ft. in height, with a fairly dense, rounded silhouette when grown in the full sun. *H. diptera* var. *magniflora* is a popular garden tree prized for its large flowers. All are very similar, especially the flowers.

Halesia diptera var. *magniflora* loaded with large silverbell flowers.

Helenium autumnale and hybrids

Sneezeweed

FORM: Perennial

HARDINESS: Zones 3–8

BLOOM PERIOD: Summer, fall

SIZE: 3–5 ft. × 2–3 ft.

Don't let the common name turn you away. This native has yellow or bronze, single, daisy-like, early fall flowers on stout, branched stems. Petals have distinct tooth-like indentations providing another common name, dog-toothed daisy. All sneezeweeds have three-lobed petals, which distinguish them from *Rudbeckia* and other coneflowers. Brown, rust-colored fruit appears in fall. If they get dry they will drop lower petals, exposing bare legs. Fine hybrid selections with red, orange, and bronze highlights include compact forms like 'Short 'n' Sassy' and Plants Nouveau's Mariachi Series, 'Morheim Beauty', 'Mardi Gras', and the intriguing 'Tie Dye', which is yellow brushed with purple and pink.

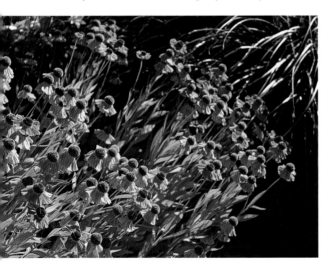

I would not be without sneezeweed like *Helenium* 'Mardi Gras' for late-season color and bloom.

Helianthus angustifolius; H. ×multiflorus; H. salicifolius

Narrow-leaf sunflower, swamp sunflower; multi-flowered sunflower; willow leaf sunflower

FORM: Perennial

HARDINESS: Zones 4–9

BLOOM PERIOD: Summer, fall

SIZE: 1–7 ft. × 1–4 ft.

Perennial sunflowers are coarse plants with simple, bristly leaves. They exhibit showy, bright, daisy-shaped flowers with cultivars in shades of yellow, orange, red, cream, purple, and bronze. *Helianthus angustifolius* 'Gold Lace' forms a bold fountain of fall gold. *H. ×multiflorus* 'Flore Pleno' boasts beefy double flowers. Most reach substantial size but not all are towering giants. *H. salicifolius* 'Low Down' is diminutive at 2 ft. and 'First Light' is compact, reaching only 3 ft.

Bold and dramatic miniature suns of *Helianthus* tower over other perennials.

FOUR-SEASON STALWARTS

A number of ornamental plants will provide four-season interest, but none are as reliable as the conifers. The trees in the group below are all indigenous to northern temperate zones so our friends in the Lower Midwest will struggle with many. But they are a boon for the rest of the region for consistent color, texture, and form when our landscapes are buried in snow. Most evolved as canopy trees, so few have any real degree of shade tolerance. Note: Conifers are unique among garden plants in that selected cultivars may be dramatically different in size from the species. Sizes listed for all conifers in this book are for the species only, with the acknowledgment that cultivars vary widely in size, growth habit, and form.

Abies
Cedrus
Chamaecyparis
Juniperus
Larix
Picea
Pinus
Pseudotsuga
Taxus
Thuja

Heliopsis helianthoides hybrids

Oxeye sunflower

FORM: **Perennial**
HARDINESS: **Zones 3–9**
BLOOM PERIOD: **Summer, fall**
SIZE: **2–4 ft. × 2–4 ft.**

Oxeye sunflower is an upright, clump-forming, short cousin of *Helianthus* with bright, large, single, medium-gold summer flowers. 'Helhan' Loraine Sunshine has interesting variegated foliage. 'Prairie Sunset' and 'Summer Nights' have purple-veined leaves with purple stems. 'Tuscan Sun' is a dense compact form up to 2 ft.

Heliopsis helianthoides 'Summer Nights' is striking, with purple stems offsetting the bright flowers.

Heliotropium arborescens

Heliotrope

FORM: **Annual**
HARDINESS: **Not hardy**
BLOOM PERIOD: **Spring, summer, fall**
SIZE: **6–12 in. × 4–8 in.**

Heliotrope is lovely with its tiny, star-shaped, deep blue, purple, lavender, or white flowers tightly packed into spikes within rounded circular clusters. But even if it was ugly I would still plant it for the intoxicating fragrance! It wafts perfume reminiscent of vanilla, particularly in the early evening, so plant it where you can appreciate the heady scent. It does not like to be crowded by other plants, and excess moisture and heat will rot it quickly, so give it space and good air circulation. 'Princess Marina', 'Marine', and 'Dwarf Marine' are popular compact cultivars with fragrant purple flowers. White forms, which are considered less aromatic, include 'Alba', 'White Lady', and 'White Queen'.

Fragrance: *Heliotropium arborescens* does it magnificently.

Helleborus hybrids and strains

Hellebore

FORM: **Perennial**
HARDINESS: **Zones 4–9**
BLOOM PERIOD: **Spring**
SIZE: **1–1.5 ft. × 1–1.5 ft.**

Hellebores are garden favorites and should be used in all gardens, but I have never seen them used more extensively than in the Lower Midwest. Southern climes have the advantage of February and March bloom when northern climes are still staring at snow banks. Hellebores bloom for long periods before humid summer heat pummels this range. Hellebores are best grown in rich, well-drained soils in shade. Cultivars will be true to description, such as creamy yellow 'Banana Cream Pie', 'Blue Lady', and 'Pink Frost'. Plants sold as "strains" means they are seed propagated, so individuals within the grouping show variations, such as the Winter Thriller and Winter Jewels Series and the Gold Collection Series.

Hellebores emerge and flower early, often through snow.

Hemerocallis hybrids

Daylily

FORM: **Perennial**
HARDINESS: **Zones 3–9**
BLOOM PERIOD: **Summer**
SIZE: **2–5 ft. × 2–2.5 ft.**

Daylilies are durable plants that tolerate poor soils, high heat, humidity, and neglect. They come in thousands of easy-to-grow cultivars. Daylilies multiply rapidly, so require regular division. The common name refers to individual flowers lasting only one day, but breeding efforts have produced cultivars with many flowers per scape. Colors include everything except true blue. Breeding for diploidy and tetraploidy has produced double flowers; some

Hemerocallis exhibits a wide range of colors and flower shapes.

cultivars exhibit "diamond dusting," ruffled petals, and contrasting throats and/or eye-zones. They feature six-petaled or double flowers on long, sturdy stems above long, arching, strap-like leaves. Due to a relatively short period of bloom, mix them with plants that provide visual interest the rest of the season. They are relatively pest free but subject to daylily rust. They make excellent ground covers for erosion control.

'Autumn Minaret' is unusual in that it blooms late, after other daylilies have finished; it shoots out butter-yellow blooms with a rosy orange wash on flower scapes up to around 5 ft. Some of my favorites among the standards are 'Primal Scream' for brilliance, 'Blueberry Breakfast' for its pastel two-tone, 'Autumn Orange Truffle' for chic double petals, 'Heavenly Curls' for unusual petal shape, and 'Raspberry Goosebumps' for ruffled edges, but there are so many cultivars I could go on endlessly describing pleasing variations.

A large number of reblooming miniature daylilies (roughly half to a third in size) are available, too. 'Stella D'Oro', which has dominated the miniature reblooming market, is a tough, durable plant but so overused that other beauties such as 'Little Dandy', 'Siloam Tee Tiny', and 'Promises Promises' are overlooked.

CLIMBERS

Vines add verticality, especially in areas with limited width for trees and shrubs. Some are lightweight enough to be managed on standard trellises, but others will develop mass and weight that require substantial pergolas, walls, or trees for support. Vines without vertical support may also be used as ground covers. Those listed below are all perennials; there are many spectacular annual vines to explore as well. They are robust to aggressive.

Aristolochia macrophylla
Campsis radicans
Celastrus scandens
Clematis species
Hydrangea anomala subsp. *petiolaris*
Lonicera ×*brownii*
Lonicera ×*heckrottii*
Parthenocissus quinquefolia
Parthenocissus tricuspidata
Schizophragma hydrangeoides
Wisteria frutescens
Wisteria macrostachya

Heuchera hybrids

Alumroot, coral bells, heuchera

FORM: Short-lived perennial

HARDINESS: Zones 5–9

BLOOM PERIOD: Spring, summer, fall

SIZE: 1–1.5 ft. × 1–2 ft.

♠ ☼

Explosion: that's the best word to describe the influx of heuchera cultivars since the early 2000s as a result of hybridization, primarily between Pacific Northwest native *Heuchera micrantha* and Southwestern native *H. sanguinea*. To date, very few *H. americana* and *H. richardsonii* (Midwest natives) have been used, which makes hybrids short-lived for us—they tend to "melt" in our summer heat and humidity. The recent introduction of southeastern hybrid *H. ×villosa* has helped that tolerance to some degree, although it has not dramatically improved winter survival. Heucheras heave in alternating spring thaws, which rips their root systems apart and causes crown rot. I call them the "Midwest shrinking violet" because they seem to shrink progressively in size every year until they disappear altogether. They are exceptional plants for the shade garden, with seemingly limitless variations in color, ruffled edges, and silver accents. Adding our native species to the bloodlines should toughen up future cultivars. I use them heavily in spite of issues and consider them short-lived perennials; if they live many years, I appreciate it as a bonus. The key to success is compost-rich, porous, well-drained, deep soil that remains evenly moist and never dries out in summer heat.

Heuchera, a plant that not many years ago existed simply with green foliage, has exploded in color choices.

Crossing *Heuchera ×villosa* with existing hybrids improved heat and humidity tolerance and increased leaf size and thickness.

×*Heucherella*

Foamy bells

FORM: Perennial

HARDINESS: Zones 4–9

BLOOM PERIOD: Spring, summer

SIZE: 12–18 in. × 8–12 in.

Foamy bells, the intergeneric cross of *Heuchera* and *Tiarella*, are becoming my favorite over heuchera. They combine foam flower size, running nature, prolific flowering, and dissected foliage with the color selections, silver overlays, and ruffled foliage of heuchera, for a wide range of variations. 'Kimono' was an early, robust selection but a number of later releases were short-lived. The introduction of *H. ×villosa* breeding has improved durability in new releases such as 'Sweet Tea', 'Alabama Sunrise', and 'Redstone Falls'. Foamy bells require the same culture as foam flower.

×*Heucherella* 'Sweet Tea' is repeated in a section of my garden's background.

Hibiscus moscheutos

Hardy hibiscus

FORM: Perennial

HARDINESS: Zones 5–9

BLOOM PERIOD: Summer, fall

SIZE: 4–6 ft. × 3–4 ft.

This shrub-like herbaceous perennial is vigorous, growing with large, glabrous leaves. The wide, tropical-looking, dinner plate–sized, five-petaled, hollyhock-like flowers range from 4 to (a whopping) 10 in. and come in colors including pink, white, red, and mixes. Individual flowers last only one day, but plants bloom continuously all season. They have hollow stems and grow so quickly that they may lodge; if they do, it is impossible to straighten their hollow stems. Cage them early or pinch growing tips of shoots 8 in. high and again at 12 in. to promote bushiness, although some cultivars branch freely without pinching. A great deal of breeding has produced many cultivars including the likes of 'Cranberry Crush', 'Kopper King', 'Plum Crazy', 'Turn of the Century', 'Jazzberry Jam', 'Berrylicious', and 'Heartthrob'.

Hibiscus moscheutos is perhaps the Midwest's hardiest plant for boldly exotic impact.

Rose of Sharon

FORM: Shrub

HARDINESS: Zones 5–8

BLOOM PERIOD: Summer, fall

SIZE: 8–12 ft. × 6–10 ft.

Rose of Sharon is a flowering, distinctively vase-shaped, deciduous shrub with large, showy hibiscus blooms of solid or bicolor, single or double flowers. In our area, Japanese beetles emerge during its bloom time and severely damage buds. This one performs well in hot, humid summers. You can increase flower size by pruning back to two to three buds in late winter. Many cultivars are available such as 'Minerva', 'Blue Satin', 'Aphrodite', and variegated 'Sugar Tip'. It is sometimes grafted on standards for single-stem forms.

Hibiscus syriacus covered in bloom is a garden treasure.

Hosta, plantain lily

FORM: Perennial

HARDINESS: Zones 3–9

BLOOM PERIOD: Spring, summer, fall

SIZE: 1 in.–4 ft. × 2 in.–6 ft.

The ubiquitous tough plant with thousands of cultivars and new releases annually shows up in more gardens than any other plant. Hostas are one of the best ornamental plants for exhibiting bold texture; they contrast nicely with the fine texture of ferns. This enormous group has expanded even more with new miniature forms that have the same wide variety of colors, shapes, and forms as traditional-sized hostas; size now ranges from delightful miniatures only inches tall to well over 5 ft. and equally wide. Foliage includes forms such as puckered, wavy, variegated, blue-gray, gold, glossy, thick, and (the recent obsession) red or purple leaf petioles. Emphasis is on foliage but hostas do produce flowers of white or purplish-lavender flared funnels; some are lightly fragrant. Even though hosta abides harsh conditions, it reaches ideal proportions with consistently moist soils. Lots of water and compost are necessary in our hot, dry Midwest summers in order to encourage the massive forms such as 'Empress Wu', 'Vim and Vigor', and the long-time favorite 'Sum and Substance' to reach their full size. Hostas are subject to slug and deer damage and southern blight. New forms occasionally suffer from reversion to a less desirable parent form—I have found many of the Mouse Series, including the original 'Blue Mouse Ears', particularly prone.

Hostas have been pegged as shade plants because the species is tolerant of low light; however, of the thousands of cultivars available, many appreciate sun over shade. When 'Great Expectations' was first released to high acclaim and price tag, consumers complained that it never gained size, even years after planting. It was being placed in the traditional shady areas reserved for hostas and actually thrived once transplanted to sunnier sites.

Advanced gardeners often exclaim that with so many cultivars, all start to look alike. Even though an element of truth exists in that statement, new forms are introduced every year that are significantly different, and those of us who have to possess the novel and different find ourselves buying yet more hostas! Some of my favorite standards include 'June', 'Paul's Glory', 'Sum and Substance', 'Sagae', and 'Guardian Angel', whereas new releases 'Wheee!', 'Curly Fries', 'Dancing Queen', and 'Autumn Frost' are finding spots in my small garden (along with more than three hundred other hostas).

Hostas are the ubiquitous garden plant and appear in most gardens for good reason.

Hostas' bold texture makes them a planting favorite.

Hydrangea anomala subsp. petiolaris

Climbing hydrangea

FORM: Vine

HARDINESS: Zones 4–8

BLOOM PERIOD: Summer

SIZE: 30–80 ft. × 5–6 ft.

Don't be fooled by size when you purchase this vine. I saw one in Toronto with a base as large as my thigh. It is one of the few shade-tolerant flowering vines. It is a climbing form of *Hydrangea*, growing upwards of 80 ft.; it won't put on a lot of growth during the first six years or so but then it takes off. It blooms in midsummer with white, flattened hydrangea flowers and has attractive yellow-gold fall color and exfoliating cinnamon bark. 'Miranda' and 'Firefly', both with gold leaf margins, are the only cultivars.

Hydrangea anomala subsp. *petiolaris* is usually used on arbors or grown up trees, but it also works well on walls.

Hydrangea macrophylla

Bigleaf hydrangea

FORM: Shrub

HARDINESS: Zones 5–11

BLOOM PERIOD: Summer, some rebloom

SIZE: 4–10 ft. × 4–10 ft.

This widely recognized species of hydrangea boasts copious cultivars. The species is divided into two groups: mopheads with globe-shaped flowers made up of large male flowers, and lacecaps with flattened flower heads and female blossoms ringed in larger male blossoms. Moist, acidic, well-drained soils in sun to partial shade and sheltered from drying winds are ideal. They flower on the previous season's wood and are maintained by cutting back to the first pair

Most of the Midwest envies any area that can grow *Hydrangea macrophylla* like this.

of buds beneath the old flower in spring. In some areas of the Midwest they suffer; as stated by renowned hydrangea propagator Tim Woods, "These plants detest the harsh continental climate of the Midwest with its wacky spring weather that ping-pongs between 85 and 20 degrees; their flower buds swell up and are zapped like flies in an electric bug killer." The Let's Dance and Endless Summer Series bloom on new wood so are sold as better alternatives for colder areas, but still prefer acidic conditions. Interesting variations include green and white foliaged 'Variegata', gold and green 'Guilded Gold' and 'Lemon Wave', gold-foliaged 'Lemon Daddy', and giant-flowered 'Big Daddy'. 'Amethyst', 'Teller Red', 'Heinrich Seidel', and 'Hamburg' are durable mopheads.

Hydrangea paniculata

Panicle hydrangea

FORM: **Shrub**

HARDINESS: **Zones 3–8**

BLOOM PERIOD: **Summer, fall**

SIZE: **4–15 ft. × 4–12 ft.**

Hydrangeas dominate the current shrub market much as shrub roses, potentilla, and spirea ruled past decades. Panicles thrive in full sun, are urban tolerant, grow quickly, and flower on the current year's new growth, so regular pruning maximizes flowering. Large, pyramid-shaped flowers start white with pink accents then darken with age, some becoming deep-rose red and drying to a pleasing papery tan, and enduring winter. They are so robust, I add at least a foot to the advertised height, especially the new cultivars and new miniature forms. Long-lived, I call them cemetery trees because that's where you

will find some of the grandest specimens. They are generally shrubby in form, but you can find some cultivars grafted on standards for a more tree-like form.

I believe I would not be alone in suggesting that 'Limelight' may well be one of the finest panicle hydrangeas to date. It produces large, tightly packed, greenish-white blossoms turning shades of vintage pink in cool weather, and now a reduced form called 'Little Lime' is offered for small spaces. 'Quick Fire' reaches more than 8 ft. and is the earliest to bloom, with robust, long-lasting white flowers turning dark magenta-pink. I am quite fond of 'Vanilla Strawberry', voted top plant of 2010 by the American Nursery and Landscape Association, beginning creamy white and turning pink to rich strawberry-red; since new flower heads continue opening into late summer, plants can display all three color stages at once. 'Fire and Ice' is a new cultivar with the same attributes and flowers ending a deep burgundy-red.

Hydrangea paniculata 'Limelight'.

Oakleaf hydrangea

FORM: Shrub

HARDINESS: Zones 5–9

BLOOM PERIOD: Summer

SIZE: 4–8 ft. × 4–8 ft.

Much like bigleaf hydrangea, oakleaf hydrangea is widely grown in the Midwest but rarely enjoys ideal acidic conditions. It produces 6- to 12-inch long, conical flower heads starting in early summer, which take on purplish-pink fall hues. The deeply lobed foliage resembles oak leaves (thus the common name) and produces outstanding autumn color. The bark displays cinnamon striping in winter but needs protection from rabbits. Cultivars range from 4-ft. 'Sike's Dwarf' to 'Snow Queen' at 8 ft. 'Little Honey' has gold foliage.

Hydrangea quercifolia.

Stonecrop

FORM: Perennial

HARDINESS: Zones 3–9

BLOOM PERIOD: Summer, fall

SIZE: 1–2 ft. × 1–2 ft.

This is the renamed genus of stonecrop sedum that included 'Autumn Joy'. Due to its success, there have been a large number of other introductions. Stonecrops flourish in average, dry, well-drained soils in full sun. The large flowers may cause the stems to drop flat under their weight, especially in good fertility. If you cut clumps back to the ground in midsummer they will grow back with shorter, stronger stems, otherwise you may need to cage them. Stonecrops are at their best in fall when their wide, circular flower heads transition from soft green to pink or magenta.

Hylotelephium turning pink in late season; the transitional period makes the flowers look multicolored.

Hypericum calycinum

Creeping St. John's wort

FORM: Ground cover

HARDINESS: Zones (5)6–9

BLOOM PERIOD: Summer

SIZE: 1–1.5 ft. × 1.5–2 ft.

This attractive evergreen ground cover widely used in the Lower Midwest is dense but not invasive. Deep green, oval leaves cover the ground en masse with 2-inch, gold St. John's wort flowers featuring pincushion-like, center-clustered stamens. It is a pleasing ground cover when in bloom and a great flowering alternative to Japanese pachysandra.

Hypericum calycinum provides bright yellow flowers in addition to serving as ground cover.

Ilex crenata 'Sky Pencil'

Japanese holly

FORM: Shrub, tree

HARDINESS: Zones 6–8

BLOOM PERIOD: Non-flowering

SIZE: 4–10 ft. × 1–3 ft.

The species of this dense evergreen holly reaches 6 to 10 ft. tall and as wide. It grows slowly but can be invasive, so it is rarely used in landscapes, giving the nod to many preferred cultivars such as 'Sky Pencil'. It is difficult to find truly narrow, columnar forms of evergreens; this cultivar fills the bill and is perfect for small gardens in the Lower Midwest. The dark green foliage holds color year-round and purple berries serve as fall accents.

Few evergreens provide truly tight, narrow structure like *Ilex crenata* 'Sky Pencil'.

Ilex verticillata

Winterberry

FORM: **Shrub**

HARDINESS: **Zones 5–9**

BLOOM PERIOD: **Summer, fall**

SIZE: **7–15 ft. × 5–12 ft.**

Although our native wetland holly is deciduous and does not produce the waxy, sharp-pointed leaf invoking Christmas, winterberry is valued for copious masses of persistent, bright red fruit and lustrous, thick, dark green leaves. Leaves drop in autumn for a fruit spectacle and late winter bird food. It adapts to a wide variety of site conditions, with compact, rounded, or vase-shaped forms and can be hedged. One male is needed for three to five females and specific male to female pairings are required; for instance 'Winter Red' pairs with 'Southern Gentlemen' whereas 'Red Sprite' needs 'Jim Dandy'.

Ilex verticillata 'Red Sprite' shows winter interest.

Iris germanica

Bearded iris

FORM: **Perennial**

HARDINESS: **Zones 3–10**

BLOOM PERIOD: **Summer**

SIZE: **.5–4 ft. × .5–2 ft.**

Bearded iris are some of the most spectacular flowers in the garden, ranging from inches-high dwarfs to 4-ft. standards. The flowers are the showstoppers, with six petals: three upright (standards) and three hanging (falls). A fuzzy line (or beard) runs down the middle of each fall. Flowers come in many colors including blue, pink, purple, reddish, white, yellow, and bi-color. But they have some issues. Even planting a selection from earliest to latest bloom, they are restricted to around a month in summer (other than a few fall rebloomers) and the rest of the season you are left with foliage only. Breeding for massive flower size creates a need for staking or the stalks will fall in rain and wind. Rhizomes are finicky to planting depth, need to be divided regularly, and are subject to iris borer, bacterial soft rot, and crown rot fungus. Foliage and flowers are sensitive to virus, mosaic, and leaf spots. Grow in full sun with well-drained soils and do not crowd, for maximum success. The primary differences are in stature and color. 'Stellar Lights', 'Splash o' Wine', and 'Earl of Essex' are a few of the reblooming cultivars. I am also fond of 'Autumn Maple', 'Bumblebee Delight', 'Gingerbread Man', and 'Cat's Eye' (standard dwarf bearded); 'Black Currant', 'Garnet Slippers', and 'Ruby Slippers' (intermediate bearded); and 'Rip City', 'Balderdash', and 'Black Knight' (tall bearded). Explore and see what colors capture your attention among the hundreds of choices.

Iris germanica thrives at Allen Centennial Gardens due to full sun and well-drained soils.

Siberian iris

FORM: **Perennial**

HARDINESS: **Zones 3–8**

BLOOM PERIOD: **Spring, summer**

SIZE: **2–3 ft. × 2–3 ft.**

Siberian iris is bearded iris's tough cousin. Easy to grow, it prefers moist, fertile, slightly acidic soils, but its thick, deep roots allow tolerance of dry to wet soils and low fertility. It has a relatively short period of bloom, so mix with other perennials. Rapid growth will require fairly frequent division. Flowers are smaller and more delicate than bearded iris and include most colors except red and orange. Arching foliage is thinner than bearded iris, developing pleasing yellowish fall color. It is susceptible to iris borer and soft rot but not nearly as vulnerable as bearded iris. 'Caesar's Brother' is overused but with its robust nature and deep purple flowers it remains a favorite. I also am fond of 'Tropic Night', 'Sultan's Ruby', and 'Chartreuse Encore', a gorgeous yellow rebloomer.

Iris sibirica is the tough, carefree cousin of bearded iris.

Virginia sweetspire

FORM: **Shrub**

HARDINESS: **Zones 5–9**

BLOOM PERIOD: **Summer**

SIZE: **2–8 ft. × 3–5 ft.**

Virginia sweetspire is a mounding, slender-branched, deciduous shrub growing to 8 ft., but you can also find smaller cultivars such as 'Henry's Garnet' (3 to 4 ft. but twice as wide) and 'Little Henry' (2 to 3 ft. by as wide). Small white flowers on long spires droop with arching branches. Flowers open from base to tip so that the plant appears to be blooming for a long time. Leaves that are semi-evergreen in the south change from striking red to purple in the fall and persist well into winter.

Itea virginica 'Henry's Garnet'.

Juniper

FORM: Tree, shrub

HARDINESS: Varies within zones 2–9

SIZE: Varies by species

Junipers vary tremendously in size and shape, from tall trees to columnar or low, spreading shrubs with long, trailing branches. Seedlings and some twigs of older trees have juvenile (needle-like) leaves; the leaves on mature plants are tiny, overlapping, and scale-like. In some species all the foliage is of the juvenile needle-like type, with no scale leaves. The needle-leaves of junipers are hard and sharp, making the juvenile foliage very prickly to handle. They prefer open, sunny locations in soils that are light, sandy, low or high pH (one of the few conifers tolerant of high-lime soils), and moderately moist. They can be very tolerant of dry, clay soils and sand, have good air pollution tolerance, and can be used as windbreaks. They do not like shade, becoming open and thin, but withstand heavy pruning and can make good hedges; in fact, many are better alternatives to deer-damaged arborvitae. Species common in the Midwest include *chinensis*, *communis*, *horizontalis*, *procumbens*, *sabina*, *scopulorum*, *squamata*, and *virginiana*. A personal favorite, 'Star Power', is a hybrid (*Juniperus chinensis* × *J. communis*) and gets its name from the blue-green, star-like, juvenile foliage, which gives it a delicate, almost sparkling texture.

Juniperus horizontalis 'Mother Lode' with *Larix kaempferi* 'Pendula'.

Kalmia latifolia

Mountain laurel

FORM: **Shrub, tree**

HARDINESS: **Zones (4)5–9**

BLOOM PERIOD: **Spring**

SIZE: **3–15 ft. × 3–15 ft.**

Mountain laurel typically grows as a dense, rounded shrub 5 to 15 ft. tall with open and gnarly branching with age. Its enchanting late spring flowers arise in terminal clusters and cover the shrub. Each flower is cup shaped with five sides, ranging in color from rose to white with purple interior markings. It is listed as hardy to zone 4 but I have never seen it grown successfully there. Cultivars vary in color and size. 'Carol' grows only to 3 ft. tall and wide, with dark pink buds that contrast well with its pale pink to almost-white flowers. 'Sarah' has bright red buds opening to pink flowers. 'Heart's Desire' flaunts cinnamon-red flowers with white edges and may grow to 4 ft. tall and wide.

Kalmia latifolia often sports eye-popping, rich colors.

Kirengeshoma palmata

Yellow wax bells

FORM: **Perennial**

HARDINESS: **Zones 5–8**

BLOOM PERIOD: **Summer**

SIZE: **3–4 ft. × 2–3 ft.**

I killed a number of yellow wax bells until I learned how important sun and soil moisture are to the health of the plant. This hardy, clump-forming perennial touts pendulous, shuttlecock-shaped, soft yellow blossoms in late summer surrounded by palmate, glossy, maple leaf–shaped leaves. Clusters of fat yellow pearl-like buds appear at the ends of the branches, opening into delicate, nodding yellow bells, further replaced in fall by intriguing three-pronged seed capsules. A happy yellow wax bell should look like a dense shrub.

Kirengeshoma palmata.

Kniphofia hybrids

Red hot poker

FORM: **Perennial**

HARDINESS: **Zones 5–9**

BLOOM PERIOD: **Spring, summer**

SIZE: **3–4 ft. × 2–3 ft.**

Aptly named, this perennial forms dense clumps of upright, finely toothed leaves with spikes of tubular flowers rising above the foliage and emerging from top to bottom. Because the buds tend to be darker, the upper portion of the "torch" can be red while the bottom is yellow. Most are hybrids of *Kniphofia uvaria* (torch lily or red hot poker). Many cultivars bloom at different times during the growing season; 'Percy's Pride', 'Malibu Yellow', and 'Yellow Hammer' bloom in spring; 'Glow', 'Gladness', and 'Cobra' in summer; and 'Light of the World' and 'Yellow Cheer' in fall. 'Bleached Blonde' blooms in late spring and again in late summer. The flowers are red, orange, and yellow. Excellent drainage is essential.

Few plants are as aptly named as red hot poker, evidenced by these 'Royal Castle' hybrids.

SOUTHERN BELLES

Gardeners in the Lower Midwest experience hot, humid summers similar to the rest of the region, but with less damaging frosts and winters, they can include plants in their palette that the rest of us try to grow with little success. Most of these listed plants prefer evenly moist, well-drained soils with good quantities of organic matter and neutral to acidic soils. They aren't all necessarily specific to that range but reach their potential better there than in northern climes. Note that I've only listed trees and shrubs, because perennials are more universal across the Midwest. They are fussy to robust.

Abelia ×grandiflora	Hypericum calycinum
Asimina triloba	Ilex crenata
Cercis canadensis	Itea virginica
Clethra alnifolia	Kalmia latifolia
Cornus kousa	Leucothoe fontanesiana
Enkianthus campanulatus	Liquidambar styraciflua
Fothergilla gardenii	Magnolia grandiflora
Fothergilla major	Magnolia virginiana
Gunnera manicata	Oxydendrum arboreum
Halesia carolina	Pieris japonica
Halesia monticola	Rhododendron hybrids
Hydrangea macrophylla	Styphnolobium
Hydrangea quercifolia	japonicum

Lamprocapnos spectabilis (syn. *Dicentra spectabilis*)

Old-fashioned bleeding heart

FORM: Short-lived perennial
HARDINESS: Zones 3–9
BLOOM PERIOD: Spring
SIZE: 2–3 ft. × 1.5–2.5 ft.

Old-fashioned bleeding heart was likely in your grandmother's garden and is a true heirloom plant. It is easy to grow, divide, and transplant; it also self-seeds. The name refers to protruding inner petals on the heart-shaped flower that appear to form a drop of blood. The flower of the species is rose-pink and white, 'Alba' is pure white, 'Valentine' is red and white, and 'Gold Heart' possesses the traditional rose-pink flower with spectacular gold foliage, brightening shade all season. Bleeding heart will go summer dormant if too dry, but foliage will persist with supplemental watering.

Lamprocapnos spectabilis 'Gold Heart' lights up shaded areas.

Larix species

Larch

FORM: Tree

HARDINESS: Varies within zones 2–7

SIZE: Varies by species

Larch is one of four deciduous conifers hardy to the Midwest (including *Metasequoia*, *Taxodium*, and *Pseudolarix*) with slender, needle-like foliage. Single, soft needles appear in dense clusters that spiral around the shoots and the delicate appearance is attractive during spring emergence. They turn yellow and fall in the late autumn, leaving the trees leafless through the winter. Larch cones are erect and small; they start green or purple and ripen brown. Care is needed in planting; they resent root disturbance and need continuous water the first year due to their swampy origins. Ideal conditions include evenly moist, well-drained soil in full sun. They are shade intolerant and detest dry or high-lime soils or polluted areas. Species common in the Midwest are *decidua*, *gmelinii*, *kaempferi*, and *laricina*. *Larix kaempferi* 'Pendula' is the definition of weeping elegance.

Larix kaempferi 'Pendula'.

Lespedeza bicolor

Bush clover

FORM: Shrub

HARDINESS: Zones 4–8

BLOOM PERIOD: Summer, fall

SIZE: 5–10 ft. × 5–10 ft.

This shrub remains underutilized in many areas of the country, which is a shame because it blooms from late summer into fall, when we are desperately seeking non-mum fall color. Arching stems are covered with pinkish-purple, pea-like blooms. The divided leguminous leaves exhibit glaucous blue color and remain attractive and free of disease all summer. Pruning is simple because plants bloom on new growth, and all stems can be sheared low and renewal pruned in early spring. 'Gibraltar' is a durable and popular cultivar with purple flowers. 'Pink Fountain' is a graceful, arching pink form that provides luscious late-season color.

Lespedeza bicolor 'Pink Fountain'.

Leucanthemum hybrids

Shasta daisy

FORM: Short-lived perennial
HARDINESS: Zones 5–9
BLOOM PERIOD: Summer, fall
SIZE: 3–4 ft. × 2–3 ft.

Shasta daisies have long been a perennial border favorite. Most are hybrids of *Leucanthemum ×superbum* cultivars, blooming through late summer with bright-white daisy petals, including single, double, fringed, and frilly forms surrounding yellow center disks. Shasta daisies prefer fertile, well-drained soils in full sun and are intolerant of wet or poorly drained soils any time; crown rot may occur under heavy winter mulch; rebloom is possible with deadheading. They may need to be staked in fertile soils where they tend to flop. 'Becky' has been a stalwart for heat resistance and I have heard excellent reports about super-compact, highly floriferous 'Daisy Duke'. Fringed, frilly, semi- to full-double forms include 'Crazy Daisy', 'Phyllis Smith', and 'Aglaia'; 'Lacrosse' and 'Silver Spoons' are a few of the forms with quilled petals.

Don't underestimate the power of white in the garden; *Leucanthemum ×superbum* fulfills that goal.

Leucothoe fontanesiana

Drooping laurel

FORM: Shrub
HARDINESS: Zones 5–8
BLOOM PERIOD: Spring
SIZE: 2–6 ft. × 2–3 ft.

The species is a multi-stemmed broadleaf evergreen shrub, growing 2 to 6 ft. tall with an arching habit. Branches appear weighed down with drooping spikes of white, waxy, urn-shaped flowers. Dark green, glossy foliage is punctuated by red emergent growth throughout the season; the dark green then turns hues of red-green to purple in winter. Cultivars have exciting foliage color patterning, such as 'Girard's Rainbow', with white, pink, or copper tricolor new growth and plum-colored fall foliage; 'Scarletta', with scarlet-purple new foliage emergent from deep green, turning reddish-bronze; and 'Rainbow', with red stems and colorful, mottled leaves.

Red new growth adds visual interest to *Leucothoe fontanesiana*.

Gayfeather, spiked blazing star

FORM: Perennial

HARDINESS: Zones 3–8

BLOOM PERIOD: Summer, fall

SIZE: 2–4 ft. × 1–1.5 ft.

Poor soils, heat, cold, and drought don't bother this durable native. It has become a standard in the cut flower industry and attracts butterflies, bees, rare moths, and hummingbirds. *Liatris* species range in size from 2 to 6 ft., but shorter *L. spicata* is most commonly used in gardens. Spikes of fluffy purple or white flowers may need staking if soils are too fertile. 'Kobold' and 'Blue Bird' are purple cultivars; 'Alba' and 'Floristan White' are white.

Liatris spicata is a native American plant that the European market vaulted to acclaim as a popular cut flower.

FUSSY CHILDREN

This designation is not meant to be a deterrent to using the plants below in your landscape, but rather a warning that they have requirements or issues that require more time, attention, and education. Many gardeners love challenging plants and feel a great sense of accomplishment when they succeed where others fail. My advice is to hold off on these until you feel confident.

PERENNIALS

Echinacea hybrids
Iris germanica
Lupinus hybrids
Papaver species
Rosa

TREES

Acer palmatum and relatives
Betula papyrifera

Ligularia dentata

Big leaf goldenray

FORM: Perennial

HARDINESS: Zones 4–8

BLOOM PERIOD: Summer, fall

SIZE: 2–6 ft. × 1.5–3 ft.

Bright orange-yellow flowers for the shade! Bold leaves are kidney- or heart-shaped and jagged along the edges. Flower shape varies by species with either golden flower spikes or flattened heads of yellow, daisy-like flowers. These moisture lovers must have deep, rich soil that remains moist. 'Othello' and 'Desdemona' were early dark-foliaged forms; dramatic 'Britt Marie Crawford' was selected for even richer dark purple stems and foliage. 'Osiris Cafe Noir' and 'Osiris Fantaisie' are chocolate with wavy serrated edges. *Ligularia japonica* (Japanese ligularia) has bold, tropical-looking, deeply dissected leaves adorned with distinctively alien-looking flower buds.

Ligularia dentata 'Desdemona'.

Ligularia stenocephala; L. przewalskii

Narrow spiked ligularia, Shavalski's ligularia

FORM: Perennial

HARDINESS: Zones 4–8

BLOOM PERIOD: Summer, fall

SIZE: 2–6 ft. × 1.5–3 ft.

Narrow spiked ligularia is a surprisingly shade-tolerant show-off with tall golden spikes ranging from compact 2-ft.-tall 'Little Rocket' to 4-ft. 'The Rocket'. Shavalski's ligularia 'Dragon Wings' and 'Dragon's Breath' have deeply dissected foliage. Even though they also prefer moist feet, I find these species the most tolerant of short-term dry conditions.

Ligularia stenocephala.

Liquidambar styraciflua

Sweet gum

FORM: **Tree**

HARDINESS: **Zones 5–9**

BLOOM PERIOD: **Non-flowering**

SIZE: **60–80 ft. × 40–60 ft.; smaller cultivars**

I remember a trip my mom made to Florida, coming back elated with bristly gum balls; her women's craft group was into pine cone wreaths and they were going to be jealous! I suspect those same gumball seedpods are negative aspects for those who grow the tree. It is a specimen tree for large landscapes. Glossy, five- to seven-pointed, star-shaped leaves achieve a brilliant mix of fall yellows, oranges, purples, and reds. Yellow-variegated forms such as 'Variegata' and 'Gold Dust' and white-variegated forms such as 'Silver King' are nearly full size. Fastigiate 'Slender Silhouette' has a tight columnar form more suited to smaller landscapes. It will achieve 50 ft. in height but only 6 ft. in width.

Liquidambar styraciflua 'Slender Silhouette'.

Cardinal flower

FORM: **Short-lived perennial**

HARDINESS: **Zones 3–9**

BLOOM PERIOD: **Summer, fall**

SIZE: **2–4 ft. × 1–2 ft.**

North Creek Nursery's description of cardinal flower is best: "It is hard to describe the intensity of a cardinal flower in bloom. It is as if the flowers catch sunlight inside some sort of crystal matrix and let it bounce around for a while until it has been stripped of all but the deepest, purest red imaginable. Then and only then is the light released to burn crimson red into our corneas." Lobelias are not true perennials because the flower stem and roots die after setting seed. They are perennial only because new offsets grow from axils of the lowermost leaves and quickly put down their own roots. It attracts hummingbirds. There are many hybrids that are short-lived and prone to disease in the Midwest, so I recommend cultivars of the species. 'Queen Victoria' and 'Fried Green Tomatoes' have purple foliage.

Lobelia cardinalis, probably the truest scarlet red in the plant world.

Lobularia maritima

Sweet alyssum

FORM: Annual

HARDINESS: Not hardy

BLOOM PERIOD: Spring, summer, fall

SIZE: 6–8 in. × 10–18 in.

Sweet alyssum has graced gardens for a long time and has hardly changed, other than increasing in heat tolerance. Another welcome change is the appearance of lovely variegated forms such as 'Frosty Knight'. I was reminded of the plant's value a few years ago when early frosts wiped out most of our annuals. Sweet alyssum remained fresh and untouched and kept churning out sweet fragrance. It provided nourishment for late-season insects and was bright and cheery until covered with snow. 'Clear Crystal Lavender Shades' is an extra-vigorous selection with fragrant, larger-than-typical lavender blooms. 'Snow Princess' is also a vigorous, heat-tolerant plant with large white flowers. 'Rosie O'Day' displays rosy lavender flowers on short stems compact to the ground, and similar-growing 'Easter Basket Blend' boasts blooms with violet, rose, or pink flowers.

Lobularia maritima thrives in heat and carries fragrance long into frost season.

Lonicera ×brownii; L. ×heckrottii

Brown's honeysuckle; goldflame honeysuckle
FORM: Vine
HARDINESS: Zones 5–9
BLOOM PERIOD: Summer, fall
SIZE: 10–15 ft. × 10–20 ft.

Ornamental honeysuckle used to be much more common as a trailing vine, growing to 15 ft. or small-shrub pruned to 4 to 6 ft. 'Dropmore Scarlet' defines Brown's honeysuckle, with rounded, semi-evergreen, blue-green leaves and terminal clusters of narrow, trumpet-shaped scarlet flowers. Goldflame honeysuckle is in reference to the yellow interiors of its tubular pink flowers, which is confusing, since there is a cultivar by the same name. For both, flowers may be followed in the fall by inedible red berries. Don't confuse these with the invasive Asian honeysuckles.

Lonicera ×brownii 'Dropmore Scarlet' is a well-behaved vine that is fairly carefree.

Lupinus hybrids

Lupine
FORM: Short-lived perennial
HARDINESS: Zones 4–8
BLOOM PERIOD: Spring, summer
SIZE: 3–4 ft. × 1–1.5 ft.

You won't find lupines where I live, because they detest our heavy soils and winter moisture. Head to sandy areas of Lake Superior and you'll realize cold is not the issue, wet roots are. Likewise, they aren't happy in heat and humidity. Cultivars sold in luscious spires of blue, purple, violet, yellow, pink, red, white, and bicolors are hard to resist. They flourish in organically rich, moderately fertile, slightly acidic, evenly moist, well-drained soils in full sun with good air circulation—but even then, they tend to be short-lived, so treat them as biennials and be pleasantly surprised if they last longer. The Russell hybrids are most commonly sold; several dwarf forms exist, including the Gallery hybrids and 'Minarette'.

Elegant flower spikes make lupine hard to resist in the perennial border.

Magnolia

FORM: Tree

HARDINESS: Varies by species

BLOOM PERIOD: Spring

SIZE: Varies by species

Magnolias are the royalty of America's native trees. They are primeval survivors of millennia of evolution, little changed from their origin, other than hundreds of cultivars. Eight species are native; their adaptability has allowed adornment in gardens all over the country. Most are perfectly hardy to areas where flower buds are winter or frost damaged, so selection shouldn't be based on plant hardiness but rather bud hardiness. *Magnolia soulangeana*, *M. ×loebneri*, and *M. stellata* cultivars bloom early. In northern climes, later-blooming cultivars such as the Little Girls Series (including the likes of 'Ann', 'Betty', and 'Jane') are more likely to avoid frost damage. *M. sieboldii* blooms in early summer as the only shade-tolerant form. All the rage in recent breeding have been many yellow-flowering forms, such as 'Elizabeth', 'Yellow Bird', and 'Butterflies', resulting from crosses of *M. acuminata* as a parent.

The pyramidal *Magnolia grandiflora* (southern magnolia, zones 7 to 9) is a beautiful native tree, which I suspect defines the South to us northerners. It is evergreen with a straight trunk, conical crown, and huge, fragrant white flowers. Flowers go through an unusual process; the blossoms open in the morning and close at night for two or three days, then when all the stamens are shed and the flower reopens it turns brown and disintegrates. Several horticultural varieties have been developed but all forms are restricted to the Lower Midwest.

Magnolia virginiana (sweet bay magnolia, zones 5 to 10) is an attractive native semi-evergreen popular for large, creamy-white, lemon-scented flowers borne over a long period; showy, cone-like fruit; handsome foliage of contrasting colors; and smooth bark. It is grown for scented flowers; clean, attractive foliage; and fast growth. It does not tolerate high pH soil.

Few trees herald spring as spectacularly as magnolias.

As a northern gardener, I am jealous of those to the south who can grow tropical-looking, large-flowered *Magnolia grandiflora*.

Magnolia virginiana is a lovely, small-scale magnolia overlooked due to splashier species.

Flowering crabapple

FORM: **Tree**

HARDINESS: **Zones 4–8**

BLOOM PERIOD: **Spring, fall**

SIZE: **12–30 ft. × 6–20 ft.**

Flowering crabapples are a common ornamental tree with hundreds of selections, from large specimens 30 ft. tall to dwarf cultivars grafted on standards; the most common shrub form, 'Sargentina', is grafted 3 to 6 ft. high ('Firebird' is the improved cultivar). Crabapples are noted for small size; prolific, fragrant, white, pink, and dark purple-magenta spring flowers; heavy fall fruiting; and cultivars with purple foliage such as 'Prairifire'. 'Royal Raindrops' has unique, dissected purple foliage. Crabapples are highly susceptible to apple scab, creating unsightly foliar spotting and leaf drop; select resistant cultivars. They are also attractive to Japanese beetles, tent caterpillars, aphids, rabbits, and deer.

Malus 'Evelyn' and 'Mackamik' are older cultivars that still please.

Melianthus major

Honeybush

FORM: **Annual**

HARDINESS: **Zones 7–11**

BLOOM PERIOD: **Non-flowering**

SIZE: **3–5 ft. × 2–3 ft.**

Honeybush provides bold, intriguing architecture with deeply toothed foliage. It has glossy, glaucous blue, pinnate leaves and small, cerinthe-colored, tubular flowers in narrow, erect racemes. Sometimes called peanut butter plant, rubbing foliage between your fingers will generate a peanut butter odor (really!). I have only achieved flowering by overwintering in a greenhouse. Honeybush will reach 6–10 ft. × 3–6 ft. when grown as a perennial.

Melianthus major adds unique color and texture to the garden landscape.

Mertensia virginica

Virginia bluebells

FORM: **Perennial**

HARDINESS: **Zones 3–8**

BLOOM PERIOD: **Spring**

SIZE: **1.5–2 ft. × 1–1.5 ft.**

Few sights take my breath away like an area covered in a spectacular mass of bluebells. Blue is still the most-sought color for gardens. Bluebells are extremely easy to grow and multiply rapidly, but this is not an issue because they disappear entirely by early summer and don't compete with non-ephemeral plants. I plant it with ferns, hostas, and other shade plants that are just emerging when bluebells are peaking, and coming into their full size as the bluebells decline.

Mertensia virginica makes a colorful statement in spring, then disappears entirely as an ephemeral.

Metasequoia glyptostroboides

Dawn redwood

FORM: Tree

HARDINESS: Zones 4–8

BLOOM PERIOD: Non-flowering

SIZE: **70–100 ft. × 15–25 ft.; dwarf cultivars significantly reduced in size**

Dawn redwood is a deciduous conifer known from fossils before it was discovered growing in China. A perfect pyramid, similar in appearance to bald cypress, its massive size relegates it to large land-scapes. The popular, eye-catching 'Gold Rush' is sold as a smaller form since it typically grows only 10 to 15 ft. tall over the first ten years, but eventually matures to 70 to 100 ft. Several dwarf cultivars are available for home landscapes, including the strongly weeping 'Miss Grace', which does not develop a true leader and will gain little height over time unless trained (if staked, 8-ft. tall × 3-ft. wide in ten years), and 'North Light' ('Schirrmann's Nordlicht'), with foliage that is creamy white frosted over green, purported to not exceed 30 in. high and wide in ten years.

Metasequoia glyptostroboides 'Gold Rush'.

Microbiota decussata

Russian arborvitae

FORM: Shrub

HARDINESS: Zones 3–7

BLOOM PERIOD: Non-flowering

SIZE: 6–18 in. × 3–12 ft.

Few conifers are shade tolerant and even fewer make excellent ground covers, but Russian arborvitae durably serves both purposes. This slow-spreading dwarf evergreen has rich green, almost filamentous, nodding foliage that reaches 12 to 15 ft.; it looks so much like waves, I inserted a leaping dolphin sculpture in a planting. It develops purplish-bronze fall-into-winter color. It is also available grafted on short standards for an entirely different weeping waterfall look. The grafted forms remain green in winter, I believe from the influence of grafting on *Arborvitae* stock.

I am quite fond of the wavelike flow of *Microbiota decussata* foliage.

Molinia caerulea

Purple moor grass

FORM: Perennial, grass

HARDINESS: Zones 5–8

BLOOM PERIOD: Summer, fall

SIZE: 4–5 ft. × 2–4 ft.

Interestingly, the entire genus thrives in full sun where it is native to European and Asian wetlands, but it tolerates light shade—purple moor grass is no exception. Large clumps of arching green foliage are somewhat bluish in hue, with tall, erect flower spikes that tower 4 or 5 ft., topped by small, airy, purplish flowers spikes. Flower stems and blooms are so fine that a dark background helps delineate them; otherwise the effect may be lost. They provide pleasing movement in gentle breezes and impact continues through fall, when flowers and foliage turn golden yellow tinged with orange and silver. Gorgeous 'Variegata' is one-third the size but less robust and popular as bunny fodder.

Molinia caerulea is a graceful grass in spite of its large size.

Mukdenia rossii

Mukdenia

FORM: **Perennial**
HARDINESS: **Zones 4–8**
BLOOM PERIOD: **Spring**
SIZE: **8–18 in. × 12–24 in.**

This fascinating plant from rocky escarpments in eastern Asia looks like no other shade plant. The foliage is shaped like a maple leaf; it was originally named *Aceriphyllum*. The white, bell-shaped flowers emerge first, almost eerily without foliage, as panicles on naked stems. Bloom is followed by palmate green leaves tinged in maroon. 'Crimson Fans' has redder tinging that deepens in fall. Plants spread by rhizomes and may self-seed. They detest high humidity and must remain relatively cool in shaded environs.

Mukdenia rossii 'Crimson Fans' is an oddity in the garden when it flowers without foliage.

Nepeta species

Catmint

FORM: **Perennial**
HARDINESS: **Zones 3–8**
BLOOM PERIOD: **Spring, summer, fall**
SIZE: **6–30 in. × 1–3 ft.**

Catmint has become a durable landscape plant for commercial use as well as home gardens. I've seen it massed in highway boulevards, surviving salt, snow, and compacted soils. Cats are not attracted to it, although the strong scent appears to deter deer and rodents; flowers attract butterflies and insect. Most are cultivars of *Nepeta* ×*faassenii*. White, blue, or mauve-to-purple flowers mass on bushy mounds of glaucous, aromatic foliage. Catmint blooms in spring with reliable rebloom through fall, especially if spent flowers are sheared. It works well in border, rock, and herb gardens, or in tough situations such as embankments. Gardeners joke about the 'Walker's Low' name because it is not prostrate at all, but the plant is tough as nails. 'Purrsian Blue' and 'Cat's Meow' are recent releases with rounded and compact forms. *N. racemosa* 'Little Titch' is very low and prostrate to the ground.

Nepeta ×*faassenii* 'Walker's Low'.

Nigella damascena

Love-in-a-mist

FORM: Annual

HARDINESS: Not hardy

BLOOM PERIOD: Summer

SIZE: 18–24 in. × 12–18 in.

It is the tangle of ferny, lacy foliage forming a mist around the flowers that gives this plant an entrancing name. Flower buds begin as interesting puffs, opening into solitary flowers with five blue or white petal-like sepals. Feathery bracts eventually form interesting, horned seed capsules. Seed mixes add pink, mauve, and purple options. There are a number of cultivars and 'Persian Jewels' is a nice mix of colors. Don't be alarmed if they start declining after eight weeks; that is the duration of their life, so stagger plantings to extend the season.

Nigella damascena will capture attention with its alien-looking flower.

Nyssa sylvatica

Black tupelo

FORM: Tree

HARDINESS: Zones 3–9

BLOOM PERIOD: Non-flowering

SIZE: 20–50 ft. × 20–30 ft.

Black tupelo is the upland form of *Nyssa*, with additional species found in wetland sites. It is a large tree with a dense and conical crown; many horizontal branches; and glossy, dark green foliage turning fluorescent yellow, orange, scarlet, and purple in autumn. Cultivars that make better shade trees for small landscapes include 40-ft. 'Red Rage' and 'Wildfire', 30-ft. 'Sheri's Cloud', with its variegated foliage; contorted, 20-ft. 'Zydeco Twist'; and spectacular, tightly weeping 'Autumn Cascade'.

Nyssa sylvatica 'Autumn Cascade' is the most splendiferous tree in autumn at Allen Centennial Gardens.

Gaura

FORM: Short-lived perennial

HARDINESS: Zones 5–9

BLOOM PERIOD: Summer, fall

SIZE: 3–5 ft. × 1–2 ft.

This wildflower is a bushy, clump-forming, vase-shaped perennial with lance- or spoon-shaped, toothed leaves on slender, wand-like stems. Leaves are occasionally spotted with maroon. Loose panicles of white flowers with four petals open a few at a time, fading slowly to pink, blooming from early summer to early autumn. It tolerates drought, heat, humidity, and even shallow soil, making it ideal for the xeriscape garden (though it flowers best when given adequate moisture). Cultivars include white-flowering 'Whirling Butterfly', pink-flowering 'Siskiyou Pink', variegated 'Sunny Butterflies' and 'Corrie's Gold', and dwarf, red-twigged 'Crimson Butterflies'.

Oenothera lindheimeri 'Corrie's Gold'.

Ironwood, eastern hop hornbeam

FORM: Tree

HARDINESS: Zones 3–9

BLOOM PERIOD: Non-flowering

SIZE: 25–40 ft. × 20–30 ft.

Ironwood is closely related to musclewood (*Carpinus caroliniana*) and shares the common name, so this is an excellent example of why you should always try to use scientific names when searching for garden plants. The two are quite similar in form and structure, cultural requirements, and seasonal interest, except that the bark of *Ostrya virginiana* presents vertical strips which exfoliate at the tips, the flowers are monoecious (forming separate male and female catkins), and the fall color of its birch-like foliage is yellow-brown.

Ostrya virginiana is a useful small-scale native tree not commonly used.

Sourwood

FORM: **Tree**

HARDINESS: **Zones (5)6–9**

BLOOM PERIOD: **Summer**

SIZE: **20–50 ft. × 10–25 ft.**

Another tree just out of my reach, sourwood is the only species of its genus named for the sour taste of its leaves. It forms a pyramidal tree with oblong-shaped, glossy leaves turning vivid maroon, yellow, or purple in fall. In late summer, tantalizing panicles of fragrant, urn-shaped flowers appear in sprays, decorating the tree in white blossoms that resemble lily-of-the-valley, followed by yellowish seed capsules that turn brown and persist into winter. It is large enough to be considered a canopy tree in most yards. Cultivars include 'Albomarginatum', with variegated white foliar margins; 'Chameleon', selected for an upright, conical habit and shades of red, purple, and yellow fall color all at one time or in sequence; and 'Mt. Charm', which is symmetrical, with early fall color. However, I have not seen any of these cultivars commonly available for sale.

Oxydendrum arboreum flaunts wavy, arching white flowers and develops outstanding fall color.

Paeonia lactiflora

Peony

FORM: **Perennial**

HARDINESS: **Zones 3–8**

BLOOM PERIOD: **Spring**

SIZE: **2–3.5 ft. × 2–3.5 ft.**

✿ ◊ ☼

Peonies establish such long-lived roots that transplanting results in divisions "pouting" several years before generating new growth. Fortunately they don't need regular division and can be left alone for years. Generations of breeding this beloved herbaceous shrub produced a myriad of choices in deliciously fragrant, single or double blossoms representing whites, yellows, reds, pinks, and multicolors. Gorgeous as specimen or massed, peony flowers are heavy and plants may require caging to prevent lodging. Foliage can develop interesting russet-purple fall color, but is extremely susceptible to powdery mildew in wet, warm springs.

I adore the coral forms, including 'Coral Charm' and 'Coral Sunset' and the luscious lemon-yellow 'Lemon Chiffon', but you may prefer the traditional red of 'Old Faithful', the pink of 'Margaret Clark', or the white of 'Eskimo Pie'. Oddities include 'Daisy Coronet', with spiky, sunray flowers of thin, semi-streaked, medium pink petals and dark maroon-red pistils; 'Raspberry Rumba', with prominent raspberry streaks and blotches on parrot tulip–like petals; plus a group of miniatures called rock garden peonies.

A classic garden plant, *Paeonia lactiflora* is so long-lived that many people own their grandmother's peonies.

Panicum virgatum

Switch grass

FORM: Perennial, grass
HARDINESS: Zones 5–9
BLOOM PERIOD: Spring, summer, fall
SIZE: 2–6 ft. × 2–3 ft.

Native switch grass is extremely adaptable to a wide range of cultural conditions, although it prefers moist, lean, and sandy; too much fertility will cause the fine-textured, arching foliage to lodge. Flowers are soft in texture and the whole plant provides pleasing movement in breezes. Popular cultivars such as 'Dallas Blues' and 'Prairie Sky' were selected for their lovely blue foliage. Some, like 'Northwind', are rigidly upright while others such as the aptly named 'Cloud Nine' are ethereally cloud-like. 'Cheyenne Sky' and 'Prairie Fire' sport reddish foliage that deepens to maroon in fall. Cultivar sizes vary.

Panicum virgatum cannot be beat for movement in the garden.

Papaver species

Poppy

FORM: Perennial
HARDINESS: Zones 5–9
BLOOM PERIOD: Spring, summer, fall
SIZE: .5–3 ft. × 1–3 ft.

Remember my earlier statement that plants don't die, we kill them? I have killed many, many poppies in attempts to establish this exotic, papery-foliaged

Both delicate and gaudy, *Papaver orientale* 'Turkenlouis' combines the two traits in showstopping fashion.

mesmerizer in the garden. It has been a popular garden plant since it was introduced to Western Europe in 1714. A long-lived herbaceous perennial with deep taproots, the trick is to get it to establish and it requires extremely well-drained soil to do so. It needs organically rich, fertile, medium-moisture, well-drained soil in full sun. It is a cold weather plant that needs a period of winter dormancy and is intolerant of high summer heat and humidity, so will not grow well south of zone 7.

So many exotic cultivars of *Papaver orientale* are available. 'Place Pigalle' sports single white flowers with a salmon-red picotee edge. 'Royal Chocolate Distinction' flaunts large, ruffled, chocolate-maroon, crepe-paper petals, each with a black mark at their base. 'Turkenlouis' has fringed, deep orange-red flowers with dark centers. Gardeners often opt for annual reseeders such as *P. somniferum* (opium poppy), *P. nudicaule* (Iceland poppy), and *Eschscholzia californica* (California poppy).

Parthenocissus quinquefolia; P. tricuspidata

Virginia creeper; Boston ivy

FORM: Vine
HARDINESS: Zones 3–9 (*P. quinquefolia*), 4–8 (*P. tricuspidata*)
SIZE: 30–50 ft. × 5–10 ft.

Virginia creeper is a native climber, growing to 50 ft. The distinctive leaves have five green leaflets tinted with red new growth, turning deep to scarlet red in fall, with blue-black attractive fruit. Critics point out that Virginia creeper can be robust to the point of overly aggressive; I would agree but it is

one of the few vines that works in difficult sites with shade. Variegated 'Star Showers' is far less rambunctious. Non-native Boston ivy is a deciduous vine with tendrils and is commonly used on stone and brick facades (which it can damage due to its adhesive disks). 'Fenway Park' is a gold form. Both species are easy to grow and tolerate site and soil conditions where other vines would do poorly; Japanese beetles plague both.

Parthenocissus quinquefolia puts on a fall show.

Passiflora species and hybrids

Passion-flower, maypop

FORM: Annual, vine
HARDINESS: Zones (5)6–9
BLOOM PERIOD: Summer, fall
SIZE: 6–8 ft. × 3–6 ft.

With blooms so weirdly exotic they look fake, passion-flower is an herbaceous vine growing to 8 ft. when grown as an annual (and 25 ft. long where perennial). It climbs by axillary tendrils or sprawls along the ground. Outlandishly intricate, 3-inch lavender flowers are short-stalked from leaf axils. The petals and sepals subtend a fringe of wavy or crimped hair-like segments with showy pistil and stamens. Sound complex? It is and you have to see it to appreciate it! Passion-flower produces egg-shaped, orange fruits with deep red, edible pulp. Most available plants are complex hybrids; the most common is plum-colored 'Amethyst', sometimes listed as *Passiflora amethystina*, *P. caerulea* 'Constance Elliot' (blue passion-flower) is a vigorous, fragrant climber with white flowers and pale blue or white filaments in the center. *P. coccinea* (red passion vine) has scarlet flowers, grows 10 ft. long in a summer season, and is not hardy in the Midwest.

Passiflora caerulea 'Constance Elliot', like all passion-flowers, is so exotic it looks almost plastic.

Fountain grass

FORM: **Perennial, grass**

HARDINESS: **Zones 5–9**

BLOOM PERIOD: **Spring, summer, fall**

SIZE: **2–5 ft. × 2–5 ft.**

✿ ◓ ☀

You can't miss the graceful, weeping mounds of fine-textured foliage on this early-season grass. It achieves 5 ft. at peak bloom, but cultivars range down in size to diminutive 'Little Bunny' at 2 by 2 ft. It is easy to grow in average to wet soils and vegetation remains as soft waterfalls for winter interest. The supple bottlebrush white flowers shine in fall, acquiring pinkish casts as temperatures drop. It is useful as specimen or massed, and is one of the most suitable plants for fine texture in the perennial border. 'Red Head' demonstrates the almost ethereal cloud of flowers typical of *Pennisetum alopecuroides*, regardless of size.

Pennisetum alopecuroides 'Red Head'.

Penstemon

FORM: **Perennial**

HARDINESS: **Zones 3–8**

BLOOM PERIOD: **Spring, summer**

SIZE: **1–3 ft. × 1–2 ft.**

✿ ☀

I adore penstemon but outside of the rock garden, the only forms I can grow long-term are *Penstemon digitalis* (beardtongue) hybrids such as 'Husker Red', 'Dark Towers', and 'Sour Grapes'. These hybrids are fine garden plants, sometimes producing robust

Penstemon 'Sour Grapes'.

forms that are more durable outside of sharply drained soils, but they are larger, coarser, and not as dramatic as numerous delicate species flourishing in the High Plains, such as *P. pinifolius* (compact pine-leaf penstemon), *P. cobaea* (prairie beardtongue), *P. crandallii* (blue pineleaf beardtongue), *P. cardwellii* (Cardwell's beardtongue), *P. davidsonii* (Davidson's beardtongue), *P. rupicola* (cliff beardtongue), *P. barbatus* (beard-lip beardtongue), *P. richardsonii* (Richardson's beardtongue), *P. fruticosus* (bush penstemon), and others. Western natives with colorful tubular flowers on tall spikes thrive in hot, sunny conditions and include pinks, blues, reds, purples, and whites. Plants grow 1 to 3 ft. tall; smaller varieties enrich rock gardens and borders, while taller types embellish wildflower plantings.

Western U.S. beardtongues like *Penstemon rupicola* need sharp drainage and good air circulation.

Petasites japonicus

Giant butterbur

FORM: **Perennial**
HARDINESS: **Zones 5–9**
BLOOM PERIOD: **Non-flowering**
SIZE: **2–5 ft. × 2–5 ft., colonizes**

This is a giant bog plant with leaves reaching 3 to 4 ft. across. It is the gunnera for the north, appreciating the same moist soils and likewise used in water-based plantings. Under ideal conditions this colossus can be an aggressive thug and should be used only in large areas or where it can be contained. The greenish-mauve flowers bloom near the ground in early spring, before alien-looking foliage pushes its way out of the ground. The stalks and flower buds are edible. Cultivar 'Variegata' has variable gold variegation.

I am standing in the tallest grove of *Petasites japonicus* var. *gigantea* I have ever seen.

Philadelphus coronarius 'Variegatus' (syn. 'Bowles's Variety')

Variegated mock orange

FORM: Shrub

HARDINESS: Zones 4–8

BLOOM PERIOD: Spring, summer, fall

SIZE: 5–6 ft. × 3–4 ft.

I adore variegation and I would not be without my variegated mock orange. But even though I can appreciate the species as one of the most fragrant flowers in spring, the rest of the season it is an unimpressive, rangy shrub. 'Variegatus' barely blooms in the shade but I give it prime space for strong, bright white variegation that does not burn (I have had nearly solid white foliage on some branches). It is much more delicate in appearance than the coarser species and grows slowly to only about 5 to 6 ft. in ten years.

Phlox divaricata

Woodland phlox

FORM: Perennial

HARDINESS: Zones 3–8

BLOOM PERIOD: Spring

SIZE: 8–12 in. × 8–12 in.

Garden phlox is a well-known plant but few people realize a lovely shade version exists. Unlike garden phlox, woodland phlox grows low to the ground, tolerating dry woodland soils. The species generally sports soft, blue-lavender, tubular flowers but cultivars add white, dark blue, pink, rose, and purple to the mix. They include 'Clouds of Perfume', with light lavender-blue flowers; 'Eco Texas Purple', sporting dark purple flowers with a violet eye; white-flowering 'Fuller's White'; and lavender-blue 'London Grove'. In good soils, it spreads as a multihued spring ground cover that allows bulbs to pop through.

Philadelphus coronarius 'Variegatus'.

Phlox divaricata.

Garden phlox

FORM: Perennial

HARDINESS: Zones 3–8

BLOOM PERIOD: Summer, fall

SIZE: 2–4 ft. × 2–3 ft.

Almost every sun gardener has grown garden phlox. This garden stalwart of the perennial border fell out of favor due to high susceptibility to powdery mildew and the resulting unsightliness of foliage dropping from lower stems. A lot of work has gone into breeding resistant cultivars. Phlox still has virtue with large, fragrant flowers that add punches of color when massed. Avoid overhead watering, mulch to keep the root systems cool, provide adequate space for good air circulation, and supply rich, moist, organic soils for maximum reward. Replacing plants with new resistant cultivars every five to six years may be beneficial. Clean, white 'David' is still a reliable resistant cultivar but newer releases include 'Peppermint Twist' (pink striped on white), 'Blue Paradise' (blue-violet), and 'Purple Kiss' (deep purple). 'Lord Clayton' is an interesting variation with cherry red blooms on purple foliage. 'Sherbet Blend' has yellow-green buds that emerge out of dark maroon bracts, opening into flowers with yellow-green edges and soft pink or white centers. 'Aureole' displays bright fuchsia flowers edged in chartreuse.

Phlox paniculata.

Common ninebark

FORM: Shrub

HARDINESS: Zones 2–8

BLOOM PERIOD: Summer

SIZE: 4–8 ft. × 3–6 ft.

As recently as around 2000, ninebark could be described as tough but uninspiring. It grows to 12 ft. tall and wide with nearly no attention; ornamental attributes were unremarkable foliage, mediocre fall color, and peeling stem bark. 'Dart's Gold' was introduced with moderate attention, but the gold dulled to dingy chartreuse-green in summer heat. Then a rogue purple seedling discovered in Germany was introduced as 'Diablo' and ninebark became a garden darling. Crosses between purple forms and 'Dart's Gold' produced gold-emergent-purple forms such as 'Amber Jubilee', 'Coppertina', and 'Center Gold', all somewhat shorter than the species as described above. Additional purple forms emerged including dwarf (4-ft.), fine-foliaged, purple 'Little Devil'.

I prefer the graceful arching habit of *Physocarpus opulifolius* 'Summer Wine' over the coarse, upright nature of popular 'Diablo'.

Picea species

Spruce

FORM: **Tree**
HARDINESS: **Varies**
SIZE: **Varies by species**

Spruces are large trees and can be distinguished by their whorled branches and conical form. The approximately ¾-inch needles are attached singly to the branches in a spiral fashion and have much more girth than the needles of pine trees, although are much shorter. The needles are also angular in cross section; the needles of hemlocks and fir trees are flat in comparison. Spruce is indigenous to cool, well-drained sites and usually found at arctic or tree lines, where they may be growing on permafrost; white (*Picea glauca*) and black (*P. mariana*) spruce are found typically in swampy areas or along the margins of streams and lakes, but all species are highly adaptable, making them very common landscape trees. Most are somewhat shade tolerant. With no taproot, they are also tolerant of transplanting, and are generally shallow rooted. None like hot, dry, polluted sites. Good drainage and air circulation around the tree is essential in the Midwest, or they are prone to fungal diseases. Species common in the Midwest include *abies, glauca, mariana, omorika, orientalis,* and *pungens.*

A grouping of various cultivars of *Picea pungens* f. *glauca*.

Japanese pieris

FORM: **Shrub**

HARDINESS: **Zones 5–8**

BLOOM PERIOD: **Winter, spring**

SIZE: **3–12 ft. × 3–8 ft.**

Another acid lover is this tidy, rounded shrub with glossy foliage, yielding drooping clusters of delicate white blossoms of abundant, bead-like flowers in winter and spring. The emerging foliage is often an attractive reddish color and many cultivars have been selected to enhance that virtue. The species can grow to 12 ft. tall and almost as wide, so it warrants researching cultivar sizes. Noteworthy cultivars under 4 ft. include compact forms 'Christmas Cheer', producing masses of pale pink, lily-of-the-valley flowers; 'Bert Chandler', with leaves that emerge bright salmon-pink but fade to paler pink and then a creamy yellow before finally turning green; 'Sarabande', which has bronze new foliage and white flowers that stand erect rather than hanging down in clusters; 'Variegata', a variegated, white-flowering form; and 'Mountain Fire', larger at 6 ft. with white flowers and bright red new growth.

Pieris japonica is an acid lover and suffers in high-lime soils.

Pinus species

Pine

FORM: **Tree**

HARDINESS: **Varies within zones 2–7**

SIZE: **varies by species**

Pines have needles that grow in bundles containing two to six needles, and are the only conifers that have their needles united at the point of attachment to the tree. Needles vary in length according to species; some pines have long, light-colored needles, while others possess short, dark ones. The cones are differentiated into male and female structures: female cones are large, long, and woody while male cones are small, long, soft projections. Pines are characteristic of areas with sandy, well-drained soils, but grow best in richer soils. They are generally intolerant of shade but are more tolerant of adverse soil, exposure, and urban conditions than firs and spruces. The two-needle types are considered more tolerant than the three-needle, which are more robust than the five-needle. Pines withstand light pruning and can be maintained as hedges and screens. They can be sheared; removing half the new candle growth will result in the formation of lateral buds below the cut. Species common in the Midwest include *aristata*, *banksiana*, *bungeana*, *cembra*, *contorta*, *densiflora*, *leucodermis*, *mugo*, *nigra*, *parviflora*, *strobus*, and *sylvestris*. *Pinus strobus* 'Pendula' is one of the most elegant weeping trees available.

Pinus strobus 'Pendula'.

Podophyllum peltatum and Asian hybrids

Mayapple

FORM: **Perennial**

HARDINESS: **Zones 3–8**

BLOOM PERIOD: **Spring**

SIZE: **12–18 in. × 8–12 in.**

☼ ◑ ☀

Mayapple's namesake is the small green fruit that arises from a single nodding, waxy, white flower tucked under foliage. The apple-like fruit is edible but the leaves and roots are poisonous. The visual interest is not flower or fruit but rather large, umbrella-like, palmate leaves with deeply divided lobes. It is easy to grow and colonizes readily. A number of hybrids of non-native *Podophyllum*, such as 'Spotty Dotty' and 'Kaleidoscope', are less hardy at zones (5)6 to 9 and require more compost and moisture than the drought-tolerant native.

Podophyllum peltatum can mass nicely over time.

Podophyllum 'Spotty Dotty' is an eye-catcher in the garden.

Creeping Jacob's ladder

FORM: Perennial

HARDINESS: Zones 3–8

BLOOM PERIOD: Spring

SIZE: 1–1.5 ft. × 1–1.5 ft.

Creeping Jacob's ladder evolved in moist areas along streams, but it adapts to dry woodland sites that have adequate organic matter. In spite of the name, it tends to clump rather than spread, although it will seed fairly freely. The dark green foliage is arranged on the stem in a ladder-like fashion. Flowers tend to be pale blue-purple bells lightly arranged on terminal stems. Two spectacular variegated forms—the coarser 'Stairway to Heaven' and the more delicate 'Touch of Class'—have generated ornamental interest in this native plant; both emerge with added pink highlights that disappear in summer.

Polemonium reptans 'Stairway to Heaven'.

Small Solomon's seal; great Solomon's seal

FORM: Perennial

HARDINESS: Zones 3–8

BLOOM PERIOD: Spring

SIZE: 1–5 ft. × 12–30 in.

Native Solomon's seal is happiest in moist conditions, but does not let dryness deter its growth. The two species are identical, except that small Solomon's seal is about half the size of greater Solomon's seal, which features 4 to 5 ft. of arching, upright, unbranched stems. Both possess small, bell-shaped, whitish-green flowers, paired and dangling from the leaf axils. These turn into dark blue berries with yellow-tan foliage in the fall. They form aggressive colonies in moist, organic-rich conditions, so adaptability to dryness helps keep them in check. They are easy to divide and transplant.

Polygonatum biflorum is a woodland floor colonizer but is fairly easy to remove in garden settings.

Polygonatum odoratum 'Variegata'

Variegated Solomon's seal

FORM: Perennial

HARDINESS: Zones 3–8

BLOOM PERIOD: Spring

SIZE: 2–3 ft. × 1 ft.

Woodland Solomon's seal is so robust, it can become a thug. However, these tough attributes have made cultivar 'Variegata' a desirable perennial. It is easy to grow in average soils with adequate moisture in sun or shade. I have seen it effectively bordering driveways—difficult sites for most plants. The upright, arching stems multiply moderately by thick rhizomes and are easy to divide and share. The white, bell-shaped flowers are lightly scented although you may have to lean close to fully arouse the nose. The flowers turn into autumn blue-black berries and the foliage becomes a pleasing, soft tan-yellow.

Polygonatum odoratum 'Variegata' tolerates a range of tough conditions.

Porteranthus trifoliata (syn. Gillenia trifoliata)

Bowman's root

FORM: Perennial

HARDINESS: Zones 4–8

BLOOM PERIOD: Spring, summer

SIZE: 2–4 ft. × 1.5–3 ft.

This lesser known woodland perennial can become almost shrub-like in size and habit if happy. It is extremely attractive when flowering, with airy, bright white, starry blooms that almost float over thin red stems, brightening shaded areas. The petals drop but leave red calyxes that hang onto the stem until fall, when the foliage turns a matching red. If its soil is overly fertile it may topple; it prefers leaner woodland soils.

The flowers of Porteranthus trifoliata appear like delicate white butterflies floating over the plant.

Primula species

Primrose

FORM: Short-lived perennial

HARDINESS: Zones 5–9

BLOOM PERIOD: Spring, summer, fall

SIZE: 6–18 in. × 1–7 ft.

Primula is a herbaceous or semi-evergreen perennial, forming basal rosettes of simple leaves. Platter-shaped or bell-shaped flowers are solitary or carried as umbels or as whorls on erect stems. They share common cultural needs of evenly moist soil in cool growing conditions; while they generally prefer moist feet, most also require good drainage, which can be a difficult combination for many gardeners. The main exceptions are *P. japonica* (Japanese primrose) and *P. denticulata* (drumstick primrose), which do well in waterlogged soil. Primroses thrive in full sun in cool summer areas but usually need partial shade elsewhere.

Massed *Primula japonica* demonstrates its preference for moist roots.

Douglas fir

FORM: **Tree**

HARDINESS: **Zones 4–6**

SIZE: **Varies by cultivar**

Douglas fir is a large evergreen tree with a compact, pyramidal crown and irregularly disposed branches; dense in youth becoming loose with age. It is a towering giant in the Pacific Northwest and grows best on the deep, moist, well-drained, sandy, neutral, or slightly acidic loams typical of that area. It has limited use and is not often found in many areas of the Midwest because it does not thrive on compacted, poorly drained, or limestone soils and is injured by strong winds. It does endure considerable drought. Cultivar sizes range from low-mounding 'Fletcheri' at around 3 to 4 ft. by 4 to 5 ft. to 'Pendula', a slightly weeping form that achieves 50 ft. in ideal conditions.

Pseudotsuga menziesii 'Pendula'.

Pulmonaria species

Lungwort

FORM: **Perennial**
HARDINESS: **Zones 4–9**
BLOOM PERIOD: **Spring**
SIZE: **1 ft. × 1–2 ft.**

☼ ◑

This ornamental will please you all season if you provide it with organically rich, well-drained, evenly moist soils. It is one of the first plants to wilt in dry soils and goes into dormancy if its plight is ignored. Blooms push up in early spring before foliage. These delicate clusters of funnel-shaped, white, blue, pink, magenta, or multicolored flowers are followed by lanceolate foliage that is often spotted or covered in a silver sheen. Foliage is prone to serious mildew damage during wet, warm springs. Simply cut them to the ground, dispose of foliage, and they will grow back fully in time for drier warmth. The flowers are a delight in early spring and the foliage is superb for summer and fall appeal. The many cultivars include 'Raspberry Splash', with raspberry and blue flowers; robust, deep blue 'Trevi Fountain'; long-time white-flowered favorite 'Bressingham White'; and many silver, overlaid forms such as 'Diana Claire', Silver Shimmers', and 'Cotton Cool'.

Pulmonaria 'Silver Shimmers'.

Pulsatilla vulgaris

Pasque flower

FORM: **Perennial**
HARDINESS: **Zones 4–8**
BLOOM PERIOD: **Spring**
SIZE: **6–12 in. × 6–12 in.**

✿ ♠ ☀

Pasque flowers are cheerful denizens of spring. Fuzzy flower buds open to bell-shaped purple flowers dancing in the breeze, before turning into silky plumed, feathery seed heads. The felted foliage has varying degrees of lacy dissection. Pasque flower self sows readily, producing petal fringing, flower colors from light lavender to dark magenta, and seedlings with differences in leaf dissection. Small plants are easily moved; mature plants have long taproots and resent transplanting. Cultivars exist but are rarely sold in stores; you are more likely to find them via mail order. 'Rote Glocke' is a robust plant sporting bright crimson-red flowers with yellow stamens, 'Rubra' is red, and 'Alba' is white. *Pulsatilla aurea*, difficult to find, is yellow but they so freely hybridize on their own, you will get variation without cultivars.

Pulsatilla vulgaris is a spring harbinger happiest in well-drained sites.

Oak

FORM: **Tree**

HARDINESS: **Zones 3–9**

BLOOM PERIOD: **Non-flowering**

SIZE: **50–70 ft. × 40–80 ft.**

Oaks are limited to large landscapes; other than fastigiate forms, there aren't dwarf forms. Oak wilt has become a serious issue, but since infection is from insects vectoring the disease into tree wounds, properly maintained specimens in home landscapes should remain issue-free. White oaks, including *Quercus alba* (white), *Q. bicolor* (swamp white), *Q. macrocarpa* (burr), and *Q. muehlenbergii* (chinka-pin) are from damp areas and prefer rich, moist, acidic, well-drained soils, but are highly adaptable. The black oaks, including *Q. rubra* (red), *Q. velutina* (black), *Q. palustris* (pin), and the underutilized *Q. ellipsoidalis* (northern pin) evolved in drier, upland sites. Oak seedlings start their growth with a "tap" root that grows downward until it finds a reliable source of water; once it does, it starts developing extensive fibrous root systems like other trees and the original tap disappears.

If there were a designated Midwest tree, I would vote for long-lived, wide-spreading *Quercus macrocarpa*.

Ratibida columnifera; R. pinnata

Mexican hat; gray-head coneflower

FORM: Short-lived perennial
HARDINESS: Zones 4–9
BLOOM PERIOD: Non-flowering
SIZE: 1–3 ft. × 12–18 in.

Mexican hat is a relatively short-lived but dependable perennial, generally growing 1 to 2 ft., but occasionally reaching 3 ft. Its fine, medium green, almost fernlike leaves are distinguished from other coneflowers by the tall, upright nature of the elongated center cone, surrounded by drooping yellow, red, or orange ray flowers. They prefer well-drained sand, loam, clay, or limestone soils. Cultivars are not common because of the amount of natural color variation, but 'Red Midget' is a compact form to less than 2 ft. Gray-head coneflower is a more durable plant, a prairie flower that flushes with masses of bright yellow flowers in the harsh heat of summer. It is surprisingly resilient, surviving heat, drought, flooding, and winter cold. It is easy to grow from seed or transplants.

Ratiba columnifera is a classic prairie flower.

Rhododendron hybrids

Rhododendron and azalea

FORM: Shrub, tree

HARDINESS: Zones 4–8

BLOOM PERIOD: Spring

SIZE: 1–20 ft. × 2–15 ft.

Midwesterners cannot visit the Southeast without drooling for rhododendron (which includes azalea). There are both native and non-native species. A few cultivars like 'P.J.M.' and the Northern Lights Series of azaleas will tough out conditions in low-pH areas lower than South of the Boreal, valiantly attempting to thrive, but only areas around the Lower Midwest will achieve maximum success. Cold temperatures are not as limiting as is high pH; rhododendron despises it and suffers in size and health as a result.

This popular genus produces large clusters of colorful pink, red, violet, yellow, and white flowers from late spring to early summer, and performs best in regions with cool, moist summers. Size varies considerably from 1 ft. to more than 20 ft. Even though they are considered a shade plant, some prefer sun. A general rule of thumb is the larger the leaf the more likely it prefers shade; smaller-leaved varieties often prefer sun. Some commonly available rhododendrons for shade include hot pink, 2-ft. 'Elvira'; 5-ft., red 'Nova Zembla'; peach-pink, 3-ft. 'Olga Mezzitt'; and 'Weston's Pink Diamond', with vivid pink, frilled, double flowers. Sun lovers include 4-ft., yellow-flowered 'Yellow Hammer'; 5-ft. 'Crater Lake' with blue ruffled flowers; and 6-ft. 'Fastuosum Flore Pleno', with double lavender flowers. As ubiquitous as bigleaf hydrangea, hundreds of cultivars have been developed from dozens of species, so your choices are almost limitless.

Rhododendron is spectacular when it is happy in low-pH conditions.

Roger's flower

FORM: Perennial

HARDINESS: Zones 5–8

BLOOM PERIOD: Summer

SIZE: 3–5 ft. × 3–5 ft.

Roger's flower thrives in moist but not water-logged soils and a happy plant provides a bold, tropical effect. It will grow in sun in humus-rich soil, but is susceptible to sun and wind scorch. New spring growth is damaged by late frosts. Height varies by species; compound leaves spread up to 3 ft. Flowering stems rise above foliage, topped with panicles of white, cream, pink, or red flowers. The most common garden species are *Rodgersia pinnata* (featherleaf rodgersia), *R. aesculifolia* (fingerleaf rodgersia), and *R. podophylla* (rodgersia). Leaves of many species emerge in spring, bronze or copper hued; some cultivars of *R. pinnata* boast reddish-purple stem and leaf, such as 'Bronze Peacock', 'Fireworks', and 'Chocolate Wings', but color fades in heat. Somewhat larger than featherleaf rodgersia, *R. podophylla* 'Rotlaub' makes a bold statement in my garden. Foliage turns attractive shades of coppery brown to magenta in fall.

I love the drama provided by *Rodgersia podophylla* 'Rotlaub' in my garden.

Rose

FORM: **Shrub**

HARDINESS: **Zones (4)5–10**

BLOOM PERIOD: **Spring, summer, fall**

SIZE: **Varies by species and cultivar**

Probably the most recognized flower worldwide, roses are spectacular garden shrubs, albeit with a large number of issues. In the late 1990s to early 2000s, the shrub rose became the dominant shrub sold in America, with claims of fewer issues over the teas and related species. However, they still require a fair amount of care, water, fertilizer, and maintenance, and rose sales have decreased significantly. Midwest rose issues include hardiness, black spot, rose rosette, mosaic, powdery mildew, deer and rabbit browsing, and many devastating insects including Japanese beetle, rose midges, thrips, aphids, scale, and spider mites. I know this list is extremely intimidating; it is not meant to deter you from growing roses, but rather to make you aware that education is necessary before you begin. The Knockout Series has been touted as Midwest durable and more disease resistant; a number of other series have been developed for tougher conditions, including Oso Easy and Drift, but keep in mind that all roses will require attention.

Roses are the ultimate garden plant for a sense of romance and for fragrance, but they require considerable effort for reward.

Rudbeckia fulgida var. *sullivantii*

Black-eyed Susan, brown-eyed Susan, orange coneflower

FORM: Perennial

HARDINESS: Zones 3–9

BLOOM PERIOD: Summer, fall

SIZE: 1–3 ft. × 1–2.5 ft.

Few plants are criticized as being overused as much as 'Goldsturm' orange coneflower. It became a standard when combined with purple coneflower and 'Autumn Joy' sedum, all planted together as a long-flowering, late-season trio. Notice that plants we deem as overused are those that perform reliably with no fuss in less than desirable conditions. 'Goldsturm' laughs jauntily at hot, humid summers, defying poor soils. It is an excellent plant for meadows and naturalized gardens and is dependable year after year. An exciting new miniature form, 'Little Goldstar', matures at a compact 14 to 16 in. tall and wide.

Rudbeckia fulgida var. *sullivantii* 'Goldsturm' has been around seemingly forever, but it is as durable as perennials come.

Great coneflower

FORM: **Perennial**

HARDINESS: **Zones 4–9**

BLOOM PERIOD: **Summer, fall**

SIZE: **5–7 ft. × 3–4 ft.**

I am quite fond of great coneflower for drama, and even in a small garden a single specimen makes a statement. A tall alternative to 'Goldsturm', *Rudbeckia maxima* flaunts huge, powder-blue basal leaves up to 2 to 3 ft. long, that are striking all season. In early summer, flower stalks shoot upward with large, deep gold, drooping ray flowers with a black center. Great coneflower attracts butterflies and birds and adapts to wet and dry while remaining more rigidly upright than most coneflowers.

Rudbeckia maxima makes a bold statement with bright yellow, cone-shaped flowers topping glaucous blue foliage.

Rudbeckia maxima.

Salix alba 'Britzensis'; S. matsudana 'Tortuosa'

Coral bark willow; dragon's claw willow

FORM: Shrub, tree
HARDINESS: Zones 5–8
BLOOM PERIOD: Non-flowering
SIZE: 20–30 ft. × 10–15 ft.

Willows hybridize freely, so we don't always know the exact parentage. They are deciduous shrubs and trees with simple leaves and tiny flowers in catkins; male and female are usually on separate plants. Their rapid growth rate, brittle branches, and moderate life spans make them "messy" trees that drop litter, but I still love the weeping willows (*Salix babylonica*) around large bodies of water. 'Britzensis' is an all-male willow cultivar with red to orange-red winter stems; 'Tortuosa' is medium-sized with narrow, twisted leaves on contorted branches. Maximize vibrancy by cutting back hard to one ft. before new growth. Many willows are grown this way, as multi-stemmed shrubs, since they grow quickly and produce sizable growth in one season.

Salix alba 'Britzensis' shines in winter.

Salix elaeagnos subsp. angustifolia (syn. S. rosmarinifolia)

Rosemary willow

FORM: Shrub
HARDINESS: Zones 4–7
BLOOM PERIOD: Non-flowering
SIZE: 8–10 ft. × 8–10 ft.

This is a well-behaved, underutilized, spectacular shrub amenable to all soil types. It was formerly known as *Salix rosmarinifolia*, because of its gray-green narrow leaves—it looks like a giant rosemary plant in the landscape! Silver colors are always welcome in the garden and this one delivers with impact. It is non-spreading and tolerates hard pruning to control size. It works equally well as specimen plant or unique hedge.

Salix elaeagnos subsp. *angustifolia*.

Salix sachalinensis 'Golden Sunshine'

Japanese fantail willow

FORM: Shrub

HARDINESS: Zones 4–7

BLOOM PERIOD: Non-flowering

SIZE: 8–12 ft. × 8–12 ft.

Splashy! Slender, gaudy, warm golden foliage retains its color throughout summer heat and humidity. Abundant 1-inch, silky, silver catkins on glossy purple stems make an appearance before the foliage. Like most shrubby and tree-sized willows, it is happy to be pruned severely each spring to control size.

Salix sachalinensis 'Golden Sunshine'.

Salpiglossis sinuata

Painted tongue

FORM: Annual

HARDINESS: Not hardy

BLOOM PERIOD: Summer, fall

SIZE: 12–24 in. × 6–12 in.

This beautiful old cottage garden plant seemed to fall out of fashion and I'm not sure why. I can't say it better than Thompson & Morgan: "Like sumptuous gold braid, the exquisite veining overlays rich, velvety hues, creating a shimmering display." The trumpet flowers on upright, bushy plants are simply stunning, although they may get straggly in excessive summer heat. Cultivars include 'Splash', 'Bolero', and the more compact-growing 'Casino'. Thompson & Morgan also offers 'Royale Mixed' if you feel adventurous enough to start from seed.

Not commonly available, *Salpiglossis sinuata* is worth seeking out.

Sage

FORM: **Perennial**

HARDINESS: **Zones 4–8**

BLOOM PERIOD: **Summer, fall**

SIZE: **1–2 ft. × 1–2 ft.**

My public garden maintains a predominantly clay stretch along the exterior length of a fence that is exposed to road salt, sand, and every imaginable street-side insult. Over time, the predominant plants in this hellstrip have become perennial veronica and salvia. Defying the odds, both of these genera bloom and rebloom several times in the season, especially if spent flowers are deadheaded. Sage flower colors range from blues to mauve-pinks to violet, fooling passersby into thinking we work hard to provide a gorgeous border in unseemly conditions. Imagine what it can do in ideal conditions! 'May Night' is a long-time favorite, for rich blue-purple flowers and 'Blauhugel' and 'Cardonna' are similar. 'Pink Friesland', 'Sensation Deep Rose Improved', and 'Rose Queen' are pink. Folks in the drier, well-drained Plains may want to try salvia straight species with airier, looser flowers such as *Salvia greggii* (Gregg's salvia), *S. sclarea* (clary sage), *S. darcyi* (Darcy's sage), and *S. cyanescens* (blue Turkish sage).

Salvia ×sylvestris 'Blauhugel' will rebloom if it is deadheaded immediately after flowering, sometimes multiple times in a season.

Salvia 'Wendy's Wish'

Wendy's Wish sage

FORM: Annual

HARDINESS: Not hardy

BLOOM PERIOD: Spring, summer, fall

SIZE: 3–4 ft. × 2–3 ft.

Annual salvias have long been summer standards, but the release of 'Wendy's Wish' a few years ago was nearly revolutionary. I planted it the year it was released and won't be without it again. This is a big, open form, up to 4-ft. high. Intriguing, oversized, shrimp-like buds emerge from soft, coral-pink bracts and open to hot-pink, tubular blooms. The attractive deep green leaves have dark maroon stems. Insects love them; I've watched sphinx moths spend entire days within them.

Not only is *Salvia* 'Wendy's Wish' vibrantly sensational, it attracts insects like this sphinx moth.

Sambucus species

Elderberry

FORM: Shrub

HARDINESS: Zones 5–8

BLOOM PERIOD: Summer

SIZE: 6–20 ft. × 6–20 ft.

I grew up with native elderberry and a mom who made elderberry jam and wine. Native *Sambucus canadensis* 'Aurea' is garden worthy and European species (*S. nigra* and *S. racemosa*) produced lovely purple, filamentous 'Black Lace'; golden cutleaf 'Sutherland Gold'; and green, deeply dissected 'Laciniata'. The natural open, scraggly look is not desirable in gardens, so I recommend coppicing them to around 8 in. every one or two years. The result is a shorter, thicker form with richly colored foliage (although it still reaches 6 ft. in a season). Elderberries are extremely durable and tolerate a wide range of soils.

Sambucus racemosa 'Sutherland Gold' makes a standout contrasting foreground to *Fagus sylvatica* 'Roseomarginata'.

Sanguinaria canadensis

Bloodroot
FORM: Perennial
HARDINESS: Zones 3–8
BLOOM PERIOD: Spring
SIZE: 6–8 in. × 4–6 in.

As farm children we were shown how bloodroot plant parts would exude a thick, blood-like sap when damaged; the source of the name. This forest floor colonizer blooms early, with clear white flowers flaunting yellow stamens; the petals fold up on cloudy days and evenings. Petals drop quickly in unseasonably warm springs, leaving palmate, silvery gray-green foliage—lovely in its own right. Cultivar 'Multiplex' is the much-revered and sought double-flowering bloodroot.

Sanguinaria canadensis.

Sanguisorba obtusa

Japanese burnet
FORM: Perennial
HARDINESS: Zones 4–8
BLOOM PERIOD: Summer, fall
SIZE: 2.5–3 ft. × 2–3 ft.

Japanese burnet is not used nearly enough in gardens. The long, pink, bottlebrush-shaped flowers are borne on tall, rather floppy spikes produced in great abundance. It forms medium-height foliar mats from which flowers rise to about 3 ft., creating a meadow-like effect. 'Red Thunder' is a large form, with a profusion of 1-in., cattail-like, deep burgundy blooms topping pinnate foliage on clump-forming, 4-ft. plants. *Sanguisorba officinalis*, the herb, forms clumps and is rhizomatous so it spreads and self-seeds.

Sanguisorba obtusa flaunts fuzzy pink tails, which work especially well when paired with soft grasses.

Schizachyrium scoparium

Little bluestem

FORM: Perennial, grass

HARDINESS: Zones 3–9

BLOOM PERIOD: Non-flowering

SIZE: 2–4 ft. × 1.5–2 ft.

Little bluestem is a well-behaved, finely textured, clumping grass with blue-green summer color and blue, wine, purple, and gold highlights from autumn through winter. In late summer, silvery seed heads float 2 ft. above foliage and are lovely when backlit by sun. It is widely adaptable to most soils, except those that are wet or highly fertile, which cause lodging. Formerly relegated to prairies and meadows, it has recently been elevated to ornamental gardening status with cultivars like 'The Blues', 'Prairie Blues', and 'Blue Heaven', all selected for color; and 'Carousel' and 'Standing Ovation', bred for rigidity.

Schizachyrium scoparium adds fall interest to the landscape.

Schizophragma hydrangeoides

Japanese hydrangea vine

FORM: Vine

HARDINESS: Zones 5–8

BLOOM PERIOD: Summer

SIZE: 20–30 ft. × 6–9 ft.

Japanese hydrangea vine is not actually a hydrangea but is in the hydrangea family. It looks and acts similar to climbing hydrangea, but true hydrangea has four petals (actually sepals), whereas Japanese hydrangea vine has one solitary, heart-shaped sepal. Japanese hydrangea vine also hugs trees or walls more closely than climbing hydrangea and is less aggressive and less winter hardy. Cultivar 'Rosea' has pink sepals and 'Moonlight' has spectacular steel-blue foliage with contrasting green veins.

Schizophragma hydrangeoides.

Senna didymobotrya

Popcorn bush, peanut butter senna

FORM: Annual

HARDINESS: Zones 8–10

BLOOM PERIOD: Summer, fall

SIZE: 3–8 ft. × 2–4 ft. depending on purchase size

Another plant with unusual scent. Rub the lush, leathery pinnate leaves for a whiff of fresh buttered popcorn! Top that with tall spikes of richly contrasting, dark, fat flower buds that pop with rich, yellow, popcorn kernel-like flowers. The flowers are supposed to smell of peanut butter as well. It can grow 6 to 10 ft. tall and wide where it is perennial. Birds, bees, and butterflies enjoy it as well.

Senna didymobotrya is often used in children's gardens because of the unique scent.

Sesleria autumnalis; S. caerulea

Autumn moor grass; blue moor grass

FORM: Perennial, grass

HARDINESS: Zones 5–8

BLOOM PERIOD: Spring, summer, fall

SIZE: 8–12 in. × 6–12 in.

This is possibly the most underutilized ornamental grass. It thrives in full sun but tolerates a great deal of shade and drought. At my public garden it is massed under a dense white ash that robs the area of moisture and sun. It is cool season early emergent and makes a lovely clump of narrow, fine foliage no more than a foot high. It is charming massed or as border specimen. Autumn moor grass blooms with small, shiny white flowers in late summer; blue moor grass has glaucous foliage flushing greenish flowers in spring. Not to be confused with *Molinia* moor grasses.

Sesleria autumnalis sited in very dry soil competes with the root system (and tolerates the shade) of a purple ash in Wisconsin.

Rosinweed; compass plant; cup plant; prairie dock

FORM: Perennial

HARDINESS: Zones 3–9

BLOOM PERIOD: Summer, fall

SIZE: 4–10 ft. × 4–5 ft.

These four species comprise tall, mostly prairie, perennial sunflowers, some with very large leaves. Rosinweed has opposite, rough, stalkless, untoothed or slightly toothed leaves, and is the shortest at 2 to 5 ft. tall. Compass plant is named for its deeply incised leaves that tend to orient north-south. Cup plant refers to its large, broad foliage forming a "cup" where it is attached to square stems; it catches and retains rainwater for insects and absorbs drowned insects. Prairie dock has large, ovate or heart-shaped, basal leaves to 2 ft. long; sparsely leaved flower stalks sometimes reach 10 ft. Butterflies use them all, and birds feed on their seeds.

Silphium laciniatum and the other three species are some of the tallest prairie plants.

Goldenrod

FORM: Perennial

HARDINESS: Zones 3–9

BLOOM PERIOD: Summer, fall

SIZE: 3–5 ft. × 4–5 ft., colonizes

Goldenrod does not cause allergies, but it does bloom at the same time as ragweed. It reliably provides end-of-season color in glowing shades of yellow and gold and works best in naturalistic plantings. Cultivated varieties are noted for showier flowers, distinctively unique habits, and a less vigorous nature. Most exhibit numerous small flowers packed into upward-facing racemes or spikey racemes on stiff, branching stems. 'Crown of Rays' is the most common *Solidago canadensis* cultivar, *S. rugosa* 'Fireworks' is an extremely popular short and arching form, and *S. rigida* is sold primarily as species. I note them here due to increased popularity, but I personally quit using goldenrod ornamentally due to aggressive rhizomatous spread and prolific seeding. Regular division helps keep it under control.

Solidago rugosa 'Fireworks'.

Spigelia marilandica

Indian pink

FORM: **Perennial**

HARDINESS: **Zones 5–9**

BLOOM PERIOD: **Summer**

SIZE: **12–18 in. × 6–18 in.**

Sometimes we fall hopelessly in love—hard—as I did the first time I saw a mass planting of Indian pink. This native is found in moist woods and along stream banks. The cheerful, red, semi-closed, trumpet-shaped flowers face upward and open enough to protrude five bright yellow, star-like lobes. Stems are rigidly upright and plants form nice-sized clumps. They are lovely in mass.

Spigelia marilandica will not fail to capture the attention of your garden guests.

Spiraea japonica

Japanese spirea

FORM: **Shrub**

HARDINESS: **Zones 3–8**

BLOOM PERIOD: **Summer, fall**

SIZE: **1–6 ft. × 1–7 ft.**

Spirea once dominated the shrub market and is considered overused and common, although sporadic new releases continue. One issue is that it gets rangy and unkempt if it isn't sheared regularly; they flower on new wood, so hard pruning maximizes bloom. Cut down to about 6 in. every fall or spring, so new growth will flush thick, dense, and with brilliant new foliage color. Japanese spirea remains a durable option for poor soils and tough sites; properly placed, it endures as a good garden plant as well. Recent releases with merit include tidier-looking dwarf forms such as 'Lavender Princess', 'Little Princess', 'Double Play Artisan', and 'Little Bonnie'; standard forms include 'Neon Flash', 'Anthony Waterer', and 'Gold Mound' with gold foliage.

Spiraea japonica 'Lavender Princess' is a recent introduction reflecting a trend in dwarf *Spiraea*.

Strobilanthes dyerianus

Persian shield

FORM: Annual

HARDINESS: Not hardy

BLOOM PERIOD: Spring, summer, fall

SIZE: 1–3 ft. × 1–3 ft.

It isn't new at all, but this is another I would not be without. Persian shield is touted for outstanding foliage, with large leaves striped in shimmering silver-blue and lilac and a majestic maroon on the underside. I join the commendation. It goes with practically any combination.

Strobilanthes dyerianus with *Torenia fournieri* 'Catalina Gilded Grape'.

Stylophorum diphyllum

Celandine poppy

FORM: Short-lived perennial

HARDINESS: Zones 4–9

BLOOM PERIOD: Spring

SIZE: 12–18 in. × 8–12 in.

Celandine poppy is native and an aggressive self-seeder; one plant will quickly become many throughout your shade garden, so it is best used to naturalize large areas. The bright yellow flowers are welcome after winter, especially when paired with the blue of Virginia bluebells, which bloom at the same time. It thrives in wet soils but will tolerate and be somewhat controlled by dry soils. It goes dormant in summer in dry conditions—but fear not, it will return next spring. It is not to be confused with a lesser celandine, *Ranunculus ficaria*, which has become a noxious plant in some areas.

Stylophorum diphyllum may be boon or bane, depending on what you think of its reseeding habit.

Styphnolobium japonicum (syn. Sophora japonica)

Japanese pagoda tree

FORM: Tree

HARDINESS: Zones 4–8

BLOOM PERIOD: Non-flowering

SIZE: 50–75 ft. × 50–60 ft.

Japanese pagoda tree is an underutilized, medium-size deciduous tree with a rounded, low-branched habit. It has rich, green, 10-inch-long pinnate leaves producing fragrant, creamy white, pea-shaped flowers, 5 in. long, in terminal panicles on mature trees. The form truly worth exalting is 'Pendulum', of which I have only seen mature specimens on the East Coast. It is a breathtaking, gloriously twisted-branched, elegant, weeping form. It is one worth pursuing further, since it is hardy to most of the Midwest.

This magnificent *Styphnolobium japonicum* 'Pendulum' at Mount Auburn Cemetery in Boston makes me wonder why it isn't used more in the Midwest.

Succulents

FORM: Annual and perennial

HARDINESS: Zone 3 to not hardy depending on species and cultivar

BLOOM PERIOD: Summer, fall

SIZE: Varies by species and cultivars

Long used in glamorous combinations on both coasts, succulents have been slow to make their way to the Midwest. In particular, non–winter hardy exotic beauties such as *Aeonium*, *Echevaria*, *Sedum*, *Crassula*, *Agave*, *Kalanchoe*, *Dorothea*, and others make fascinating combinations that take little care, next to no water, and zero fertilization. Prices have dropped, so Midwesterners can treat them as annuals; however, they are also easy to overwinter by bringing indoors if you have the room. Mix with hardy *Sempervivum* (hen-and-chicks) and sedums for an almost infinite selection of combinations. Since an enormous assortment of succulents is available, they are often sold as mixed succulents and many times not even labeled by name. They work well in containers or the ground and will add punch and pizzazz to traditional Midwest combinations.

Explore myriad fascinating succulents for easy-care, unique planters.

Asters

FORM: **Perennial**

HARDINESS: **Zones 3–10**

BLOOM PERIOD: **Summer, fall**

SIZE: **1–6 ft. × 1–4 ft.**

Aster was a large genus, now being reevaluated and reclassified by taxonomists. A few, such as *Symphyotrichum cordifolium* (blue wood aster) and *Eurybia divaricata* (white wood aster), are shade tolerant. Most, like *S. novae-angliae* (New England aster) and *S. ericoides* (heath aster) prefer full sun. *S. lateriflorum* 'Lady in Black' and 'Prince' have layered purple foliage. As a rule they are tough plants that bloom reliably in spite of drought, clay soils, and severe winter. Over-fertility causes lodging; cutting asters back hard in early summer will force development of shorter, more compact plants. All are native to various areas of North America.

Symphyotrichum lateriflorum 'Lady In Black' provides a unique horizontal branching pattern in dark purple.

Shredded umbrella plant; umbrella plant

FORM: **Perennial**

HARDINESS: **Zones 4–8**

BLOOM PERIOD: **Summer**

SIZE: **1.5–3 ft. × 1.5–2 ft.**

Umbrella plants are foliage accents since their tiny flowers are interesting close-up, but not very visible from a distance. They emerge like folded umbrellas covered in silvery pubescens. The tomentose surface turns glossy green as each plant opens like an umbrella. *Syneilesis aconitifolia* opens to large, palmate, dissected leaves; *S. palmata* does the same with palmate leaves that lack the shredded appearance. They are excellent plants for adding textural interest to mixed plantings.

Syneilesis aconitifolia couldn't have a more apt common name: shredded umbrella plant.

Syringa meyeri

Meyer lilac

FORM: Shrub

HARDINESS: Zones 3–7

BLOOM PERIOD: Spring

SIZE: 4–8 ft. × 6–15 ft.

The most popular form of Meyer lilac is 'Palibin', otherwise known as dwarf Korean lilac. It has a smaller, glossier leaf than common lilac (*Syringa vulgaris*) and is resistant to powdery mildew. It blooms in late spring, immediately after common lilac. It is grown as a shrub or grafted on standards to create small, round-headed crowns, although I have seen it easily 15 ft. wide. The delicate, lilac-shaded flowers are strongly fragrant and cover the shrub to the point that no foliage is visible. It is lauded for its rebloom, especially the recent release, purple 'Bloomerang'—although repeat bloom is sporadic and produces far fewer flowers. Pink forms include 'Tinkerbelle', 'Thumbelina', and 'Fairy Dust'. 'Prince Charming' opens wine red and 'Sugar Plum Fairy' is the most compact, with a rosy lilac bloom. Another common shrub form of lilac is *S. pubescens* subsp. *patula* 'Miss Kim', which is more upright and can reach 9 to 12 ft. high (I have seen it used as hedge), but has similar flowers to 'Palibin'.

Syringa meyeri 'Tinkerbelle' exhibits more delicate flowers and foliage than *Syringa vulgaris*.

Syringa reticulata; S. reticulata subsp. pekinensis

Japanese tree lilac; Pekin lilac

FORM: Tree

HARDINESS: Zones 3–7

BLOOM PERIOD: Summer

SIZE: 20–30 ft. × 15–25 ft.

Japanese tree lilac became a popular ornamental with cultivar 'Ivory Silk'. This showy ornamental is valued for its small size and urban tolerance, so it now lines streets under power lines. It produces large, showy panicles of creamy white blooms with musky scent after common and dwarf Korean lilacs; the species tends to bloom every other year. Its smooth, brown bark resembles cherry. It tolerates lower pH and drier soil than its shrubby cousins and is highly resistant to powdery mildew. I prefer Pekin lilac, with similar flowers but peeling, gold-bronze bark. Several outstanding cultivars include 'Copper Curls', 'Beijing Gold', and 'China Snow'.

Syringa reticulata subsp. *pekinensis* 'China Snow' provides multi-season interest due to beautiful exfoliating bark.

Syringa vulgaris

Common lilac

FORM: Shrub

HARDINESS: Zones 3–7

BLOOM PERIOD: Spring

SIZE: 6–15 ft. × 4–12 ft.

Common lilac is a single-season interest shrub, but one of the few plants that our friends in hot climates can't grow—and thus envy. It has many cultivars, featuring outstandingly fragrant flowers. Some that excel include bicolored purple and white 'Sensation'; creamy yellow 'Primrose'; blue-purple 'Henri Robert'; double-flowering, dark purple 'Royal Purple'; pink, opening to blue 'Wedgewood Blue'; semi-dwarf (6-ft.), purple 'Yankee Doodle'; and dwarf (4- to 5-ft.), blue 'Little Boy Blue'. A roommate who was allergic to them stayed away from school for two weeks every spring because fragrance could not be avoided. They make excellent cut flowers. Regular maintenance is required since they sucker rampantly; renewal pruning is necessary to keep them flowering prolifically. They are very prone to powdery mildew, but are extremely durable and long-lived; it is not uncommon to find them standing solitary on long-abandoned properties.

Syringa vulgaris has graced gardens for centuries, providing some of the strongest fragrance of any plant.

Taxodium distichum

Bald cypress

FORM: Tree

HARDINESS: Zones (4)5–9

BLOOM PERIOD: Non-flowering

SIZE: 50–70 ft. × 20–40 ft.; numerous dwarf cultivars

This massive tree is native to the southeastern United States primarily, but has surprising zone 5 and perhaps 4b hardiness. Bald cypress is generally found in wet, swampy areas, even in standing water, but adapts to dry, upland sites. It is a deciduous conifer with beautiful soft foliage that turns autumn bronze, then drops entirely in winter. Its massive size limits use to large properties, but dwarf forms exist for smaller landscapes. 'Cascade Falls' and 'Falling Waters' are graceful dwarf weepers but did not survive in our area, so I suspect they are more accurately zone 6 than 5. Hardier dwarf forms include dense compact 'Secrest', columnar 'Peve Minaret', gold 'Peve Yellow', feathery 'Cody's Feathers', and round-headed 'Cave Hill'.

Taxodium distichum 'Secrest'.

Taxus species

Yew

FORM: Tree, shrub

HARDINESS: Varies within zones 4–7

BLOOM PERIOD: Non-flowering

SIZE: Varies by species

These evergreen trees and shrubs have reddish to brown bark and spreading, ascending branches. There is a wide variation in habit, size, growth rate, and textural effects. Foliage color is dark green with some variations to lighter greens and a few cultivars with gold foliage, such as *Taxus cuspidata* 'Dwarf Bright Gold' and 'Nana Aurescens'. Yews are easily transplanted and require fertile soil, sufficient moisture, and excellent drainage. With poor drainage they will suffer or die (a clue is yellowing foliage). Yews prefer full sun but are shade tolerant; they need to be kept out of sweeping winds as the needles will turn brown or die due to winter desiccation, and they do not tolerate extreme heat. They have been heavily used in landscapes—maybe overly so--since they are very tough, reliable, and adaptable and they tolerate heavy shearing. Species common in the Midwest include *baccata* (south only), *cuspidata*, and ×*media*.

Yews are one of the most commonly sheared conifers.

Thalictrum aquilegiifolium

Columbine meadow rue

FORM: Perennial
HARDINESS: Zones 5–9
BLOOM PERIOD: Spring
SIZE: 1–3 ft. × 1–3 ft.

✿ ◆ ☀

Several genera go by the common name meadow rue and you might mistake it for columbine (*Aquilegia*), since it has similar foliage. It tolerates high pH and grows easily in average soils from full sun to shade, even though it is indigenous to wetter sites. The drooping greenish-white flowers appear in panicles and look like tiny starbursts as they open. (Flowers are not actually flowers, but rather incredibly showy, tufted, white or purple stamens.) The best attribute of the plant is the lasting bluish foliage with lacy form, which makes an exquisite fine texture mixed with coarser woodland plants. The only readily available cultivar is 'Thundercloud' which grows to the 3-ft. range and exhibits fuzzy, lavender double blooms on deep purple stems.

Thalictrum delavayi; T. rochebruneanum

Yunnan meadow rue; lavender mist meadow rue

FORM: Perennial
HARDINESS: Zones 4–7
BLOOM PERIOD: Spring
SIZE: 3–6 ft. × 1.5–3 ft.

✿ ◆ ☀

Ethereal? Cloud-like? Adequate terminology is impossible to find for the delicate effect of massed tiny flowers on fine stems, appearing to flutter like tiny butterflies. Lavender mist meadow rue features airy spikes of lilac-purple flowers with lemon-yellow stamens. Round, glaucous blue leaves are finely textured and the wiry stems are rich, dark purple. Shorter Yunnan meadow rue blooms in clusters of large, fluffy-looking flowers with lilac to white petals and pale yellow stamens, atop wiry purple-tinted stems and delicately textured foliage. 'Album' is a white-flowering form and 'Hewitt's Double' has double flowers. Both bloom midsummer to fall.

Thalictrum aquilegiifolium.

Thalictrum rochebruneanum is a hard perennial to photograph because the flowers are so airy, light, and ethereal.

Arborvitae

FORM: **Tree**

HARDINESS: **Varies within zones 2–7**

SIZE: **Varies by species**

Arborvitae are extremely common and low-cost landscape conifers, generally available as small to large evergreen trees with stringy textured, reddish-brown bark. The foliar shoots are flat with side shoots only in a single plane, making them easy to identify; leaves are scale-like. The male cones are small, inconspicuous, and are located at the tips of the twigs; female cones grow to about ½-in. long at maturity. They prefer fertile, moist, well-drained soils. They have shallow root systems that make them easily transplanted from containers or ball-and-burlap wraps about any time of year, but those shallow roots also make them intolerant of drought. Although they perform best in full sun they are moderately shade tolerant, opening up and losing dense form in heavy shade. They tolerate light shearing and pruning prior to growth in early spring; heavy pruning into their interior may kill living tissue permanently. They are used often as wind breaks and fences, but the winter wind side may severely burn, causing brown foliage. Species common in the Midwest are *occidentalis* and *plicata*. *Thuja occidentalis* is highly susceptible to deer and rodent browsing.

Thuja occidentalis 'Yellow Ribbon'.

Thunbergia alata

Black-eyed Susan vine

FORM: **Annual, vine**

HARDINESS: **Not hardy**

BLOOM PERIOD: **Summer, fall**

SIZE: **3–8 ft. × 3–6 ft.**

Sunny cheerfulness in the garden. You can't help but smile when around merry black-eyed Susan vines, with hundreds of star-shaped, yellow, orange, and apricot flowers with dark, finely etched eyes scattered along slender, trailing vines. Naturally vining, this plant is perfect for hanging baskets, trellises, or arbors. As examples, 'Orange A-Peel' is a striking orange; 'Lemon A-Peel', a rich lemon yellow; 'Spanish Eyes' comes in shades of red with a majority of paler oranges and yellows (both with and without dark eyes); 'Sunrise White' is pure white with a black eye, and 'Apricot Smoothie' is apricot.

Thunbergia alata flowers are small but so very bright and cheerful.

Tiarella cordifolia

Foam flower

FORM: **Perennial**

HARDINESS: **Zones 4–9**

BLOOM PERIOD: **Spring**

SIZE: **8–12 in. × 12–24 in.**

☼ ◑ ☀

I would not be without foam flower. Flowers emerge early spring as bright, reflective-white racemes of tiny flowers that literally shine as sunlight penetrates still-leafless trees. Flowers blooming in cool spring last a fairly long time, until they disappear with emergence of interesting foliage. Breeding has produced variants of deeply lobed to rounded leaves, many with red "blood spots" or reddish veins that fade out or disappear in summer heat. Organically rich, moist soils are essential. The group includes clumping and running (stolons) forms. Some lovely clumping forms are 'Spring Symphony', 'Iron Butterfly', 'Elizabeth Oliver', and 'Sugar and Spice'; running forms include 'Jeepers Creepers', 'Lace Carpet', and 'Running Tapestry'.

Running forms of *Tiarella cordifolia* make excellent ground covers.

Tiarella cordifolia 'Spring Symphony' lights up my garden in early spring with brilliant white foam flowers.

Tilia cordata; T. heterophylla (syn. T. americana); T. tomentosa

Little-leaf linden; American basswood; silver linden

FORM: Tree

HARDINESS: Zones 3–7 (*cordata*), 2–8 (*heterophylla*), 4–7 (*tomentosa*)

BLOOM PERIOD: Non-flowering

SIZE: 50–80 ft. × 30–50 ft.

Tilia includes species that are primarily canopy shade trees but are important to American horticulture. American basswood (*T. heterophylla*) is the northernmost basswood species used as a handsome shade and street tree. When flowering, the trees are full of bees. 'Redmond' was selected for a dense habit, 'Boulevard' was selected for a narrow pyramidal form with ascending branches, and 'Fastigiata' is columnar, although it still reaches 50 to 70 ft. tall and 30 to 40 ft. wide. Non-native littleleaf linden (*T. cordata*) is a common shade or specimen tree, symmetrical in shape, pyramidal to rounded, with densely dark green foliage in summer. It is often incorrectly planted as a street tree and is prone to heat- and drought-induced leaf scorch. 'Greenspire' outsells the species; it grows faster, has a dense pyramidal-to-oval crown, and the leaves are smaller, which adds a delicate touch. Silver linden (*T. tomentosa*) is also not native but bears merit with attractive, fuzzy, heart-shaped, dark green leaves with silver undersides that turn outstanding gold in the fall; 'Sterling' is the most notable cultivar.

Tilia tomentosa 'Sterling' has a silvery look when breezes expose the tomentose leaf undersides.

Torenia fournieri

Wishbone flower

FORM: **Annual**

HARDINESS: **Not hardy**

BLOOM PERIOD: **Spring, summer, fall**

SIZE: **6–12 in. × 6–12 in.**

This stalwart is my reliable replacement for impatiens in shady areas during the heat and humidity of summer. Flowers bloom all season and come in various shades of blue, rose, yellow, pink, purple, or white, depending on variety. Most have purplish-blue flowers with a yellow throat. The name wishbone flower comes from two short, curved, wishbone-shaped stamens. As with many annuals, wishbone flowers are often sold in series such as Summer Wave Bouquet, that includes 'Gold', 'White', 'Blue', 'Deep Blue', 'Deep Rose', and 'Cream Yellow', or the 'White', 'Rose', 'Yellow', 'Magenta', 'Blue', 'Punky Violet', 'Purple', and 'Velvet' cultivars in the Indigo Moon Series. The Catalina Series also has a number of colors.

Torenia fournieri 'Catalina Violet Flare'.

Tricyrtis species and hybrids

Japanese toad lily

FORM: Perennial
HARDINESS: Zones 4–8
BLOOM PERIOD: Summer, fall
SIZE: 2–3 ft. × 1.5–2 ft.

Its autumn-flowering boon is also its bane in cold climes. Extremely long bloom is possible, however it is very cold sensitive, so early frost can wipe it out before finishing entire bloom periods. *Tricyrtis hirta* hybrids and related species have very long arching stems from center crowns, exhibit coarse, somewhat tomentose, foliage, and have large orchid-like flowers emerging from numerous leaf axils. 'Lightning Strike', with gold-streaked foliage, has proved quite durable for me; other cultivars include 'Miyazaki', 'Togen', 'Blue Wonder', gold-foliaged 'Golden Gleam' and 'Moonlight', and gold-variegated 'Variegata'.

T. formosana and related species have fine-textured foliage, upright structure, and smaller, more delicate, mostly terminal, orchid-like bloom. Lovely cultivars include 'Dark Beauty', 'Samurai', 'Empress', 'Golden Festival', and 'Gilt Edge'. *T. macrantha* subsp. *macranthopsis*, which has no cultivars, has long arching stems with glossy leaves and long, tubular, rich, waxy, yellow flowers sprinkled with red spotting in

Tricyrtis hirta 'Golden Gleam' displays arching branches, coarse foliage, and large flowers in leaf axils the length of the stem.

Tricyrtis formosana 'Dark Beauty' exhibits the fine-textured foliage, upright nature, and more delicate terminal flowers of this species.

the interior. Unfortunately, this stellar beauty is the last to bloom and first to be damaged by frost. *T. latifolia* begins to flower in mid- to late summer, much earlier than the fall-flowering selections. It forms upright stems of light green leaves and loose clusters of butter-yellow star flowers, with delicate, cinnamon-brown spots or freckles. I grow this one in case my fall bloomers freeze early. 'Yellow Sunrise' and 'Golden Leopard' are cultivars. Toad lily colonizes by stolons. Deeply composted, well-drained, evenly moist soils are necessary; they cannot dry out in summer, yet an overly wet winter/spring will rot them.

Tricyrtis macrantha subsp. *macranthopsis* elegantly cascades, so I like using it over rocks.

Trillium

FORM: **Perennial**
HARDINESS: **Zones 4–8**
BLOOM PERIOD: **Spring**
SIZE: **12–18 in. × 8–12 in.**

We are blessed with a number of native trilliums flourishing in woodlands and meadows. They are slow to start and need rich, evenly moist soils to establish, but then multiply if undisturbed. Some boast fully open, erect flowers (pedicellate); others have blooms with petals partly folded upright like hands in prayer (sessile). Species include large, white-flowering *Trillium grandiflorum*; richly red *T. cuneatum* (sweet Betsy) and *T. sessile* (toadshade), with mottled foliage and partly folded flowers; *T. luteum* (yellow trillium), with mottled, folded yellow flowers; dark red, open-flowered *T. erectum* (wakerobin); nodding, white-flowered *T. flexipes* (nodding trillium); and more than forty other native species.

A pedicellate form of *Trillium grandiflorum*.

A sessile form of *Trillium luteum*.

Tsuga canadensis.

Tsuga canadensis; T. diversifolia

Eastern or Canadian hemlock; northern Japanese hemlock

FORM: Tree

HARDINESS: Zones 3–7

SIZE: 40–70 ft. × 25–35 ft. (*T. canadensis*), 30–40 ft. × 15–20 ft. (*T. diversifolia*); dwarf cultivars significantly reduced in size are available

The most commonly used shade-tolerant conifer is native eastern hemlock. A large number of dwarf forms include weeping, layered, white- or gold-tipped new growth, globose, nest, and others. They are absolutely intolerant of drought. They prefer cool temperatures, but desiccate easily in winter wind and summer sun. Pampering early on is worth it for the beautiful, fine-textured form of the mature plant. Northern Japanese hemlock is smaller and slower growing, with dark green needles resembling yew. They tend to burn less, although they are not immune. 'Gracilis' and 'Loowit' are very dwarf cultivars.

Tsuga diversifolia.

Uvularia grandiflora

Merrybells, large-flowered bellwort

FORM: **Perennial**

HARDINESS: **Zones 4–9**

BLOOM PERIOD: **Spring**

SIZE: **1.5–2 ft. × 1–1.5 ft.**

It seems a rule that ephemerals naturalize easily in shaded areas and merrybells are no exception. This plant forms tight, dense clumps of upright foliage with clear yellow, downward-facing pendant flowers with twisted tepals. It blooms for a fairly long time for a spring woodland plant and tolerates drought once established.

Uvularia grandiflora can be ephemeral, but puts on a lovely show before it disappears.

Verbascum hybrids

Mullein

FORM: **Short-lived perennial**

HARDINESS: **Zones 5–8**

BLOOM PERIOD: **Summer**

SIZE: **2–4 ft. × 1.5–2 ft.**

This large genus of more than three hundred species has a multitude of common names, including beggar's blanket and old man's flannel. (In England, the poor put thick leaves into shoes for warmth.) Some are dwarf, others are towering giants, but nearly all have fuzzy stamens, lamb's ear–like foliage, and prefer well-drained sandy or rocky soil. Most garden forms are hybrids of *Verbascum chaixii*, although large, woolly, 8-ft. forms such as *V. olympicum* (candlewick) are gaining popularity as statement plants. Hybrid mullein produces tall flower spikes in white, yellow, gold, tan, purple, pink, red, and more.

Verbascum olympicum.

Verbascum bombyciferum is often used in dry, well-drained sites for architectural structure and height.

New York ironweed

FORM: **Perennial**

HARDINESS: **Zones 5–9**

BLOOM PERIOD: **Summer, fall**

SIZE: **3–8 ft. × 2–4 ft.**

New York ironweed is quite possibly one of the largest natives, reaching 8 ft., while providing nectar to foraging bees, butterflies, and beneficial insects midsummer through fall. Large, iridescent, flat-topped, fluffy, red-violet flower heads apex tall, sturdy stems. It adapts well to any moist to normal soil, punching corners in the perennial border with mass and late-season bloom. 'Richard Simon' is a dwarf form, growing 3 to 4 ft. tall. A cross with another native, *Vernonia lettermanii* 'Southern Cross' fits small gardens at 3 ft x 3 ft., and masses in flowers.

Vernonia noveboracensis makes a statement in the English Garden at Allen Centennial Gardens.

Veronica spicata and hybrids

Spiked speedwell

FORM: Perennial

HARDINESS: Zones 4–9

BLOOM PERIOD: Spring, summer, fall

SIZE: 1–2 ft. × 1 ft.

Spiked speedwell is as durable as sage and similar in appearance, except that sage possesses soft, herbal-scented, glaucous foliage compared to the thick, glossy, dark green of speedwell. It lends itself well to mass plantings. Commonly used cultivars include white 'Alba' and 'Icicle', blue 'Sunny Border Blue', purple 'Purpleicious', and dwarf fuchsia-pink 'Red Fox'. Veronica flourishes under the same cultural conditions as sage and also reblooms when spent flowers are removed.

Veronica spicata.

Veronicastrum virginicum

Culver's root

FORM: Perennial

HARDINESS: Zones 3–8

BLOOM PERIOD: Spring, summer

SIZE: 3–6 ft. × 2–4 ft.

This plant considers full sun ideal but appears in many Wisconsin woodlands, so it manages with dappled sun. Too much shade will deter rigidity, so it works well in the woodland border. It is easy to identify because the leaves are arranged in whorls on the stem and margins are finely serrated. The long-lasting flowers appear in extended multiple spikes described as candelabras. The species has white flowers, but you can also find color in cultivars such as bluish-purple 'Fascination' and pink 'Roseum'.

Veronicastrum virginicum 'Roseum'.

Viburnum carlesii

Koreanspice viburnum

FORM: Shrub, tree
HARDINESS: Zones 4–7
BLOOM PERIOD: Spring
SIZE: 4–8 ft. × 4–8 ft.

Fragrance is an elusive attribute in modern gardens. Few garden plants achieve the scent of Koreanspice viburnum, as its snowball-like white flowers emerge from waxy, red-pink buds. They are on garden perimeters in our public garden, yet on a warm spring day, visitors comment on the pleasing omnipresent scent. It flowers best in full sun, but tolerates light shade and develops striking red to purple fall color. Several new selections are more compact in form and more florific, such as 'Spiced Bouquet' and 'Spice Island'.

Viburnum carlesii.

Viburnum native species

Viburnum

FORM: Shrub, tree
HARDINESS: Zones 3–9
BLOOM PERIOD: Summer
SIZE: 4–15 ft. × 4–12 ft.

Many of our native viburnums are overlooked for flashier trees and shrubs but those don't have the advantages of Midwest durability, wildlife food source, and resistance to pests and diseases. Explore blackhaw (*Viburnum prunifolium*), arrowwood (*V. dentatum*), maple leaf (*V. acerifolium*), nannyberry (*V. lentago*), possumhaw (*V. nudum*), and highbush cranberry (*V. trilobum*) for spring flowering, heavy fruiting desired by wildlife, and excellent fall color. They will please native plant enthusiasts and ornamental gardeners alike!

Viburnum dentatum 'Autumn Jazz' reliably displays excellent fall colors of red, yellow, and orange.

Weigela florida

Weigela

FORM: **Shrub**

HARDINESS: **Zones 4–8**

BLOOM PERIOD: **Spring, fall rebloom**

SIZE: **6–10 ft. × 9–10 ft.**

Another old-fashioned plant, weigela has long been appreciated for its light shade tolerance, durability, and profuse spring flowering, with potential late-season rebloom (less prolific). Most flowers are bright rose-pink. Foliage variations include green-yellow variegated 'Nana Variegata'; purple-foliaged 'Wine & Roses' and 'Spilled Wine'; gold-leafed 'Rubies N' Gold', 'Gold Rush', and 'Rubidor'; and creamy foliaged 'Ghost'. Because it is a large, coarse, and rangy shrub with no significant fall color, dwarf colored forms have gained popularity, such as tricolor 'My Monet' and wine-purple 'Midnight Wine'.

Gold-foliaged *Weigela florida* 'Rubidor' provides foliar interest after spring bloom fades.

Wisteria frutescens; *W. macrostachya*

Wisteria

FORM: **Vine**

HARDINESS: **Zones 3 to 9**

BLOOM PERIOD: **Summer**

SIZE: **15–30 ft. × 4–8 ft.**

A common question is why doesn't my wisteria bloom? In most cases it is because the gardener has a non-native species rather than native. American-native wisteria blooms reliably, with lavish clusters of pale, lilac-purple flowers. Native wisteria flowers are not as fragrant as Asian wisterias, but they bloom later in summer so blossoms are less prone to late frost damage. They grow to 30 ft. or more when trained to climb over arbors or shaped into small trees or standards. Cultivars in light blue, purple, and white include 'Amethyst Falls', 'Longwood Purple' (*Wisteria frutescens*), 'Blue Moon', 'Aunt Dee', 'Betty Matthews', and 'Clara Mack' (*W. macrostachya*).

Wisteria might be the most lovely of vines, but selection in the Midwest is important for flowering.

Adam's needle

FORM: **Perennial**

HARDINESS: **Zones 5–10**

BLOOM PERIOD: **Summer**

SIZE: **4–8 ft. × 2–3 ft.**

Bring the Southwest look to the Midwest with Adam's needle. The evergreen foliar clumps sport arching, sword-like leaves radiating from dense, fibrous stems. Dramatic branched clusters of nodding, creamy white bells open in midsummer on stout stems that reach 4 to 8 ft. Many beautiful variegated yuccas are available, with leaves featuring bold stripes of bright canary-yellow alongside rich celadon, defined by whether gold or green is the margin color. In cool weather, leaf margins often tinge pink and the yellow stripe turns to rose. 'Color Guard', 'Bright Edge', and 'Golden Sword' are striking examples.

Yucca filamentosa 'Golden Sword' emerging from winter.

Yucca filamentosa often surprises gardeners with its tall spires of gorgeous, creamy flowers.

Acknowledgments

MANY PEOPLE HAVE influenced and continue to influence my horticultural career and continued education. It has been an interesting journey to make horticulture a second career, but my route to that ultimate profession started early. I spend a fair amount of time in the preface talking about my parents' influence that inspired my love of the natural world and gardening. Douglas and Irene Lyon were so closely linked in love that they passed twenty days apart but their inspiration will remain with me for the rest of my life. Margaret Dunbar, the years we spent immersed in growing field crops, vegetables, and ornamentals was the start of my true passion and love affair with ornamentals and even distance doesn't keep us from continuing to share that. I returned to college at age forty to embark on a new vocation with the intent of becoming a college professor. Dr. Dennis Stimart, my graduate advisor, was instrumental in giving me the opportunity to learn that my true calling was public garden administration—mentor, advisor, and friend, I miss you daily in the very gardens where I got my start. I am fortunate to have so many horticultural friends; three of the finest horticulturalists I know—Jeff Epping, Mark Dwyer, and Dan Benarcik—have inspired me with their work, supported me in my endeavor, and continue to allow me to lean on their expertise. Peggy Anne Montgomery, nobody I spend time with generates as much excitement over life and plants as you. When I was deciding who should write the foreword to this book, I felt it should be a Midwest horticulturalist whom I respected, and whom I knew others did as well. Richard Hawke is what I call a quiet horticulturalist, managing one of the best plant evaluation programs in the country, never boasting about his deserved accomplishments and contributions to the field of horticulture. I feel honored to have him introduce the book.

I have to thank Timber Press for giving me this opportunity. A book is a horticulturalist's legacy so I hope I leave a good one. I thank them for their patience with a first-time author, and especially my editors Julie Talbot and Mollie Firestone, who were always encouraging, even when I wasn't realistic about deadlines! Finally, the most important person who helped make this book a reality is not a gardener. You can't spend hours on end immersed in writing without a supportive partner and Dylan provided me with encouragement and attended to necessary daily tasks to allow me to accomplish one of my life's goals.

I am only able to write a book in a most humble fashion knowing that I don't have all of the answers myself, but I can encourage readers and gardeners to do what I have done. I am only knowledgeable and able to impart advice because of the superb gardener and horticulturalist peers who are part of my career and friendships. This book is a compilation of knowledge I have learned over time; as a result, the information comes from many minds greater than mine. To everyone who has encouraged and supported my gardening efforts and horticultural career, I give my sincere thanks. To my readers, I encourage you to surround yourself with the same type of people because the gardening family is embracing and supportive.

Recommended Reading

I did a quick perusal and I believe I have more than three hundred books related to gardening, from in-depth botanical science to personal stories. I confess, I still prefer actual books to the Internet and e-books. To me, there is nothing like the ability to easily and quickly thumb through pages with excellent images and illustrations. I think every horticulturalist has certain volumes that are worn from use; the reliable go-tos that we reach for first. Michael Dirr's *Manual of Woody Landscape Plants*, often referred to as the bible for woody plants, might very well be the most famous example. This section includes some of the most-used books in my personal library (as well as some Internet resources) with the caveat that your resource availability is almost limitless, and this is in no way meant to be anything near all-inclusive. However, each has served as a valuable resource to my personal gardening education and reference and will make a great addition to your own collection.

Botany

Capon, Brian. 1990. *Botany for Gardeners: An Introduction and Guide*. Portland, OR: Timber Press.

Elpel, Thomas J. 2013. *Botany in a Day: The Patterns Method of Plant Identification*. 6th ed. Pony, MT: Hops Press.

Harris, James G. and Melinda Woolf Harris. 1994. *Plant Identification Terminology: An Illustrated Glossary*. Spring Lake, UT: Spring Lake Publishing.

Smith, A. W. 1997. *A Gardener's Handbook of Plant Names: Their Meanings and Origins*. Mineola, NY: Dover Publications.

Culture

Lanza, Patricia. 1998. *Lasagna Gardening*. Emmaus, PA: Rodale.

Lowenfels, Jeff and Wayne Lewis. 2010. *Teaming with Microbes: The Organic Gardener's Guide to the Soil Food Web*. Portland, OR: Timber Press.

——. 2013. *Teaming with Nutrients: The Organic Gardener's Guide to Optimizing Plant Nutrition*. Portland, OR: Timber Press.

Design and General Landscaping

Austin, Sandra. 1998. *Color in Garden Design*. Newtown, CT: Taunton Press.

Darke, Rick. 2002. *The American Woodland Garden: Capturing the Spirit of the Deciduous Forest*. Portland, OR: Timber Press.

DiSabato-Aust, Tracy. 2003. *The Well Designed Mixed Garden*. Portland, OR: Timber Press.

Hodgson, Larry. 2005. *Making the Most of Shade*. Emmaus, PA: Rodale.

Maconovich, Janet. 2000. *Designing Your Gardens and Landscapes: 12 Simple Steps for Successful Planning*. North Adams, MA: Storey Publishing.

Internet

These are the Internet sites I use on a regular and consistent basis:

The Missouri Botanical Garden Plant Finder: missouribotanicalgarden. org/plantfinder/plantfindersearch

USDA Natural Resources Conservation Service PLANTS Database: plants.usda.gov/java/

Plants of Canada Database: plantsofcanada.info.gc.ca

Maintenance and Management

Deardorff, David and Kathryn Wadsworth. 2009. *What's Wrong with my Plant (And How do I Fix It?)*. Portland, OR: Timber Press.

Gillman, Jeff and Meleah Maynard. 2012. *Decoding Gardening Advice: The Science Behind the 100 Most Common Recommendations*. Portland, OR: Timber Press.

Gillman, Jeff. 2008. *The Truth About Garden Remedies: What Works, What Doesn't, and Why*. Portland, OR: Timber Press.

——. 2008. *The Truth About Organic Gardening: Benefits, Drawbacks, and the Bottom Line*. Portland, OR: Timber Press.

Grisell, Eric. 2001. *Insects and Gardens*. Portland, OR: Timber Press.

Hill, Lewis. 1986. *Pruning Simplified*. North Adams, MA: Storey Publishing.

Royer, France and Richard Dickinson. 1999. *Weeds of the Northern U.S. and Canada*. Edmonton, Alberta, Canada: Lone Pine Publishing.

Tychonievich, Joseph. 2013. *Plant Breeding for the Home Gardener*. Portland, OR: Timber Press.

Natives

Armitage, Allan M. 2006. *Armitage's Native Plants for North American Gardens*. Portland, OR: Timber Press.

Burell, C. Colston. 2007. *Native Alternatives to Invasive Plants*. Brooklyn, NY: Brooklyn Botanic Garden.

Cullina, William. 2000. *The New England Wildflower Society Guide to Growing and Propagating Wildflowers of the United States and Canada*. Boston, MA: Houghton Mifflin.

Junker, Karan. 2007. *Gardening with Woodland Plants*. Portland, OR: Timber Press.

Ladd, Doug. 1995. *Tallgrass Prairie Wildflowers*. Helena, MT: Falcon.

Peterson, Roger Tory and Margaret McKenny. 1996. *A Field Guide to Wildflowers: Northeastern and North-central North America*. Boston, MA: Houghton Mifflin.

Perennials

Armitage, Allan. M. 2000. *Armitage's Garden Perennials: A Color Encyclopedia*. Portland, OR: Timber Press.

Darke, Rick. 2007. *The Encyclopedia of Grasses for Livable Landscapes*. Portland, OR: Timber Press.

Cullina, William. 2009. *Understanding Perennials: A New Look at an Old Favorite*. Boston, MA: Houghton Mifflin.

Grenfell, Diana and Michael Shadrack. 2004. *The Color Encyclopedia of Hostas*. Portland, OR: Timber Press.

Heger, Mike, Debbie Lonnee, and John Whitman. 2011. *Growing Perennials in Cold Climates*. Revised and updated ed. Minneapolis: University of Minnesota Press.

Mineo, Baldassare. 1999. *Rock Garden Plants*. Portland, OR: Timber Press.

Olsen, Sue. 2007. *Encyclopedia of Garden Ferns*. Portland, OR: Timber Press.

Toomey, Mary and Everett Leeds. 2001. *An Illustrated Encyclopedia of Clematis*. Portland, OR: Timber Press.

Sustainability

Christopher, Thomas, ed. 2011. *The New American Landscape: Leading Voices on the Future of Sustainable Gardening*. Portland, OR: Timber Press.

Tallamy, Douglas W. 2011. *Bringing Nature Home*. Updated and expanded ed. Portland, OR: Timber Press.

Grenlee, John. 2009. *The American Meadow Garden: Creating a Natural Alternative to the Traditional Lawn*. Portland, OR: Timber Press.

Haeg, Fritz. 2007. *Edible Estates: Attack on the Front Lawn*. 2nd ed. New York: Metropolis Books.

Trees and Shrubs

Bitner, Richard. 2007. *Conifers for Gardens: An Illustrated Encyclopedia*. Portland, OR: Timber Press.

Bloom, Adrian. 2002. *Gardening with Conifers*. Buffalo, NY: Firefly Books.

Cullina, William. 2002. *Native Trees, Shrubs & Vines*. Boston, MA: Houghton Mifflin.

Dirr, Michael A. 2009. *Manual of Woody Landscape Plants*. 6th ed. Champaign, IL: Stipes Publishing.

Snyder, Leon C., Jr. 2000. *Trees and Shrubs for Northern Gardens*. Revised ed. Minneapolis: University of Minnesota Press.

Sternberg, Guy and Jim Wilson. 2004. *Native Trees for North American Landscapes*. Portland, OR: Timber Press.

Metric Conversions

INCHES	CENTIMETERS
¼	0.6
½	1.3
¾	1.9
1	2.5
2	5.1
3	7.6
4	10
5	13
6	15
7	18
8	20
9	23
10	25
20	51
30	76
40	100
50	130
60	150
70	180
80	200
90	230
100	250

FEET	METERS
1	0.3
2	0.6
3	0.9
4	1.2
5	1.5
6	1.8
7	2.1
8	2.4
9	2.7
10	3
20	6
30	9
40	12
50	15
60	18
70	21
80	24
90	27
100	30

TEMPERATURES

$$°C = \frac{5}{9} \times (°F - 32)$$

$$°F = (\frac{9}{5} \times °C) + 32$$

Photography Credits

Photographs are by the author except for the following:
Darrell Hart, pages 10, 315
Mark Dwyer, page 245
Pixabay, page 31

Index

About the Author

Ed Lyon is director of Reiman Gardens, Iowa State University, Ames, Iowa. He has worked for Allen Centennial Gardens in Madison, Wisconsin; Chicago Botanic Garden; Olbrich Botanical Garden; and Rotary Botanical Gardens. Through Spellbound Garden Writing & Consultation, he writes and speaks nationally for public and professional audiences. He writes the Ask the Expert column and feature articles for *Wisconsin Gardening* magazine, and a regular regional report and feature articles for *Chicagoland Gardening*. He teaches and lectures and is a frequent keynote speaker. His partner, Darrell Hart, has fully embraced Ed's plant addiction, which ultimately inspired Hart-N-Home & Garden Decor. Ed is emphatic about gardening, with regionalism as a primary focus. Most important, he is an avid gardener with dirt under his nails.